Interdisciplinary Courses and Team Teaching
New Arrangements for Learning

by
James R. Davis

AMERICAN COUNCIL ON EDUCATION ★
ORYX PRESS ★
Series on Higher Education
1995

The rare Arabian Oryx is believed to have inspired the myth of the unicorn. This desert antelope became virtually extinct in the early 1960s. At that time several groups of international conservationists arranged to have 9 animals sent to the Phoenix Zoo to be the nucleus of a captive breeding herd. Today the Oryx population is over 1000, and over 500 have been returned to the Middle East.

© 1995 by American Council on Education and The Oryx Press
4041 North Central at Indian School Road
Phoenix, Arizona 85012-3397

Published simultaneously in Canada
Printed and Bound in the United States of America

∞ The paper used in this publication meets the minimum requirements of American National Standard for Information Science—Permanence of Paper for Printed Library Materials, ANSI Z39.48, 1984.

Library of Congress Cataloging-in-Publication Data

Davis, James R., 1936–
  Interdisciplinary courses and team teaching: new arrangements for learning/by James R. Davis.
      p. cm.—(American Council on Education/Oryx Press series on higher education)
  Includes bibliographical references and index.
  ISBN 0-89774-887-5
    1. Education, Higher—United States—Curricula.
2. Interdisciplinary approach in education—United States.
3. Teaching teams—United States. 4. College teaching—United States. I. Title. II. Series.
LB2361.5.D38   1995
378.1'99—dc20   95-19858
                                                                              CIP

To the "Little Women" in my life:

Adelaide Bouchardet Davis
brilliant, understanding, and always
supportive wife

Marcela Bitarães
hard-working, witty, smart,
has-it-all-together stepdaughter

Annalise Davis
brave, inspiring, physically
challenged, but never-defeated
daughter

Julianne Davis Robinson
simultaneously committed
professional psychologist and
dedicated mother

Lauren Rachelle Robinson
bright, sensitive, and
artistic granddaughter

Lindy Meghan Robinson
eager, energetic,
ready-to-go granddaughter,
the littlest woman of them all,

who have given me purpose and meaning—someone to nurture—and who,
in turn, in their various ways, have returned my love many times enlarged
and enriched.

CONTENTS

• • • • • • • • •

FOREWORD

· · · · · · · · ·

by Julie Thompson Klein

*I*nterdisciplinary Courses and Team Teaching is a welcome addition to the ever-expanding literature on interdisciplinary studies. The past decade has been a bountiful one for interdisciplinary studies, with the appearance of an updated directory, a new handbook, and numerous state-of-the-art accounts. Although team planning and team teaching are recurring topics in the literature, James Davis's work is welcome as the first sustained focus on the subject. The structure of Davis's book is equally welcome.

Generalizations about interdisciplinary studies are too often based on single examples, hallowed but dated models, or small samples. Beyond updating the stock of course models, the dialogue of micro- and macro-context in Davis's work unites the advantage of close study with a large comparative base. The micro-context of five closely studied examples fosters in-depth understanding of interdisciplinary courses, from conception and planning to evaluation and revision. A rich ethnographic picture emerges, enhanced by a wealth of concrete techniques and strategies.

The macro-context documents the current variety and extent of examples across general, disciplinary, professional, and interdisciplinary contexts. Older fields of interdisciplinary interest exist alongside new subjects and problems that blur traditional categories of knowledge and institutional structure. The boundaries they cross are equally multiple, spanning content and skills in the syllabus; courses, programs, and their institutional hosts; disciplines, professions, and interdisciplinary fields; and the university's relationships with its many communities.

The diversity of contexts in which interdisciplinary studies are appearing today is affirmed by the breadth of examples. In general education, they encompass development studies, humanities, the sciences, and social sciences. They include older integrative approaches to the humanities and liberal arts as well as contemporary models of international studies, American multicultural and gender studies, historical consciousness, and ethical understanding. The science examples echo this variety, incorporating the history of science, the nature of scientific inquiry, and contemporary problems of science and society.

In disciplinary contexts, interdisciplinary approaches are now being mainstreamed in the form of topical first-year seminars, required core courses, advanced courses on problems and intellectual themes, and senior seminars and projects. The inclusion of examples from the professions is especially significant. Pre-professional and professional degree programs increasingly involve courses or course elements focused on integration, complex issues, and the day-to-day problems of practices. The examples included here document that trend in business, the health sciences, law, commercial art and design, natural resources management, and education.

The book is timely in an added respect. The need for integrative skills, awareness of multiple perspectives, the ability to work collaboratively, and the capacity to cope with complexity are leitmotifs of reform across the academy, industry, government, and public life. Team planning and teaching are ideal settings for addressing these widely felt needs. Unfortunately, teachers often arrive ill-prepared for the task. The knowledge of group dynamics and organizational theory that James Davis brings to bear on the topic provides both a theoretical perspective and practical advice.

Interdisciplinary Courses and Team Teaching is a book, as Davis intends, for busy faculty, who have multiple roles as teachers, committee members, department chairs, deans, and other administrative officers. It is a *vade mecum*, a handbook of know-how and reflection to carry for ready reference. The most productive use of the book will be long-term. Teachers, curriculum committees, and administrators will find it valuable background reading. It will be particularly beneficial for the often neglected new members of interdisciplinary teams. Everyone will return to the book again and again. Its many definitions, taxonomies, criteria, guidelines, checklists, and clustered questions will be valuable discussion points at all stages of course and program life cycles.

The clustered questions that guide the discussion from chapter to chapter are especially useful. These questions are not always completely formed in everyone's mind, and they do not always arise in ordered sequence. Yet, they are the heart of interdisciplinary practice. On a weekly, monthly, and annual basis, the questions can be used to build a shared sense of how teams interact with each other and with their students. Davis speaks insightfully of "inventing the subject." There is, we are assured, no *a priori* logic that courses have to be set up in particular ways, no one way of doing it. Yet, as individuals and teams go about creating interdisciplinary courses, they can now do so with the benefit of the comparative wisdom and models this book so amply provides.

Julie Thompson Klein
Wayne State University

PREFACE

• • • • • • • • •

This book is written for faculty who are engaged in team teaching or who, as committee members, department chairs, or deans, are contemplating or planning interdisciplinary team-taught courses. Although most courses in colleges and universities have traditionally found their home within a particular discipline—biology, history, art, sociology—or a professional specialization—accounting, constitutional law, pediatric nursing, school administration—many colleges and universities today are discovering the limits of specialization and are experimenting with alternatives to the traditional format of discipline-based courses. Although disciplinary and professional specializations are still useful for discovery of knowledge, presentation of foundational concepts, and introduction of the specialized methods of the discipline, many institutions find this structure inadequate as the only method of organizing knowledge for instruction. Unfortunately, problems in the "real world" seldom present themselves in tidy, disciplinary packages; there is much that needs to be explored in other formats.

Today, interest in developing courses that provide interdisciplinary perspectives is increasing. Offering these courses often requires two or more faculty members to plan and carry out instruction as a team, thus breaking a traditional norm: one professor presenting, for the duration of the course, one perspective, his or her specialization.

In Part I of this book, I explore in depth the definition and rationale for interdisciplinary courses and the dynamics of team teaching. I have selected five examples from my own institution, the University of Denver, to use as illustrations. Because the courses are the focus in Part I, I decided not to select examples from several institutions, but rather to hold constant (or eliminate) the variables associated with differences in setting. Instead I chose five very different courses from the same institution to illustrate how interdisciplinary courses are planned and executed. I interviewed the faculty who taught in these courses to understand their struggles and satisfactions, and I also surveyed the students in these courses to understand student responses to team teaching. The five courses used as illustrations are:

Making of the Modern Mind. Designed for freshmen and sophomores and meeting the core curriculum requirement in the humanities, this course provides students the opportunity to explore the central assumptions, attitudes, and cultural expressions of Western Culture that determine how we view ourselves and our "modern" world. The course is team taught by faculty from philosophy, literature, music, religious studies, and art history. The course offers a year-long sequence of lectures and demonstrations in conjunction with small seminars of approximately 20 students each.

Multiple Voices of America. Designed as a new way of presenting the study of American history, this course provides an opportunity for undergraduates to gain an appreciation of the role of Native Americans, African Americans, Hispanics, and various immigrant groups in shaping American culture and political forms. The course brings together specialists from history, religious studies, literature, and art, who are assisted by teaching assistants with diverse cultural backgrounds.

The Origin and Evolution of Life. Developed for nonscience majors, this course allows undergraduate students to explore Charles Darwin's thesis that all life on earth has evolved from a common ancestral form by means of a naturalistic process. The course is centered around three organizing themes: (1) evaluating why scientists believe evolution happened, (2) evaluating how scientists believe evolution occurs, and (3) evaluating plausible answers to some of the major questions still posed by the theory. The faculty are drawn from the fields of biology and anthropology.

The Lawyering Process. This course is required of all first-year law students, both day and evening divisions, and is designed to introduce students to the three sources of law—case law, legislation, and administrative law—and to provide a context in which students can develop the skills used in legal practice, for example, interviewing clients, locating relevant case law, writing briefs, taking depositions, preparing for trial, requesting motions, and filing appeals. The entering class is divided into 16 simulated law firms paired to work on opposite sides (plaintiff and defendant) of carefully elaborated problem cases. The firms are staffed by the students and a senior partner (practicing attorney), a junior partner (upper division student), a writing consultant, and a librarian consultant. A core of four faculty organizes the course, provides lectures, trains participants, generates case material, selects readings, develops assignments, and evaluates student progress.

The Quality Panorama. This team-taught course in the newly developed Integrated Master's in Business Administration (MBA) program focuses on Total Quality Management (TQM). The course draws on the expertise of faculty in accounting, marketing, and management, as well as on the real world experience of a new faculty member formerly employed by a local telecommunications corporation.

The focus of Part I, therefore, is on the structure of interdisciplinary courses and the delivery of team teaching at the micro-context level.

In Part II, interdisciplinary courses are examined within the contexts of the programs where they most frequently reside. To gain this broader perspective, I collected a file of examples of interdisciplinary courses drawn from a broad list of institutions in the United States, Canada, and Mexico. A list of "promising prospects" was compiled and an invitation was sent to the presidents of selected institutions to nominate examples of interdisciplinary team-taught courses at their institution. For the courses that were selected, a faculty contact person at the institution was asked to send a packet of materials from which annotated descriptions were developed. The courses were then clustered for discussion according to various contexts, for example, general education, interdisciplinary studies, gender studies, international studies, etc. The courses are introduced with brief discussions of the context, and are then elaborated in some detail to provide a stimulus for further thought about how interdisciplinary team-taught courses can be used to accomplish different goals in different contexts.

Written with the busy faculty member in mind, this book is designed to be a useful guide, with practical illustrations, to planning for interdisciplinary courses and delivering them through team teaching. As such, it is a sympathetic treatment of the subject, and contains some advocacy. The advocacy is supplemented, however, with a significant amount of discussion of the obstacles to creating and sustaining interdisciplinary courses and the problems involved in team teaching. Furthermore, interdisciplinary courses are not presented here as a panacea for all of the ills of postsecondary education today. Team teaching is a good alternative to traditional teaching, but it is not the only alternative. It will flourish best in the right setting and only with proper nurture by those who are committed to the educational values it best facilitates.

In the first chapter of Part I, I explore various types of arrangements for teaming and establish a tentative definition of team teaching. I introduce the five examples and measure their similarities and differences against four criteria of collaboration. In the second chapter, I set forth the historical and philosophical foundations of the disciplines and professions and examine the limitations of specialization. I also develop a rationale for interdisciplinary courses and team teaching as a response to the problem of specialization. In the third chapter, I provide a menu of what to consider for those planning to approximate the "ideal" interdisciplinary team-taught course. The examples of the previous chapters serve, with other suggestions and ideas, as illustrations for this chapter. In the fourth chapter, I explore the opportunities and problems of working in teams by drawing on the literature on groups and teams and applying it to the stresses and strains that naturally develop when faculty members work together in teams. The fifth chapter contains the results of the interviews with faculty about their experiences with and responses to interdisciplinary courses and team teaching and the results of the student survey. In the sixth chapter, I summarize what has been learned and discuss future prospects for interdisciplinary courses and team teaching.

In Part II, I set forth the methodology for gathering and arranging the selected examples, describe various contexts for interdisciplinary courses, and present the selected examples. Collectively, the examples provide a stimulating accumulation of ideas about interdisciplinary courses and team teaching that should be useful to those planning such courses at their own institutions.

I found myself in a unique position to write a book on team teaching. First, I was involved as a faculty member in an undergraduate, team-taught, core curriculum class entitled "Social Science as a Craft." I served as a member of the team that developed, revised, and offered that course over a period of five years; from that experience I have personal, first-hand knowledge of what is involved, intellectually and emotionally, in team teaching. I've been there.

Second, I am currently serving as Special Assistant to the Provost for Academic Quality and Assessment of Student Learning. In this position I am responsible for coordinating the work of our institution in faculty development and assessment, but I also serve as a roving consultant on curriculum planning and course development. In other words, the University makes me available (free) to our various colleges, schools, and departments as a consultant. In this role, I have become acquainted with the team teaching taking place at our institution across many levels and fields of study. In one instance, I have served as the facilitator of the faculty team responsible for planning, revising, and implementing our largest and most complicated team-taught course, the required first-year course in the College of Law.

Third, I work at an institution that has had, over the years, an extensive involvement with interdisciplinary courses: the University of Denver, an independent, doctoral-granting institution with an enrollment of approximately 7,000 students, evenly divided among undergraduates, graduates, and nontraditional students. As early as the 1950s, the faculty in the arts and sciences divisions had experimented with interdisciplinary courses for general education, including a course in the sciences entitled "Science in the Modern World." In 1973, the University attracted a multi-year grant of over $1 million from the National Endowment for the Humanities to support a program of "block courses" designed to allow students to meet one of their general education requirements through an interdisciplinary 15-credit hour course in one term. Through grant support, the University developed a series of nine block courses around critical eras of particular civilizations, such as classical Athens, twelfth-century Paris, Gupta India, Elizabethan England, Sung China, Weimar Germany, and twentieth-century Black America. Unfortunately, at a critical moment in the development of the program, undergraduate enrollment began to decline, and as grant support for "soft money" specialists disappeared and the number of faculty was reduced, the block option faded out. The University was left, however, with useful experience in producing interdisciplinary courses. Nonetheless, arrangements for meeting general education requirements reverted to a distributive system. Although many members of the faculty wanted to do something more interesting and effective, the committee charged with review of the general education curriculum had difficulty marshalling support for changes. In 1984, after years of faculty indecision about how to reform general education, a new chancellor mandated an interdisciplinary core curriculum as part of a wider reorganization of the University. He didn't mandate the content of that core curriculum, just that there would be one. After much faculty resistance and venting of anger about perceived intrusion in the curriculum, some senior faculty took the lead in developing a magnificent series of interdisciplinary, team-taught courses from which students could choose to meet their general education requirements. The sources of team teaching at the graduate professional level are more recent and are more self-directed. All in all, the University of Denver now has some excellent examples of team teaching and a growing reputation for it, and I am in the fortunate position of being able to draw on these examples as illustrations in the chapters that follow.

Fourth, I have thought about teaching over most of my career and written about it elsewhere. I am the author of a recent, more comprehensive book on teaching entitled *Better Teaching, More Learning: Strategies for Success in Postsecondary Settings* (Phoenix: American Council on Education/Oryx Press, 1993). In that work, I presented in detail five teaching strategies based on corresponding paradigms of learning. Much of what good teachers do can also be done by teachers working in teams, and I assume that effective team teachers will also consciously select teaching strategies and use them in appropriate ways. The focus of this book, however, is on the critical characteristics of the team setting and the particular opportunities and problems that grow out of this unique instructional configuration.

There is much serious and useful conversation today about the improvement of teaching. The pressure is on us as teachers to do a better job whenever we step into the classroom. There is growing documentation of a huge gap between where society has moved—more information-based, global, complex, and confused—and what institutions of higher education do to prepare students for life in that society. What many professors do, persistently without much self-reflection, is go into classrooms (alone because it is *their* classroom), start talking, and write things (as the spirit moves them) on the chalkboard. The days are over when any conscientious professor can be satisfied with this as the dominant mode of teaching, when there are really so many viable, well-elaborated alternatives. Team teaching, when effectively implemented, is one of these alternatives. It not only changes the arrangements for learning, it engages the team members in serious and continuous reflection on what they are doing. Ultimately, this reflection may be the most important contribution of team teaching, allowing and requiring instructors to articulate and justify before their colleagues the choice of activities that take place in their classrooms.

I owe a debt of gratitude to many people for helping to make this book possible. I certainly want to thank Sharon Irwin at the University of Denver for typing and proofing the manuscript, for maintaining the file of course examples presented in Part II, and for communicating with institutions about details. Her work has been accurate and her judgment sound, and without her efforts the manuscript would never have taken form. Todd Olson, a graduate student in Higher Education, provided valuable assistance in conducting literature searches and providing useful ideas about classifying the examples of courses in Part II. I also want to thank John Wagner at Oryx Press for another great job of editing, and Susan Slesinger at Oryx and James Murray III at the American Council on Education for their support of the project. Thanks also to those anonymous readers out there, whoever you may be, for suggestions that truly changed the scope of this work and enriched the final product.

At the University of Denver I want to thank the faculty who gave of their time and expertise to teach me about their involvement with interdisciplinary courses and team teaching. This includes the coordinator of each of the five courses and the faculty who were interviewed. The coordinators at the time of the research were:

Dr James Platt, "Origin and Evolution of Life"

Dr. Anne Culver, "Making of the Modern Mind"

Dr. Annette Stott, Dr. Will Gravely, "Multiple Voices of America"

Dr. James Sorensen, "Quality Panorama"

Dr. John Reese, "The Lawyering Process"

Additional faculty members interviewed were:

Mike Monahan, Dean Saitta, M.E. Warlick, Richard Klemmer-Smith, Don Bacon, Lynn Goering, Mary Wilder, Barbara Greenspahn, and Jere Surber.

I want to thank all of the persons who submitted course examples, and the contact persons who agreed to list their names with the courses ultimately selected for Part II. I also want to thank our Provost, Dr. William Zaranka for his support of my office, The Center for Academic Quality, and Dr. Elinor Katz, the Dean of the College of Education, for her support of my teaching and scholarship. I appreciate their permitting me to divide my time among administration, scholarship and teaching. It goes without saying, but needs saying anyway: the University is the only place I know of that pays people to think and to express their thoughts freely.

PART

I

Structure and Delivery of Courses

CHAPTER 1

Interdisciplinary Courses and Team Teaching: Definitions and Examples

"Liberating education consists in acts of cognition,
not transferrals of information."

—Paulo Freire

DEFINING INTERDISCIPLINARY

Many colleges and universities today are developing and offering interdisciplinary courses taught by teams of faculty members. What are interdisciplinary courses and what is the best way to define team teaching?

The dictionary defines "interdisciplinary" as "combining or involving two or more academic disciplines or fields of study." This definition raises the question: What is a discipline? *Missions of the College Curriculum*, a publication of the Carnegie Foundation for the Advancement of Teaching, provides the following "academic" definition of discipline. A discipline is

> a discrete subject and its characteristic regimen of investigation and analysis—geography, political science, psychology and English are examples. In most American colleges and universities, such realms are structurally accommodated in departments, which administer the teaching and research in the individual disciplines.[1]

Interdisciplinary connections assume, therefore, a disciplinary structure to begin with, that is, a prior arrangement of knowledge according to patterns that have traditionally come to be called "the academic disciplines." In the more narrow definition, a discipline usually refers to a subject specialization in the arts and sciences; a broader definition, one more widely used today, would include the specializations that also occur within professional fields. Thus, one might think of the specializations within business as disciplines, such as accounting, marketing, and management; or within law, such specializations as constitutional law, torts and contracts, and international law. There are those who for good reason would object to calling professional specializations "disciplines," but for the purposes of this book, such specializations are also referred to as "disciplines" and are included within the concept of "interdisciplinary studies." Thus, interdisciplinary courses are those involving the subject matter and faculty expertise of two or (usually) more disciplines or professional specializations.

Unfortunately, this simple definition is insufficient; too much rests in the word "involving." The key question is this: Exactly how are disciplines related in interdisciplinary courses? It wouldn't be so difficult to make a definition if scholars had not also invented, and then used rather carelessly, the terms "cross-disciplinary," "multi-disciplinary," and "trans-disciplinary." Do these terms all mean the same thing, or do they provide a vehicle for making useful distinctions?

The most comprehensive treatment of the problem of making the definitions is found in *Interdisciplinarity: History, Theory, and Practice* by Julie Thompson Klein.[2] Klein suggests that there are important distinctions to be made by the varying terms. "Cross-disciplinary," though used in many ways refers to efforts to view one discipline from the perspective of another, often subordinating the phenomena from one discipline to the other, as in the physics of music. There is little effort to integrate and no intent to generate a new subject or paradigm. "Multidisciplinary" refers to several disciplinary specialists working side by side in an additive way. For example, in child development, members of a "multidisciplinary team," composed, for example, of a social worker, a counselor, and a school psychologist, might work together in making a diagnosis and suggesting interventions for a child with special problems; but the team members probably would not spend much effort or feel the necessity to integrate their "disciplinary" perspectives. Each would contribute a point of view. "Transdisciplinary," on the other hand, suggests themes or issues that transcend or cross over several disciplines. Marxism, phenomenology, or general systems theory, for example, can be said to be "transdisciplinary" concerns, conceptual frameworks that go beyond the domains of particular disciplines and their methods. "Interdisciplinary" is usually the term that is used to imply higher levels of integration and greater amounts of teamwork. But the word "interdisciplinary" is often used in different ways.

Sometimes the word "interdisciplinary" refers to a peculiar kind of activity that has grown up between two specific disciplines. After scholars in two disciplines have worked together over a period of time, often in an area of specialization, they come to a crossroads and discover that both are standing in the same intersection. A new area of study begins to develop out of this fertile collaboration. From the work of biologists and chemists, a new specialization called "biochemistry" has arisen, and from the collaboration of psychologists and sociologists, the field of "social psychology" has evolved. The word "interdisciplinary" can be used in this more narrow sense to refer to the body of knowledge that emerges from the productive synthesis of scholarship in two related disciplines. The term "interdisciplinary" is not used in that sense in this book; to the contrary, we shall see that the disciplines brought together in most team-taught courses are often somewhat *unrelated*, and some of the more interesting arrangements for team teaching involve distant fields.

An individual professor teaching alone in his or her course may also do "interdisciplinary" teaching by making connections to areas outside of the primary discipline. For instance, an art historian might have the background and desire to teach the history of art by making connections to important contemporaneous movements in literature, music, and philosophy. Professors teaching alone can learn to make interdisciplinary connections, but this form of interdisciplinary teaching is not what is meant in this book by the terms "interdisciplinary courses" and "team teaching." The courses examined here involve two or more professors collaborating in significant ways.

"Interdisciplinary" is used in this book to refer to the work that scholars do together in two or more disciplines, subdisciplines, or professions, by bringing together and to some extent synthesizing their perspectives. Interdisciplinary courses involve efforts, at least to some degree, to bring about mutual integration or organizing concepts and methodologies. As Julie Klein points out, there are different opinions about what constitutes "genuine interdisciplinarity," but she stresses the importance of at least some efforts at intregation, what Piaget referred to as reciprocal assimilation among the participating disciplines.[3]

In the efforts that have been made to describe the "inter" prefix of "interdisciplinary," the reader often finds the words "integration," "incorporation," "assimilation," or "interpenetration."[4] Perhaps most useful is a metaphor generated in an article by Paul Haas, Barbara Hursh, and Michael Moore on interdisciplinary work in general education.[5] If four pieces of fruit are set before us side by side on a table, for example, an apple, orange, pear, and peach, the first impulse is to describe each one separately. "Their existence," the authors indicate, "invites . . . discrimination." At the next level, one might actually compare the four fruits, noting the similarities and differences among them. At this point the interdisciplinary conversation is only beginning. "If, however, these four entities are collected into a basket, our specialists must shift their perspectives to recognize that a new entity was created, a fruit basket." The assemblage of the fruit in the basket creates a new order, a new set of relationships. What was previously four entities has been synthesized into a new construct. Although not all interdisciplinary efforts achieve this kind of integration, the concept, as it is generally defined in the literature, and as it is used in this book, implies the goal of integration.

Although the concept of "interdisciplinarity" is usually thought of as a recent idea, and one that logically would seem to come chronologically after the emergence of the disciplines, the larger issue addressed by interdisciplinarity, namely, the relations among various forms of knowledge, is an old problem, one with which both Plato and Aristotle grappled. As Julie Klein points out, Francis Bacon, Descartes, the French Encyclopedists, Kant, Hegel, and Comte all expressed concern about the fragmentation of knowledge, and developed their peculiar vision of the unity of knowledge.[6] In modern times, after the rise of the disciplines, concern for the unity of knowledge has most often been expressed in curricular efforts to establish general education programs, area studies majors, and the emerging ethnic studies concentrations. Interdisciplinarity has its own history, though, which Klein has summarized well in her chapter on "The Evolution of Interdisciplinarity."

The key historical markers include the establishment of the Social Science Research Council in the 1920's; the beginning of geographical area studies programs in the 1930's; an important book entitled *Integration: Its Meaning and Application*, published by the National Education Association in 1935; a typology of definitions that emerged in the 1970's from *Interdisciplinarity: Problems of Teaching and Research in Universities*, a work by the Organization of Economic Cooperation and Development (OECD); several "mission-oriented" research projects in agriculture and national defense, including the famous Manhattan Project; numerous National Science Foundation initiatives; and the founding of two professional associations in 1979, the Association of Integrative Studies (AIS) and the International Association for the Study of Interdisciplinary Research (INTERSTUDY).

Defining "interdisciplinary" is not easy, but the phenomenon of interdisciplinary efforts is surly there, taking many forms and calling for clearer understanding. If there is a key characteristic of interdisciplinary courses, it is "integration," scholars working together to pool their interests, insights, and methods, usually with the hope of gaining and presenting new understandings that could not be derived from working alone.

DEFINING TEAM TEACHING

"Team teaching," likewise, is not easy to define. It refers, most often, to the teaching done in interdisciplinary courses by the several faculty members who have joined together to produce that course. The arrangements vary considerably among teams, however, and it is not always easy to agree on what constitutes the "team" part of team teaching. Although most of the courses described in this book follow the pattern of "one course with several faculty," there are some interesting variations on this arrangement that might also be called "team teaching." Recently, several institutions have begun to experiment with what have come to be called "cluster courses." These involve a series of courses linked together in planning and in student enrollments. Students are required to register for a sequence of courses, so that all of the students are in the same cluster of courses. The faculty work together to plan and deliver the cluster, and the individual courses in the cluster may or may not be taught by teams of faculty. In some cases, a series of cluster courses may follow a comprehensive theme or may make up an entire concentration, sometimes referred to as a "federated learning community." Because an excellent monograph published by Faith Gabelnick et al. in 1990 already covers learning communities, these course concentrations will not be the focus of this work, although Part II lists several cluster courses and federated programs. Sometimes these arrangements even involve the intentional clustering of *students* from different disciplines. For the most part, however, the definition of team teaching used in this book is "single courses taught by two or more persons."

But what does it mean for faculty to teach as a team? To what extent does the team actually function as a team? On what do they collaborate and in what ways? Consider some extremes.

At one end of the continuum are courses planned by a group of faculty and then carried out in serial segments by the individual members of the group. For example, three faculty members might plan a course to be delivered over the three quarters of an academic year, with the first faculty member taking responsibility for the first quarter, the second for the second quarter, and the third for the third quarter. They plan the general content of the three quarters together to avoid overlapping and ensure continuity, but once this general planning is done they teach "their own" sections serially, one after the other. They do not attend each other's classes, they devise their own teaching strategies, and they employ their own evaluation procedures. Is this "team teaching?" There are many who would say "no." The degree of collaboration is low and the amount and kind of interdisciplinary interaction is limited. The enrichment that comes from the interrelationship of multiple perspectives is minimal.

On the other end of the continuum are courses both planned and delivered by a group of faculty working together closely as a team. They develop a common syllabus, they struggle to integrate their various perspectives, they come to agreement about the ordering of topics, and they intermingle their teaching activity throughout the course. They take primary responsibility for individual class sessions, but sometimes two or more faculty are involved in planning and delivering the instruction for a particular class. They attend each other's classes and provide feedback and support for each other in their teaching. They agonize together over grading and evaluation procedures. When the course is evaluated, they sink or swim together. The degree of collaboration is high and the amount and kind of interdisciplinary integration is extensive. The enrichment that comes from the synthesis of their multiple perspectives is what gives the course its distinctive character.

Are the courses at both ends of this continuum worthy of the designation "team teaching?" Well, perhaps, yes, if it is clearly understood that the differences are significant. Most team-taught courses will fall somewhere between these extremes. For the purpose of definition, it will be useful to include within "team teaching" all arrangements that involve two or more faculty in some level of collaboration in the planning and delivery of a course. On the other hand, it should be understood that optimal arrangements for interdisciplinary integration and for team teaching involve higher levels of collaboration. The reason for this, of course, is linked to the goal of providing *integrative interdisciplinary perspectives*. If the reason for team teaching—its justification—is to create and deliver interdisciplinary courses, then the achievement of that goal, in ways that are significant and not superficial, will require collaboration. In fact, one might generate the following principle: *The greater the level of integration desired, the higher the level of collaboration required.*

ESTABLISHING CRITERIA

The question to ask about team teaching, therefore, is not: Is this team teaching? The more important question is: If this is team teaching, what is the type and level of collaboration among the team members? To help answer this question, a list of criteria is provided. These criteria can be applied to any team-taught course, whatever the mix of disciplines, and will serve as useful guidelines both for analyzing existing courses and for making decisions about the level of intended collaboration for interdisciplinary courses in the planning stage. The criteria for judging degree of collaboration are as follows:

> *Planning.* What is the involvement of the faculty in planning this course? Are all members of the team involved in planning or do some members of the team play a more important role in planning the course than others? Does the leader of the course (its coordinator) have more responsibility and more authority for planning the course than other team members? To what extent does the team use collaborative decision-making (democratic) processes in planning the course? How much time and effort have gone into planning the course? How well have the goals of the course been elaborated and to what extent do the goals of the course reflect the views of all the participants?
>
> *Content Integration.* In what ways, and to what extent, have the multiple disciplinary perspectives of the faculty been represented? Are the

differing perspectives seen as contradictory or complementary? Do the various disciplines provide different lenses for viewing the same phenomena, or do the disciplines examine different phenomena? Are the perspectives distinct and related in some logical way, such as serial or chronological order, or have the perspectives been integrated to produce some new way of thinking about the substance of the course? Is some unifying principle, theory, or set of questions used to provide unity and coherence to the course?

Teaching. Who will do the teaching and how will it be done? Do all team members participate more or less equally in the delivery of the course? Is there a core of key faculty who teach regularly but are supplemented by less frequent guests? Are there assistants or consultants who play roles that are different from faculty roles? Are teaching responsibilities broken into identifiable time segments, such as a term or a unit of instruction, or do faculty intermingle their instruction day by day? Do faculty sometimes work together during a single class session? How are decisions made about what teaching strategies to employ and what readings and other materials to use?

Testing and Evaluation. How is agreement reached about what kind of learning outcomes are to be measured and how they are to be measured? What kinds of tests, papers, and other devices are used to measure student achievement? How are the various components of the testing and evaluation process weighted? Who writes and who grades the exams and papers? How do the course faculty involve themselves in this process? Who is included and who is left out? Who takes charge of this process and where is the highest court of authority when students challenge the process, including their grade? In addition, who decides what mechanisms will be used to get faculty feedback about the course, not only on what students appear to be learning, but on their satisfactions and concerns about the course?

EXAMINING EXAMPLES

It is useful in attempting to define "interdisciplinary courses" and "team teaching" to move from the abstract to the concrete. The concepts come alive when specific courses are considered. For purposes of illustration, I selected five examples of interdisciplinary, team-taught courses for elaboration throughout Part I. These examples are introduced here now to illustrate the issues raised in settling on definitions. These courses fall at different places on the continuum developed above, and they employ different forms of collaboration. The examples are drawn from a single institution, the University of Denver, thus holding constant the variation that might come from differences in institutional setting, while highlighting differences among subject fields and desired educational outcomes. All of the examples are sufficiently complex to provide a high level of interest and are different enough, one from the other, to provide points of contrast and a basis for comparison. Readers from various types of institutions and different fields of study should be able to profit from reflection on these examples; that is because the courses are the focus of this study and the arrangements for interdisciplinary learning are our primary interest. (Other examples, from other fields and different types of institutions, are presented in Part II.)

As the examples are examined, try to apply the criteria presented above and try to place the courses on the continuum of collaboration. What decisions appear to have been made about planning, content integration, teaching, and testing and evaluation? The key question to ask about these courses is this: What is the type and level of collaboration that is taking place?

"Making of the Modern Mind"

"Making of the Modern Mind" is an interdisciplinary team-taught course available to freshmen and sophomores to select in meeting their 12-hour core requirement in the humanities. Offered for the first time in 1984, it is among the oldest of the continuing courses in the core curriculum, although it was "off line" (on sabbatical) in the 1992-93 academic year. With roots that go back to the Coordinated Humanities Block, funded by a grant from the National Endowment for the Humanities, and an earlier team-taught coordinated humanities course, "Making of the Modern Mind," was originally conceived by Jere Surber, a philosophy professor. He saw the need for a strong course in the humanities to serve as an alternative to the typical Western civilization course taught by an historian. The intent was to bring the various disciplines of the humanities together—art, music, literature, philosophy—to explore how the modern world view developed. In the words of the current syllabus,

> the aim is to trace the development of the lens through which we view the world. . . . Different cultures equip their people with different lenses. You have been equipped with the lens of what is often called the *Modern* (and Western) Mind. In this course we will explore the origins and meaning of those central assumptions, attitudes, and cultural experiences that determine how you view yourself, your society, and your "modern" world.

The course is organized chronologically, beginning with the seventeenth and eighteenth centuries in the fall, and moving through the nineteenth and twentieth centuries in the winter and spring, exploring the broad categories used to describe the intellectual movements associated with those periods—

the enlightenment, romanticism, and modernism. To bring together the disciplines and to break out of purely disciplinary perspectives, the instructors introduce other conceptual frameworks; for example, in the fall quarter, selected "dichotomies" serve as organizing principles—sacred and secular, reason and the senses, mind and body, the old religion and the new science, Protestant and Catholic.

The course is structured at two levels, as a lecture series and as a seminar. Students enroll for a seminar of their choice, knowing that the seminar has the content focus of one of the disciplines, for example, art, literature, religion, philosophy, or music. Each of the seminars has its own ongoing agenda—about music or art. But the purpose of the seminar is to link the ideas of the lecture with the ideas of the seminar, for example, to continue to explore the development of music in the broader context of the cultural themes presented in the lecture. Thus the 11 sections of about 20 students each function in one sense as separate seminars on the development of art, music, literature, religion, and philosophy, but are also "glued together" by the lecture series, which is designed to demonstrate the interrelationships of these various cultural expressions. Anne Culver, a music historian from the School of Music, coordinates the course, and the seminar leaders include (counting Culver) two each in music, English, and foreign languages; four in religious studies; and one in philosophy. All of the seminar leaders lecture, and special guest lecturers supplement the roster of seminar leaders. The lectures are intended to be engaging presentations of the ideas of key thinkers and the works of important creators, and are usually accompanied by slides, video clips, film segments, or stereo CDs. At least once in each term an artist or ensemble performs live for the class.. A teaching assistant is available to arrange the schedule and support faculty use of media.

The team consists of the 11 seminar leaders and regular guest lecturers, and all are welcome and usually attend the planning sessions in the spring and summer. The team also meets every three weeks during the quarter to fine tune the coordination and to hammer out questions. Lecturers all contribute "objective" questions to the general exam (70% of the exam), and the seminar leaders prepare an essay question appropriate to their own seminar (30%). The exams are given in the seminar and graded by the instructor.

Because the seminars draw upon the content of the lectures and conduct their disciplinary discussions in the wider context of the themes explored in the lectures, all of the seminar leaders attend all of the lectures. "This creates a stimulating intellectual comradery," notes Culver. "We talk to each other, in front of each other; we learn from each other, not only about what we present, but how we present it. It raises our expectations, but also our support for each other." Is this a team-taught course? "We maintain the thread of continuity in the disciplines, which is good," says Culver, "but I have to look at my music in a broader cultural perspective." The main problem for Culver is organizing this "cast of thousands" and making sure that all the players are ready to enter and exit at the right time.

"The Origin and Evolution of Life"

"The Origin and Evolution of Life" is an interdisciplinary team-taught course offered to undergraduate nonscience majors as an option for meeting their 12-hour core requirement in science. The course had its origins in a conversation between two biologists. Bob Dores walked into the office of Jim Platt one day and said, "We ought to do a course on evolution for the core curriculum." Platt took up the challenge and began searching for subject matter specialists who could present the evolution of earth structures, life forms, and human origins. First offered in 1989-90 with six faculty, "Evolution," as the course has come to be called in shortened form, originally focused on the description of processes and the naming of forms. Interestingly enough, "Evolution" has itself *evolved*, so that the primary emphasis now is on the development of critical thinking skills for the freshmen and sophomores who are attracted to the course.

Today the course is planned and carried out by three faculty, James Platt, the course coordinator, a biologist with research interests in comparative endocrinology and amphibian metamorphosis; another biologist with broad interests in environmental sciences; and a cultural anthropologist with special interests in the archaeology of the Southwest, particularly the Anasazi culture of the Mesa Verde cliff dwellers. The faculty are aided by three teaching assistants.

The course meets three times each week for 50-minute lectures. Students also register for a two-hour laboratory, which is further subdivided into several learning/discussion groups. In the autumn quarter, students explore the earliest forms of life by examining cells and reflecting on what cells require to live. The instructors then introduce the problem of the classification of diversity, the relationships of classification categories, and the idea of species. They demonstrate for students how animal and plant forms can be said to have evolved and introduce the "hard evidence" for evolution in fossils. Students then explore how the theory of evolution itself has evolved, and how recent interpretations of fossil evidence in Canada's Burgess shale have changed the way scientists think of evolution. Today scientists believe that evolution involved a lot of chance as well as "survival of the fittest," but the question of "how much" each of these factors contributed to the evolutionary process is unresolved. The issue is illustrated by asking whether the dinosaurs were flawed, or just unlucky. During the winter quarter, students are introduced in more depth to Darwinian theory, its logic and adequacy, and to the mechanisms of evolution—cell division, rules of inheritance, genetics, and molecular evolution. During the spring quarter, students are introduced to theories of human origins, to paleoanthropology as a science for exploring the interesting issues of humanity's place in nature, and to the prospects for survival of the human species.

Although the faculty team meets to plan and develop the course periodically, the teaching is conducted by the individual assigned primary responsibility for a particular quarter. In the autumn, Platt does almost all the teaching; in the winter, the second biologist does it; in the spring, Platt and the anthropologist split it, although at the end the two teach some class sessions together, capstoning the year and reviewing, summarizing, and dealing with unanswered questions. Each professor, with help from teaching assistants, handles the grading and evaluation for his quarter, although there are serious team discussions about what learning outcomes are valued and how they are to be evaluated.

Platt insists that the main purpose of the course now is to use evolution as a "topic" for teaching critical thinking. That goal is captured well in the course syllabus:

> We want to change the way you think (i.e., not *what* you think, but *how* you think). We want to help you to understand how scientists think so that you will experience this kind of thinking for yourself. . . . It is not our goal to convert you to science majors, but rather to give you a clear understanding of how science works and—we hope—a life-long interest in keeping track of what scientists are doing in our society.

Only gradually, over the development of several years, did the course come to have such a strong emphasis on thinking skills. Almost by chance, Platt attended an NSF-sponsored Chautauqua course taught by Craig Nelson on how to modify science courses to emphasize critical thinking. As Platt notes, the course was a critical turning point, almost a "religious experience," that encouraged him to find ways to close the gap between how he and his colleagues think—after years of training—and how students think. To help deepen his own thinking about thinking Platt wrote a grant application and received NSF funding of $85,000 over two years to study and develop two core science courses, one of them being "Evolution." The grant, Platt admits, was another "lucky event:" "I wrote the grant and almost forgot about it, then one day the people at NSF called me and said they wanted to fund it." The third lucky event was that Karen Kitchener, a nationally known scholar on reflective judgment and critical thinking, was working, literally, right across the street from Platt's lab.

The course continues to be studied heavily and to evolve, and although Platt is still deeply committed to it, he acknowledges some problems. One problem is student heterogeneity. If thinking is developmental, then students are at different places in their cognitive development. It's not easy to deal with that. Furthermore, the teaching of thinking skills involves new forms of evaluation—putting an end to multiple choice tests, grading a lot of writing assignments, and giving sophisticated feedback. These forms are time consuming and not all TA's are good at them. Finally, Platt's biggest discouragement is the difficulty encountered in changing faculty teaching methods—his own and that of his colleagues. "Not everyone" he notes, "wants to put forth the effort it really takes to break old habits and rethink what you are doing."

Is this a team-taught course? "In some ways yes and some ways no," Platt responds" We work together closely in planning the course but not in delivering it; and because students almost never see us working together, it is unlikely that they would even identify what we do as team teaching."

"Multiple Voices of America"

"Multiple Voices of America" is an interdisciplinary, team-taught course available to freshmen and sophomores as an option for meeting their 12-hour requirement in the humanities in the core curriculum. "Multiple Voices," as the course has come to be known, was the "brain-child" of philosophy professor Jere Surber; Will Gravely and John Livingston later helped to shape it as a new way to approach American studies. The course has operated for three years now within the core curriculum, and has two sections, one coordinated by Annette Stott and one by Gravely. The team is made up of an anthropologist with special interests in Native Americans and the cultural anthropology of the Southwest; Gravely, a member of the Department of Religious Studies with special interests in American religious history and social movements; a member of the Department of English; a professor with a joint appointment in History and Religious Studies with special interests in Ghandi's philosophy of nonviolence; and Stott, an art historian. In addition to this group of regularly appointed faculty, the team includes several teaching assistants who participate both as lecturers and section leaders, and also bring to the course some interesting ethnic diversity.

To plan the course, the team met every two weeks for a year and throughout a summer under the sponsorship of an internal planning grant, and by the fall of 1992, the syllabus and course materials were ready. The course now has two sections, 11 discussion groups, and 221 students, with each faculty member or TA leading a section for class discussion. Often, but not always, the first hour is used for a large communal lecture, film, or demonstration, followed by discussion sections that meet twice a week.

Intellectually, the course operates at two levels, and is aimed at goals usually associated with the liberal arts. At one level, the faculty is interested in providing a context in which students can explore diversity in the American experience, and further appreciate the way in which many different kinds of people—Native Americans, Blacks, Hispanics, Asians, and European immigrants—have contributed to the history and culture of the United States. At another level, the faculty is interested in helping students develop certain basic skills for further study in the humanities: how to look at art and artifacts, how to read a map, and how to read texts, critique films, and write papers with appropriate attention to purpose, voice, and audience.

During the first quarter, the lectures, readings, and discussion explore the land—the people who were already in the land, how and why people came to the land, and how they perceived the land, settled it, and fought over it. During the second quarter, the class explores social and political relations, how some people came to dominate, how some were enslaved, and how various political structures were developed and used for oppression or to gain freedom and cope with diversity. The third quarter is devoted to exploring American identity. Students research their personal "family trees" of ethnic inheritance, and in one of the sections engage in service learning opportunities arranged through the course that allow them to experience an ethnic culture different from their own.

Students write short papers each quarter, some in class and some out, and take a mid-term, and a common final exam for all students prepared by the faculty but administered and graded in the sections by the teacher for that section. The faculty learned the hard way to develop common grading procedures and criteria: In the first year the course was offered, one student and three friends submitted the same paper under four different names to four different faculty, and the "selfsame paper" received an "A," "B," "C," and "D" a "B" and BIG TROUBLE for the original author and friends. Now the faculty collaborate in setting standards and identifying examples of good and poor work.

Will Gravely, one of the founders of the course, is very up-beat about what he believes is a successful venture in team teaching. "It becomes a cumulative effort, doing all this planning and hearing one another lecture. The course is more than the mix; it's something larger than the sum of its parts."

"The Quality Panorama"

"The Quality Panorama" is an interdisciplinary, team-taught course offered to graduate students in business at the University of Denver. One of eight core modules within the newly designed Integrated MBA Program, it was offered for the first time during the 1993-94 academic year. The course is part of a totally reconceived MBA, which resulted from three years of discussion among business faculty and employers about how to educate graduate students in business in light of mounting public criticism nationally. The new MBA is part of a larger planning effort led by (then) Dean Bruce Hutton to break out of departmental structures and address issues that colleges of business, generally, have been reluctant to address. "We knew," says Hutton, "that we needed to make some changes. Employers are still looking for people who have firm skills, who are able to balance the books and close sales, but they also are looking for critical thinkers who can look at marketing and finance issues and know how they relate."

After many months of study the faculty voted to institute the "Integrated MBA." A planning committee agreed that the cornerstone of the program would be eight modules of interdisciplinary team-taught courses. The committee outlined in some detail what these courses would contain, and also established a process initiating planning for these courses. After some consultation and negotiation, the Dean appointed eight seasoned faculty to head the teams—good teachers with successful records and high respect from colleagues. The faculty were then invited to express interest in working on the team for a particular course, and after a period of negotiation, the teams were assembled. The detailed planning was begun in earnest over the summer of 1993 and was supported by special funding, part of a larger development effort supported by a private donor.

The planning phase involved two tiers, a group of faculty and outside consultants who designed the course, and, eventually, a smaller implementation group of faculty who would actually teach the course. Planning also involved two steps, getting the course sufficiently elaborated to have it approved by the central planning committee that provided oversight for all eight modules, and fleshing out the details for implementation. The planning team was led by James Sorensen and the implementation team is now composed of Sorensen, who is a professor of accountancy, and a professor of marketing, a professor of statistics and operations research, a professor from management, a management information systems specialist and computer expert, and a new professor from the communications company, U.S. West.

"In planning the course," Sorensen notes, "we didn't begin with academic disciplines; we began with the concept of quality and the topics, and then asked who could contribute what. For example, one day we were thinking about Mitsubishi's idea of customer focus—how to get the customer involved up front in developing products and services. So we asked, who knows something about customer focus? What about the people in marketing; they know about these things." The same was true when the team began thinking about quality driven processes. Sometimes processes are driven by the information people get within the company, rather than by what would contribute to a better product. "We decided," Sorensen says, "that we needed to let students know that sometimes accounting information can cause people to behave in crazy ways. And it was my job, as the accountant on the team, to illustrate this."

The course opens with real life examples of consumer choices, a class period devoted to choosing, tasting, and making quality decisions about "real" ice cream served to the students. Students are introduced to the history and basic principles of the TQM movement and the reasons why it developed. The "Six-

Circles Model" is presented and an objective assessment of TQM is developed, emphasizing failures as well as successes. Most of the course is focused on presenting various components of the TQM model: stressing the importance of having a systems perspective, providing mechanisms for focusing on the customer, exploring methods for establishing quality-driven processes, providing techniques for establishing and measuring ongoing improvement, using the right kind of management and leadership, and providing incentives for engaging and increasing the commitment of employees. The second quarter of the course, "Putting Quality to Work," delves into illustrations of applications of TQM in various organizational settings. Here the focus is on long-term changes that need to be made to affect organizational culture and bring about lasting change.

Although much of the information about TQM is presented through traditional lecture by the various team members, the students are heavily involved in reading and writing about cases. The class is divided into teams of students who work on three different cases during the quarter. For each case, the teams are assigned to writing (2 cases) or oral presentation (1 case), so that students have an opportunity for different modes of response to the cases. Their writing and presentations are judged according to criteria for evaluating cases established and approved by the central planning committee for all eight modules. One of the cases grows out of an application for the Demming Award generated by the Samsonite Corporation; the discussion of that case is coordinated with a field visit to Samsonite, which provides students an opportunity to visit with employees and view production operations.

Is "The Quality Panorama" a team-taught course? "Let's put it this way," notes Sorensen, "nobody on the team could teach the course alone. It takes the team. One person in a classroom can generate maybe 50 watts of light; five or six team members working together make a 1,000 watt spotlight."

"The Lawyering Process"

"The Lawyering Process" is an interdisciplinary team-taught course required of all (day and evening division) first-year law students at the University of Denver. Most law schools are notorious, at least by reputation among students, for their "difficult" first year. In addition to offering substantive courses on law—usually courses on torts, contracts, and civil procedure—most law schools face the difficult challenge of helping students build certain specialized skills—for example, researching cases and legal writing—and introducing students to the legal profession in general. These things are most commonly done through separate courses, and the skills course, usually a legal writing course, often has a "bad reputation," both for being hard and boring. Furthermore, students often plunge directly into the academic study of law without much opportunity for socialization into the profession. "The Lawyering Process" course is an interdisciplinary effort to address these needs in one course: to introduce law as a field of study, to help students gain a sense of what lawyers do, and to build the essential skills needed to practice.

The course had its roots at the law school of Gonzaga University in Spokane, Washington; when Professor Jeff Hartje joined the faculty at the University of Denver some years ago, he persuaded the faculty to consider "his version" of this earlier idea for a team-taught, first-year course. Although Professor Hartje is no longer associated with the course, having moved on to other interests, the course continues, now in its third year, and has been thoroughly redesigned during the past year by the faculty team responsible for planning and delivering the course. The "genius" of the course is in its structure: students are divided into 16 simulated law firms of approximately 20 students each, and the firms are paired—plaintiff and defendant—to work on opposite sides of the same problem, a detailed, carefully written case (a total of 8 different cases for 16 firms), that unfolds throughout the course. Each firm is headed by a "senior partner," a practicing attorney from the community; a junior partner, a carefully selected upper division student (who functions somewhat like a teaching assistant); an adjunct writing consultant, one for each pair of firms; a consulting librarian from the library staff for each of four firms; and a client. The team of faculty responsible for planning and delivering the course is coordinated now by John Reese, an experienced senior professor with interests in constitutional and administrative law. The team is made up of Reese plus a librarian of the law library who lectures on and develops exercises involving legal research, a legal writing specialist who creates the ideas for and writes the problems used throughout the course by the paired law firms, a specialist in alternative dispute resolution and client relations who organizes the selection and training process for the junior partners and supervises their work with the firms, and a full-time administrative assistant assigned exclusively and permanently to the course to provide organizational, logistic, and communications support.

Because the students are divided into 16 simulated law firms of approximately 20 students each, the total number of people working together as "the team" for this course is 57, distributed as follows:

$$
\begin{array}{rl}
4 & \text{core faculty} \\
16 & \text{senior partners} \\
16 & \text{junior partners} \\
8 & \text{writing consultants} \\
4 & \text{law librarian consultants} \\
1 & \text{administrative assistant} \\
\underline{8} & \underline{\text{clients}} \\
57 & \text{Total team members}
\end{array}
$$

During the past two years, I served as a "consultant" from the Center for Academic Quality to help the core faculty reexamine the entire course, including overall purposes, goals, and objectives; selection and ordering of topics, readings, and materials; and development of assignments and evaluation methods. The reexamination began with a "focus group" of students who had just completed the course; their recent experience provided insights about what was strong and what was weak about the course.

The content of the course, that is, the academic substance, is delivered through lectures and demonstrations presented to the first-year class (separate but identical lectures for day and evening students) and through regular meetings of the simulated law firms, in a two-semester, two-credit-hour block. Conceptually, the course is designed to introduce students to the three primary sources of law as a field of study: case law (sometimes referred to as common law), legislation, and administrative law. The course opens, therefore, with a series of lectures on jurisprudential perspectives. These lectures are followed with more skill-oriented lecture-demonstrations on legal research, issues of authority, case reports, finding cases, citation methods, and blue-booking, as well as legal writing style. During the first week of the course, students are given their first research assignment as well as a diagnostic pre-test on legal writing. The course proceeds with additional lectures on case law, as students and faculty begin to meet for the first time to get acquainted (with each other and with their problem cases) in their simulated firms. After a lecture on client-based law practice, the firms begin to work on their first "real life" task—interviewing the client for their particular case. The course continues with lectures on law as legislation, statutory interpretation, statutory research, legislative history, and legislative intent. As the case unfolds in the law firm, students are given the opportunity to develop skills in client counseling and decision making and are introduced to alternatives to the litigation process—negotiation and other dispute resolution techniques. By this time, students are becoming involved in some fairly difficult research and writing assignments—a fact memo, a case synthesis, an employment letter, a counseling plan, a closed memo, an opinion letter, and a negotiation plan. All of these items are hammered out with assistance from consultants and from junior and senior partners, and through a reflection process in the firm, where students are given opportunities to practice specific written and oral communication skills in the context of their case. The assignments are graded in various ways and with varying weight; feedback, with occasional opportunities for rewriting, is provided by the writing consultants. The first semester ends with lectures on administrative law, the preparation of an administrative law counseling plan, and assignments for the second semester.

During the second semester, the firm focuses on the decision to litigate, and students are guided through the process of preparing for trial. Although the case never goes to trial—litigation is a separate, upper division course—students learn about preparation for litigation, including fact-finding, drafting discovery requests, taking depositions, and filing pleadings and motions. Even though the case is not tried, the outcomes of a hypothetical trial are unfolded through the problem case and students are taught how to file appeals. The course ends with students writing appellate briefs and practicing oral appellate arguments within their firms.

Is this team a team? "Well, we've had our struggles," notes Reese. "But if this isn't team teaching, I don't know what is."

APPLYING THE CRITERIA

Earlier I suggested that interdisciplinary courses and team teaching might be examined with regard to where they fall on a "continuum of collaboration." It may, indeed, be possible to locate such a course on this continuum in making an overall judgment about it. When the courses are examined more closely, however, to determine the degree of collaboration in specific areas—planning, content integration, teaching, and evaluation—it turns out that there is not just one continuum of collaboration, but four.

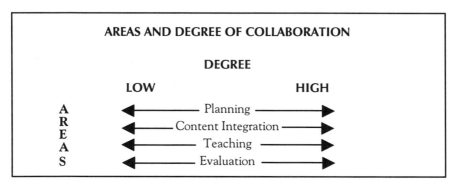

Thus, in the diagram above, an "x" might be placed on each of the continua in different places, depending on the degree of collaboration in that area. The degree of collaboration may vary within a course in these four areas; a course may, for example, have a high degree of collaboration in planning, but a low degree of collaboration in teaching; a high degree of collaboration in content integration, but a low degree of collaboration in evaluation.

In the area of planning, in the examples elaborated above, "Quality Panorama" and "Multiple Voices" have a high degree of collaboration because they are in their earlier stages of development and have formal structures created for planning. The team works closely in planning "Evolution," but not in delivering it. The large team for "Making of the Modern Mind" operates fairly loosely because the course is old and well-established, and planning at this point has more to do with implementation than with substance. Because it is complicated and involves many people, "The Lawyering Process," requires high levels of collaboration not only in planning the substance of the course but also for delivery of the course.

With regard to content integration, the faculty of "Multiple Voices" are collaborating closely to create an entirely new way of teaching American history and few remnants of traditional disciplines remain. The same is true of "Quality Panorama," where the focus is on TQM, not accounting, marketing, and management. In "The Making of the Modern Mind," the disciplinary structure is consciously preserved, but enriched through the themes of the lectures. The concept of "professional practice" becomes the unifying theme for "The Lawyering Process" and the case problems are used to achieve integration. On the other hand, "Evolution" has minimal content integration except to make sure that topics are presented in a logical serial order.

With regard to teaching, instruction is delivered in rather different ways in each of the courses. In "Evolution," the teaching is serial with some integration at the end. In "Making of the Modern Mind" and in "Multiple Voices," sections become important and the faculty all participate in a large lecture experience, being aware of each other's contributions. "Multiple Voices" has some collaborative lectures. "The Quality Panorama" doesn't have sections and the faculty participate in some class sessions together, sometimes commenting on each other's lectures. The faculty in "The Lawyering Process" attend each other's lectures some of the time, but the law firms operate semi-autonomously under the direction of the senior partner.

Collaboration levels also vary with the task of evaluation. In "Making of the Modern Mind," section leaders develop some of their "own questions" and grade their own exams. In "Multiple Voices," section leaders administer and read their own exams and papers, but collaborate in designing questions and setting criteria for good and poor answers. In "Quality Panorama," student responses to cases (oral and written) are evaluated according to criteria and processes established by a central coordinating committee for the Integrated MBA. The core faculty determines evaluation procedures for "The Lawyering Process," but assignments (written and oral) are evaluated within the firm by writing consultants and junior partners.

One can conclude, just from these few examples, that there are many ways to build interdisciplinary courses and to engage in team teaching. There is not one continuum of collaboration; there are many. There is not "one way to do it."

Thus, defining team teaching is not as simple as it appears at first. Devising a definition certainly requires looking beyond appearances (conveyed in catalogue descriptions and course syllabi) to examine the behaviors of the team members more closely. If the examples provided above are typical, or at least illustrative, there may be not one definition of team teaching, but many; not one kind of collaboration, but several. Indeed, there may be many ways for faculty to work together to achieve the enriching outcomes associated with interdisciplinary courses and team teaching. What are these outcomes? Why do faculty colleagues go to all this trouble to generate interdisciplinary courses? What is the rationale for team teaching? We will address these questions in the next chapter.

NOTES

1. Carnegie Foundation for the Advancement of Teaching, *Missions of the College Curriculum* (San Francisco: Jossey-Bass, 1978), p. 100.
2. Julie Thompson Klein, *Interdisciplinarity: History, Theory, and Practice* (Detroit: Wayne State University Press, 1990). The discussion of the terms here is based on Chapter 3 "An Interdisciplinarity Lexicon," p. 55ff. The brief historical treatment at the end of this section is drawn also from Klein, Chapter 1, "The Evolution of Interdisciplinary," pp. 19–39. For those who are seeking a more detailed historical and philosophical treatment of the concept of "interdisciplinarity," Klein's work is highly recommended. See also Carl R. Hausman, "Introduction: Disciplinarity or Interdisciplinarity?" and Joseph J. Kockelmans, "Why Interdisciplinarity?" in Joseph J. Kockelmans, *Interdisciplinarity and Higher Education* (University Park, PA: The Pennsylvania State University Press, 1979), p. 10, where these terms are also defined, although sometimes in different ways. See also William Newell and William Green, "Defining and Teaching Interdisciplinarity Studies," *Improving College and University Teaching* 30:1 (winter 1982): pp. 23–30.
3. Julie Thompson Klein, "An Interdisciplinary Lexicon," *Interdisciplinarity*, p. 63.
4. For a fuller discussion of "interpenetration" see Steve Fuller, "The Position: Interdisciplinarity as Interpenetration" in *Philosophy, Rhetoria, and the End of Knowledge* (Madison: University of Wisconsin Press, 1993), pp. 33–65.
5. Paul Haas, Barbara Hursh, and Michael Moore, "An Interdisciplinary Model to Implement General Education," *Journal of Higher Education*, 54 (1983): 42–49. The illustration and quoted passages are on p. 47.
6. Julie Thompson Klein, "The Evolution of Interdisciplinarity," in *Interdisciplinarity*, pp. 19–39.

CHAPTER 2

The Rationale for Interdisciplinary Courses: The Problem of Specialization

"The solution which I am urging is to eradicte the fatal disconnection of subjects which kills the vitality of our modern curriculum."
—Alfred North Whitehead

How is it that knowledge came to be organized into academic disciplines and professional fields? If interdisciplinary courses are in some sense a reaction to the disciplinary structure, where did the disciplines come from and how did they become such a stronghold in academia? Certainly there must be other ways of organizing knowledge for presentation in classes and cumulatively as a curriculum. Why disciplines?

ORGANIZING ALL THE KNOWLEDGE OF THE WORLD

What if one were given the task of organizing all the knowledge of the world? How might one go about it? If it were possible to collect the accumulated knowledge of the world and lay it out on a table—this might, indeed, be possible today with CD-ROMs and microfiche—how might one approach the task of organizing it? What principles would be used? What categories would evolve?

This is not just a hypothetical task. Some people spend a major portion of their professional lives struggling with this problem. Librarians, for example, have developed systems for organizing the knowledge of the world, so that people can locate the information they want. The earlier Dewey decimal system, based on 10 categories has gradually given way to the more comprehensive Library of Congress classification system, with its complex system of descriptors. When scholars go to a library to locate a book, they can be sure that the book they are looking for will be located among books on a similar subject; and it is possible to "browse" through the related books, either physically by going to the shelf and looking at the books that are classified together, or electronically (in most modern libraries) by examining the titles that appear directly before or directly after a particular source. A similar problem exists for people who organize periodical literature for databases. What they have done is to evolve a system of descriptors for computer access.

People who write encyclopedias are also concerned about organizing all the knowledge of the world. Although the topics in an encyclopedia are usually arranged alphabetically, some prior decision has been made about which topics to write about and to include. How many articles are to be written, and how is the knowledge in one article related to that in another in such a way as to avoid gaps and overlaps? When the most recent edition of the *Encyclopedia Britannica* was being developed, the editors produced a scheme—an outline— for organizing all the knowledge of the world, which they named *The Propaedia*. It employed 10 parts and numerous divisions that eventually provided the organizational framework for including the essential knowledge for an encyclopedia. Both of these systems for organizing knowledge, the classification and database systems used by librarians and the organizational schemes of encyclopedists, are essentially access systems; they are designed to help us find knowledge that already exists.

ORGANIZING KNOWLEDGE FOR RESEARCH

In the academic world, knowledge is also organized for research and instruction. What is the best way to organize knowledge in order to generate more of it? That is an interesting question, and the answers to it have changed over the centuries. In the modern era, roughly since the last quarter of the nineteenth century, knowledge has been organized for research according to various disciplines and professional fields of study; and indeed, judging by both the quantity and quality of what was produced, the output of this system has been impressive. How these disciplines emerged is described below. First, however, it is important to get a better grasp of what a discipline is, that is, how it is thought about today.

Academics use the word "discipline" in a specialized way, but they are not the sole proprietors of the word. Parents and teachers use it to describe what they do to children—alas, some would say, not frequently enough—and clerics use it in describing the foundations of religious orders. Thus one may be the member of an order, a discipline, and under a discipline, that is following the rule of that discipline. Discipline, then, implies both a domain to be investigated and the methods used in that domain.[1]

In what is perhaps the most extensive effort to conceptualize and elaborate the nature of the academic disciplines, Arthur King and John Brownell have outlined 10 characteristics of a discipline. Their descriptions are quoted and paraphrased as follows:

- A *discipline is a community of persons.* It is a "corps of human beings with a common intellectual commitment . . . a community of individuals whose ultimate task is the gaining of meaning."
- A *discipline is an expression of human imagination.* It is an activity of the imagination involving the creation of "novel mental images in a variety of forms: ideas, sentences, concepts, sequences, harmonics, rhythms, figures, among others."
- A *discipline is a domain.* It is a bounded realm in the "larger territory known as the intellectual life . . . on which the members of the disciplines focus their attention."
- A *discipline is a tradition.* It has a history with "intellectual heroes" and is "built on the discourse of its forebears."
- A *discipline is a syntactical structure.* It has not only a content, but a way of gathering and evaluating data and the evidence to support its assertions.
- A *discipline is a conceptual structure.* It employs a system of fundamental ideas, principles, and propositions and organizes them into meaningful categories.
- A *discipline is a specialized language or other system of symbols.* It uses "an intellectual shorthand" of technical terms (jargon) and symbols, and it invents new terminology as needed.
- A *discipline is a heritage of literature and a communication network.* The members of a discipline produce a heritage of "writings, paintings, compositions, musical scores, artifacts, recorded interviews and other symbolic expressions" which become available in "libraries, galleries, lecture halls, theaters, museums, and studios." Scholars stay in touch through books, professional meetings, scholarly journals, and a network of informal communications.
- A *discipline is a valuative and affective stance.* It involves prior assumptions about reality and human nature and includes intellectual passions and commitments.

- A *discipline is an instructive community*. It provides the underlying principles that structure a subject for instruction.[2]

By using these criteria, it is possible to identify in academia today separate
and distinct disciplines. Although there will always be some overlap, some
fuzziness in the boundaries, and some change over time, the disciplines have
provided the key mechanism for structuring knowledge for research.

Although some recent evidence suggests that interdisciplinary efforts are
now being employed more widely in the discovery of new knowledge,[3] thanks
in part to the encouragement of collaboration by funding sources, the disciplines have been and continue to be the primary way to organize knowledge
for research. As Phillip Phenix notes:

> The most impressive claim the disciplines have upon education is that they
> are the outcome of learning that has actually been successful. A discipline is
> a field of inquiry in which learning has been achieved in an unusually
> productive way. Most human efforts at understanding fail. A very few
> succeed, and these fruitful ways of thought are conserved and developed in
> the disciplines. Every discipline is simply a pattern of investigation that has
> proved to be a fertile field for the growth of understanding.[4]

Whatever criticisms might be made of the disciplines, it is important to
acknowledge at the outset that the disciplines and professional fields of study
have been enormously successful in generating new knowledge.

ORGANIZING KNOWLEDGE FOR INSTRUCTION

In the academic world, scholars are also faced with the problem of organizing
knowledge for the purposes of instruction. Once knowledge has been generated, what is the best way of transmitting it? Consider the following as the
"root question" of all curriculum planning: Of all of the things that could be
taught, which things should be taught and how might they best be organized?
The question has been answered in many ways, of course, but the following has
been the dominant response in the twentieth century: Through the academic
disciplines and professional fields of study. The primary vehicle for organizing
knowledge through the disciplines has been the academic major or professional concentration.

There are alternatives to academic disciplines, and in recent years modest
experimentation with these alternatives has taken place at certain institutions
interested in innovation. Most notable is the effort to develop competency-
based curricula, the operationalizing of specific skills and abilities necessary for
the performance of professional tasks. Competency-based education has been
employed to some extent in the health sciences, particularly nursing, and in
education. Some small colleges have successfully employed a competency-
based curriculum in liberal arts education (Alverno College in Wisconsin,

Sterling College in Kansas, Mars Hill College in North Carolina, and others). The "Great Books Curriculum" is another alternative to the disciplinary format. St. John's College, with campuses in Annapolis, Maryland, and Santa Fe, New Mexico, organizes instruction around small seminars in which students systematically explore the accumulated wisdom of the past by reading and discussing the "great books." Other colleges take the position that the organizing principle for instruction resides within the student. Examples of a "student-centered" curriculum can be found in Antioch University in Ohio, Sarah Lawrence College in New York, and The Evergreen State College in Washington. The "curriculum" at such institutions contains stimulating and "developmentally relevant" courses from which students may choose those that best fit their needs for intellectual and emotional development. One might add to this list of alternatives a problem-centered curriculum, designed to foster the exploration of contemporary social problems.[5] The University of California at Santa Cruz provides an example of this alternative in some of its theme colleges, as does the College of the Atlantic in Maine with its emphasis on human ecology.

What is most striking about these alternatives is that they have received so little attention. They have remained, for the most part, on the periphery of higher education, surviving as unique "experiments" that give particular institutions, usually smaller colleges, a distinctive identity and a way to express a unique mission. Why are these alternatives so little known and so little used, and why are they perceived by some as "suspect" with regard to quality? How did the disciplinary structure come to be the dominating organizational principle for both the discovery and the transmission of knowledge?

THE ORIGINS OF THE DISCIPLINARY STRUCTURE

The idea of breaking knowledge into subjects has its origin in Greek and Roman antiquity. Even the word "discipline" has roots in a Latin phrase, *disciplinae liberae*, "the liberal disciplines," which parallels in meaning the Greek phrase *enkuklios paideia*. The Roman scholar Varro, writing between 50 and 25 B.C. used *disciplinae liberae* to refer to the trivium (grammar, rhetoric, and dialectic) and quadrivium (arithmetic, music, geometry, and astronomy)[6]. As Ernest Boyer and Martin Kaplan note in their brief historical sketch of the origins of the postsecondary curriculum, these seven subjects descended from antiquity, via the Middle Ages, Renaissance, and Reformation, through the English universities, Oxford and Cambridge, to Harvard College in the seventeenth century. When these subjects were studied in the early days of Harvard, they were regarded as a "fixed and known body of knowledge" and as "absolute and immutable truth" to be "absorbed—not criticized or questioned—by every student."[7]

The Harvard curriculum of the seven liberal arts, however, was nothing like the curriculum of subject specialties that emerged in the late nineteenth and early twentieth centuries, or the disciplines and professional fields as we know them today. To the contrary, the Harvard curriculum was characterized by its unity rather than by specialization, and this traditional unified curriculum of the liberal arts remained solid for centuries. Strong forces held the curriculum in place. As Boyer and Kaplan note, it was "the intellectual mirror of the divine mind. It was eternal, not subject to revision, and education diligently pursued would lead students to the knowledge of God that was its highest aim."[8]

There were some early efforts to open up the curriculum to more subjects. Benjamin Franklin, as early as 1749, recognized the need for "a parallel, utilitarian track that students might choose instead of the Greco-Latin course."[9] As Boyer and Kaplan point out, well before the federal legislation of 1862 establishing the land grant colleges, Francis Wayland, the president of Brown University, had suggested that "traditional curriculum be expanded to prepare men to be the farmers and mechanics and great production managers for the future."[10] Intellectual support for the traditional curriculum, however, held firm in the often-quoted *Report on the Course of Instruction in Yale College* of 1828, even as new subjects were in fact being added at Yale and elsewhere.

Charles William Eliot, president of Harvard from 1869-1909, "sounded the death knell of the mandatory classical curriculum" by introducing over his long presidency what came to be known as "the elective system."[11] In a famous speech on the elective principle, Eliot remarked:

> When a young man whom I never saw before asks me what studies he had better take in college, I am quite helpless, until he tells me what he likes and what he dislikes to study, what kinds of exertion are pleasurable to him, what sports he cares for, what reading interests him, what his parents and grandparents were in the world, and what he means to be. In short, I can only show him how to think out the problem for himself with such lights as he has and nobody else can have.[12]

As students at Harvard during Eliot's administration gained the freedom to choose the subjects in their course of study, the school introduced more subjects. The elective principle gave rise to new courses and under Eliot's successor, Abbot Lawrence Lowell, these courses came to be configured in a concentration called "the major."[13] Meanwhile, disciplines, departments, and professional associations began to emerge.

The best recent description of the evolution of the disciplines and emergence of professional fields is found in Burton Clark's *The Academic Life: Small Worlds, Different Worlds*.[14] As Clark notes, the disciplines had their roots in the pre-Civil War period and some were beginning to develop well before the coming of universities based on the German model. The development of new subjects and separate disciplines came first in the sciences. Chemistry appeared as a distinct field by 1820, and was soon followed by astronomy, physics, and biology, although the number of professors and scholarly books in these fields was at first quite small.[15] In a process that Clark refers to as "parturition" (childbirth), better established fields gave birth to new ones. At mid-century, biology brought forth genetics and microbiology and produced two cross-disciplinary fields—biochemistry and biophysics.[16] Moral philosophy produced political economy and then political science. Political economy, renamed economics, produced sociology.[17] These fledgling disciplines were nourished and supported by three parallel developments—the emergence of graduate programs, scholarly associations, and departmental structures.

As Clark notes, "the universities that took hold in just four decades after 1870 became dominant over the small colleges that had held the stage for over two centuries."[18] One way they did this was through the development of another tier of study built upon the baccalaureate. The awarding of graduate degrees expanded from fewer than 50 students in 1870 to nearly 6,000 by the turn of the century.[19] "This separate sphere for advanced degrees—the master's, the doctorate, the special degrees of the professional schools—gave the American structure a strong vertical thrust in the systematic preparation of disciplinary specialists and professional experts."[20] The universities now prepared the specialists who became the college teachers. What took place was a "gradual shift in all leading and ambitious institutions from teaching to research. Where teaching once had been the only task that counted, it became an activity whose rewards could be made subsidiary to research."[21]

To support this new emphasis on research and growing interest in disciplinary specialization, numerous disciplinary associations were founded. Although some of these associations have roots that go back before 1800—e.g., the American Philosophical Society, the American Academy of Arts and Sciences—the "takeoff occurred during the last two decades of the nineteenth century, when more than 25 associations formed along disciplinary lines."[22] The growth continued steadily through the twentieth century and "provided yet another powerful condition and force for the ascendance of the disciplinary point of view."[23]

Disciplinary specialization was also strengthened by the development of a departmental system of organization within the colleges and universities. Although the concept of "departments," or something very like it, goes back to the University of Paris in 1213, and although Harvard reorganized into six "departments" in 1825, the real development of departmental structure in the modern sense came in the 1890s under the leadership of Harvard, Yale, Columbia, Princeton, and the University of Chicago, the latter organizing into 26 departments and 3 faculties.[24]

As Clark notes, the development of associations and departments provided strong support for the disciplines. "One macro and external, and other micro and internal, the association and the department became powerful organizational instruments. One pulled together a discipline across all local boundaries; the other served to support small clusters of disciplinarians at the operating levels of institutions."[25]

A similar pattern of development took place for the professions. Three professions had ties to the medieval universities: divinity, law, and medicine. Thus it is possible to speak of "old professions" and "new professions" and to distinguish those with ancient roots from modern arrivals.[26] But in the United States, even the old professions were slow to find their niche in the colleges and universities, and apprenticeship systems—even in divinity, law, and medicine—preceded the development of professional schools. Under the apprenticeship system, a professional candidate worked under an "able and mature minister, lawyer, or doctor and hoped by observation and imitation to be admitted subsequently to professional status."[27] The apprenticeship involved a theoretical as well as practical side, and aspiring clergy chose a minister who also had a good library, and law candidates clerked in a good law office so that they could also read law.[28] Gradually, some professionals began to mentor several candidates at once. For Judge Tapping Reene of Litchfield, Connecticut, "the teaching of apprentices in his office came to predominate over the carrying on of law practice," and eventually the first law school came into being, although it is hard to date the event exactly.[29]

These schools were proprietary schools, as yet unattached to universities, and they supplemented, but did not supplant, apprenticeship training.[30] The professions as we know them today emerged in the United States in the 1880s and 1890s, about the same time as the development and expansion of the disciplines. During this same period, some of the proprietary schools attached themselves to the universities and some of the universities began new professional schools.[31] Under Eliot (again) at Harvard, a lasting innovation was begun: candidates for professional training were required first to complete a bachelor's degree.[32] A rush to affiliate soon followed; any self-respecting profession needed a legitimate academic curriculum and ties with a university. In a process that Clark calls "dignification," the universities opened their doors to, and thus legitimized, a host of new fields of instruction—some professional, some vocational—including the fine arts, music, home economics, education, business, physical education, and military science.[33]

The important thing that happened, both in the development of the professions and of the disciplines, is specialization. The unified curriculum of the "liberal disciplines" of the colonial college became the fragmented curriculum of the specialized subjects of the disciplines and professions. Specialization did not end with the discipline; it continued into sub-disciplines and highly specialized areas of scholarly inquiry. Thus, the modern university, as Clark points out, offers not only biology, but its many subfields; UCLA, for example, has separate departments and doctoral programs in biology, microbiology, immunology, biomathematics, biochemistry, and molecular biology. History, at many large universities, has specialists in European and American history, as well as ancient history, Japanese history, history of science, history of religions, the American West, etc. The professional schools also foster this "permutation of subjects"; education schools will have specialists in "early childhood education," "special education," and "school administration."[34]

One counter movement to the trend of specialization has been the effort to establish programs for "general education," the required portion of the bacca-laureate designed to achieve the goals of liberal education. General education has usually been delivered in one of two ways: through a distribution system, requiring students to take a specified number of courses in various divisions of the curriculum, a concept dating back to Lowell at Harvard, or through a core curriculum of courses especially designed to achieve the purposes of general education. Although such courses were not necessarily team taught, some were, and many were interdisciplinary in nature. However, with the exception of these general education courses and a few integrated courses in professional fields, most courses in the major and in the catalog of electives are today taught in the traditional manner as disciplinary or professional specializations. The norms have been quite clear, certainly for the last half of the twentieth century: "true scholars" are specialists.

THE HISTORICAL ROOTS AND CONTEMPORARY PRACTICE OF TRADITIONAL TEACHING

What are the implications of this historical development of the disciplines and professions for teaching? How do specialists teach?

In the earliest days of the colonial college, teaching was tutoring; teachers were able to tutor in the subjects of the liberal arts that they themselves had mastered. The ministers of Harvard's board of overseers appointed a cleric as president, who assembled the tutors, usually young inexperienced clergy waiting for a pulpit. As Clark notes, "there were no dominating masters, no chaired professors, no pretenses to a self-defining professorate. With the trustees, the elders of the church and state, fully able to decide what would be taught and who would teach it—and how much the tutors would be paid and how they would live—the instructional staff were hired hands."[35]

What these early tutors did in the classroom was to conduct recitations and monitor disputations. Recitation was "a process in which students repeated from memory, often verbatim, textbook assignments. For disputation, stu-dents defended or attacked a proposition in Latin, the required language both in and out of class."[36] In the recitation, the students proved that the lesson had been learned, while concealing what had not been learned sometimes became a game of wits. Despite the strong emphasis on rote memory, recitation sometimes involved a true inquiry, even some Socratic dialogue, about the content and meaning of the text.[37]

Through reading, recitation, and disputation, the students worked their way through the whole four-year curriculum as one class. "Everybody took the same subjects at the same time of the day in the same room under the same tutor."[38] The tutor took the class through the whole curriculum of a given year, and some tutors took a class through all four years.[39] Even as professors became masters of a specific subject, they continued to teach several subjects. "It would not be at all unusual, for instance, to find the same man teaching mathematics, natural philosophy, astronomy and geography."[40]

As the German university began to exercise its influence on American colleges, and as new, more specialized subjects began to enter the curriculum, the recitation and disputation, the predominant forms of instruction in the seventeenth and eighteenth centuries, gave way to the lecture. As Brubacher and Rudy note, "lecturing had an ancient lineage extending back at least to the medieval university. It was customary then to lecture, on account of the scarcity of books. Indeed, as the etymology of the word should suggest, a lecture was a reading."[41] ("Lecture" derived from the Latin, *lectura*, meaning reading.)   The earlier lectures were delivered slowly enough for students to copy them down verbatim. Although the medieval tradition of lecturing in moral philosophy, metaphysics, and logic had continued sporadically in the American colleges, the emerging sciences gave the lecture new life as an instructional method. Lectures in the sciences were supplemented with experimental demonstrations employing ingenious devices to illustrate scientific principles.[42] The most important source of invigoration for the lecture method, however, came from the German universities during the second quarter of the nineteenth century and into the twentieth. As Brubacher and Rudy note:

> Pre-eminent in scholarship, the German professors were lecturing to their students as the means par excellence for informing them of the latest research, for helping them organize wide ranges of information, for giving them an overview of the domains yet to be conquered, and finally for electrifying them with the professors' enthusiasm for their specialties.[43]

By the early twentieth century, the norms had been established for discipline-based courses and traditional teaching, patterns that have dominated instruction throughout most of the rest of the century.

What is "traditional teaching" and how widespread is it today? Although numerous exceptions and some innovative, nontraditional examples of instruction exist in many diverse institutions today, there is still an easily identified and frequently practiced approach to classroom instruction that might be called "traditional teaching."

Once the disciplines and professions emerged and specialization came to dominate, a pattern developed where professors would lecture on *their* subjects in *their* classrooms, as disciplinary specialists. With traditional teaching, whatever integration takes place across separate and discrete subjects is achieved by students, usually on their own, if at all. Professors lecture on what they know, and, if possible, only on the special area that they know best. The classroom is the professor's castle, buttressed to some extent by the rhetoric of academic freedom, and encircled by the wide moat of specialization. No dean or department chair, or colleague for that matter, need enter, because no one will be qualified to judge what takes place there except other experts in the same specialization. As for teaching methods, these are hardly a matter for discussion, because it is presumed at the postsecondary level that expertise in one's specialty is the only prerequisite for effective teaching.

Individual faculty members are clearly in charge of their classrooms and have the power to determine what takes place there. The extent of this power, and the reasons for it, are summarized well by Burton Clark in these words:

> What changed within the local hierarchies to give influence to faculty was their gathering control of knowledge brought about by research-driven specialization. Once the research ethic was in the driver's seat, there could no longer be a common curriculum taught by men of general learning whose responsibility in the first instance would be the moral character of the young. When the universities sought the rewards of research, they also moved toward a modern profession of academics in which self-government would be strengthened. They created settings in which professors would acquire primacy in determining the precise nature of their own work—what they would teach and what they would research—and would have more than a passing influence, subject by subject and classroom by classroom, in determining who they served. The academic guild came late to American higher education, but come it did, and on the back of fragmenting bundles of knowledge that allowed "teachers" to become "professors" by acquiring the authority of arcane knowledge.[44]

The traditional classroom is today so familiar, so much a given, that it is difficult even to gain perspective on its characteristics. But seen in contrast to classrooms where interdisciplinary courses are offered and team teaching is practiced (or other types of innovations are introduced), traditional classrooms are settings where individual teachers:

- determine what subjects they are competent and willing to teach.
- select the subject matter to be included in a course, based on some mix of what they once studied, what the best textbooks contain, and what the disciplinary or professional association recommends.

- organize the course syllabus according to units and classes based on their own best judgment.
- determine the best means of evaluating learning, usually some combination of "objective" tests, term papers, and (maybe) class participation.
- lecture to large groups of students sitting quietly in rows and using tablet arm chairs to take notes on what is being said.
- use little or no supporting media, such as slides, video, overheads, or projected computer images, but rely on the availability of a chalkboard to write (usually illegibly) names, dates, and technical terms spontaneously as they may occur to the lecturer.
- employ course evaluations usually at the end of the course, partly to get student feedback about how to improve the course the next time it is offered, but more frequently to support (if the evaluations are good) the acquisition of promotion, tenure, and annual merit increases at institutions where the quality of teaching is valued in such decisions.

If the above description seems harsh and to border on caricature, one need only ask: Have you seen it and how frequently?

How wide-spread is "traditional teaching?" In *College: The Undergraduate Experience*, a comprehensive report written on behalf of the Carnegie Foundation for the Advancement of Teaching, Ernest Boyer notes, with a tone of discouragement, that traditional teaching was encountered frequently and almost exclusively during site visits of the 29 colleges and universities in the study:

> Today the lecture method is preferred by most instructors. With few exceptions, when we visited classes, the teacher stood in front of rows of chairs and talked most of the forty-five or fifty minutes. Information was presented that often students passively received. There was little opportunity for positions to be clarified or ideas challenged . . . When discussion did occur in classes we visited, a handful of students, usually men, dominated the exchange.[45]

Boyer opens chapter nine of *College*, entitled "Creativity in the Classroom," with this description:

> At a freshman psychology lecture we attended, 300 students were still finding seats when the professor started talking. "Today," he said into the microphone, "we still continue our discussion of learning." He might as well have been addressing a crowd in a Greyhound bus terminal.[46]

But what is wrong, one might ask, with discipline-based courses and traditional teaching? Certainly this approach to instruction has a long history and justifiable rationale. Why are professors seeking alternatives today in interdisciplinary team-taught courses?

THE CASE FOR INTERDISCIPLINARY COURSES

The ancient Greeks were wise in seeing that bad things can result from an excess of virtue. Sometimes there is "too much of a good thing" or harmless things "get carried too far." It can be argued that this is the situation with disciplinary specialization. What began as a reasonable effort to delineate domains of study and methods of investigation has ended in the infinite regress of specialization. Today academics are charged with "knowing more and more about less and less." Can interdisciplinary courses help to correct the excesses of disciplinary specialization?

Disciplinary specialization produces some important problems. First, there is the problem of isolation. As disciplines and professional fields become more and more specialized, they tend to become isolated and proliferate their own findings and their specialized language. What was intended as "intellectual shorthand" becomes incomprehensible gobbledegook to the uninitiated, and induction into the discipline becomes more and more difficult. Disciplinary specialists find it difficult to introduce their field to beginners, and beginners are impatient with having to learn so much jargon. Established specialists, who might want to know more about another's field, grow increasingly frustrated in trying to communicate with other scholars who don't speak their language, and vice versa. This is true not only of the language, but also of the concepts and theories the language is designed to depict. Equally frustrating is the problem of getting to know, let alone master, the huge amount of knowledge being generated in a discipline. Many scholars have the sense that they have no time for their discipline, let alone learning another, a concern that leads to even more isolation.

One way to address the problem of isolation is to develop scholars who are initially competent in two or more fields. This is happening, as students increasingly "double major" or earn dual or joint graduate degrees. Given the explosion of knowledge, however, and the difficulty of approaching mastery in even one field, this effort to learn more than one field—becoming the modern-day quasi-Leonardo—may or may not meet with success. Joseph Kockelmans suggests an alternative.

> What we need today is not a number of Leonardos, but rather groups of interdisciplinarians . . . Now it becomes clear that the focus of scientific knowledge is shifting from individuals to groups. Scientific knowledge has become a collective product that is only imperfectly represented in isolated individuals.[47]

One response to this new reality is to train scholars in how to work in the community of scholars. If it is no longer possible, or at least unlikely, that anyone today can become the true renaissance scholar, mastering a vast accumulation of findings and research techniques, then the task becomes "learning where, what, and how to borrow from other disciplines." Scholars today, says Kockelmans, need to know what the major developments are in other disciplines, and how to appropriate, adapt, and incorporate those findings. This provides a strong rationale for interdisciplinary studies designed to build the badly-needed bridges to overcome isolation.

Second, specialists have a tendency to absolutize method. Having found a method that is particularly useful for gaining certain kinds of knowledge, scholars are inclined to give that method greater priority, to create a hierarchy of methods, and in some cases to present their method as "the method"—the only way (or at least the preferred way) of looking at the world. For example, sociologists are quick to criticize psychologists for not being sufficiently aware of how social patterns and movements tend to determine or at least greatly circumscribe what individuals do. Psychologists, in turn, note that sociologists never get down to the complexities of individual behavior driven by personality, stages of development, or reinforcement history. The observations may be appropriate, but in making them, both groups of social scientists tend to absolutize the method of their disciplines, leaving the apparent conflict unresolved and in the hands of their students. Neither group is able to step back sufficiently from "the method" to develop, first for themselves and then for their students, a "critical perspective" on the discipline. As the saying goes, "give a person a hammer and all they see is nails."

A recent publication on the major by the Association of American Colleges and Universities, *The Challenge of Connecting Learning* underscored the importance of fostering critical perspectives:

> Any proposal from any community as to "what is the case" is necessarily partial and bounded; any proposal is necessarily simpler than the complexity it attempts to describe or explain. This is simultaneously the source of its cognitive power and the grounds of its critique.[48]

Recently, some scholars have begun to acknowledge the "constructed" nature of the disciplines. Disciplines use different paradigms, rules, and terminologies to construct different reflections of reality. As David Haliburton points out, "because (a discipline) is something made up—an invented set of assumptions and practices—it selects reality; and selecting means leaving things out—perhaps a lot of things. Thus, while the discipline *reflects* reality it also *deflects* reality. This is why no single discipline can be equal to all tasks."[49] This recognition of the constructed nature of all disciplines introduces a healthy relativism that challenges the absolute claims of some disciplinary specialists. Interdisciplinary courses provide an opportunity to explore in some detail the strengths and limitations of the participating disciplines and their constructed nature.

What disciplinary specialists often fail to do is to "come clean" about both the limitations and the advantages of their method, and the constructed nature of their discipline. As Joseph Schwab noted in an old but prophetic essay on this subject, the "answers" that disciplines get depend heavily on the questions they ask, the phenomena they chose to study, and the rules they develop about "evidence." In Schwab's words:

> A given body of knowledge, arising under the aegis of a given substantive structure, contains only as much of the richness and complexity of the subject matter as the structure admits. Consequently, no body of knowledge is other than incomplete. Further, substantive structures succeed one another as the knowledge acquired through the use of one structure permits the conceiving and use of another which is presumably more nearly adequate to the complexity of the subject matter . . . It follows then that it is desirable, if not necessary, that we so teach that students understand that the knowledge we impart may be incomplete, is relatively ephemeral, and is not mere literal, "factual" truth.[50]

Interdisciplinary courses provide a vehicle for creating this critical perspective for students. In the curricula of some institutions, there is no place where this happens, except in interdisciplinary courses.

Third, disciplinary specialization tends to ignore or downplay broader issues and holistic perspectives. At their worst, the disciplines can be reductionistic, seeing the whole world through their own lens; more likely, they simply ignore the phenomena that exist outside their purview, leaving them to other specialists. Missing is the integration of knowledge that leads to a more comprehensive description of reality. Surely it is true that complex phenomena are often better understood by breaking these phenomena into their constituent parts for study. As described above, this has been one of the strengths of specialization. One of the excesses of specialization, however, is that the constituent parts under study become smaller and smaller; subsequently, less time is devoted to reassembling the information and drawing conclusions about the whole. Who puts Humpty-Dumpty back together again? In many fields today, the holistic perspective is critical to the advancement of knowledge. For example, as scientists work on some of the "big questions," such as the origins of the universe, the beginning of life, and a unified physical theory, they draw together teams of biologists, geologists, molecular physicists, astronomers, and mathematicians. The big picture is at least the sum of the parts and usually much more. Specialists are not good at seeing the whole, unless they have had some practice at it. Interdisciplinary courses can be a vehicle for providing holistic perspectives.

Fourth, specialization can lead to trivialization. At worst, the disciplinary specialists can lose sight not only of the big picture, but of the little picture as well, thus failing to establish any value at all in what they are studying—or even seeing the need to do so. This is not the issue of applied versus theoretical scholarship; this is the question of fundamental utility—whether the study has *any* ultimate worth—for the advancement of knowledge, for aesthetic appreciation, or for the amelioration of humanity or the broader social and physical environment. Some scholars today find themselves under pressure to conduct research and publish in areas they privately deem trivial, and they regard much of the work of their colleagues as worthless. The accumulation of trivialization, some would say, has led to a more general crisis of confidence in higher education. As Robert Scott has written

> Much of the current literature setting forth the case for interdisciplinarity has a decidedly millennial flavor. . . . higher education, as it is now constituted, has entered its last days. Its external connections with the society that sustains it have been allowed to atrophy by a self-indulgence that has increasingly made the production of knowledge esoteric rather than relevant to the very real problems besetting society.[51]

Interdisciplinary courses may be not only a healthy response to overspecialization, but to the trivialization that has alienated the modern university and society.

The concerns about the disciplinary structure developed thus far might all be classified under the general category of "excesses," as something gone wrong with the disciplines, primarily because of excessive specialization. Another set of criticisms suggests that the disciplinary structure itself is inadequate and that this structure is today no longer the best way of organizing knowledge for instruction in postsecondary education.

First, there is a growing belief that the goal of education today should no longer be dominated by the concern for transmitting information. In the "information society," so well documented by the authors of *Megatrends* and *Megatrends 2000*,[52] the teacher's role is not so much to transmit information, but to help students locate, retrieve, understand, and use information. What the disciplinary structure has done, ironically through its unusual effectiveness, is to create a deluge of information, so overwhelming in its volume and detail that most people, including the scholars who produced it, don't know what to do with it. What students need today is considerably more help than they usually get in learning to find and retrieve the right information, to analyze it critically, to synthesize it, to relate it to other appropriate information, and to apply it to a given situation. These functions are best carried out, it can be argued, in interdisciplinary courses, where the focus is on developing critical thinking skills, employing multiple perspectives, and relating information to some larger conceptual framework than the concerns of a specific discipline. When Piaget conducted his now well-known experiments on conservation, asking young children if the water in a short and wide beaker was less than that in a tall and narrow one, he introduced the concept of decentering, being able to move from the height to the width dimension and back again. In developing a model for interdisciplinary general education, Haas, Hursh, and

Moore remark: "The term decentering is still appropriate to denote the ability to shift deliberately among alternative perspectives or frames of reference and to bring them to bear upon each other or upon the problem at hand."[53] Thus, interdisciplinary courses and team teaching become more appropriate means of organizing instruction in a society where information now functions in a qualitatively different manner from the way it did in the past. Having knowledge is different from having information, and gaining knowledge today involves multiple perspectives and complex processes that students learn best in classrooms where interdisciplinary courses are offered and traditional teaching is augmented by other strategies.

Second, students today live in a world, and will probably continue to live in a world, where problems appear to pile up faster than solutions. Furthermore, many of these problems are "world" problems, that is, they are global in nature. One only need think of urban decay, crime, hunger, disease, ethnic warfare, and environmental pollution as the beginning items on a long list of growing problems that seem to defy solution. Unfortunately, none of these problems come in the tidy packages of disciplines. In fact, sometimes the approach used by applying knowledge from a single discipline can create more problems. As Wolfram Swoboda has explained, many short-term solutions, such as using pesticides like DDT, chemical scavengers to clean the air, and fire retardents in children's nightware, have created long term problems involving cancer-producing agents. "All of these instances," he points out, "exemplify the dangers that accrue from dealing with problems from too narrow a point of view," from "an overly restricted, specialized perspective."[54] Although the fundamental research created by the disciplines may be indispensable in addressing certain aspects of these problems, ultimate solutions require people who are skilled in using many kinds of knowledge in a problem-solving context. Educated people today will become parts of problem-solving teams whose efforts are organized and coordinated by large-scale organizations. As members of these teams, they will bring various types of specialized expertise, but they must also bring the skills and abilities to relate this expertise to all aspects of the problem-solving endeavor and to the likely consequences of proposed situations. Problems come in "layers" that need to be separated and analyzed, but solutions usually need to be comprehensive, addressing the problem as a system, not as pieces. Effective problem solvers today have skills in seeing the "the big picture," in creating webs of interrelated knowledge, and in working in teams. Thus, interdisciplinary courses, it can be argued, are well-suited to developing the problem-solving skills most needed in today's society because they emphasize the development of comprehensive perspectives. Team teaching demonstrates how specialists work together in teams, functioning some of the time as specialists, but at other times as generalists, capable of creating the broad understanding needed for solving problems.

Third, today students increasingly need exposure to cultural diversity, both in its historical roots and in its contemporary expressions. This exposure takes two forms on most campuses: one involving efforts to develop new appreciations of the history, political struggles, and current needs of traditional American minority populations; the other involving efforts at internationalization, that is, to prepare students more adequately for their encounter with people from other countries and cultures. Both tasks require and are enriched by interdisciplinary courses. Deepening appreciation of cultural diversity often involves the infusion of new material into traditional courses, but may more often involve rethinking a course completely to develop entirely new perspectives. Understanding what happened to Native Americans on the frontier or Black people under slavery involves not only what happened to "them," but also to the "others" who took the land or enslaved them. This understanding often requires a retelling of the whole story, with a completely different emphasis. Although cultural historians are beginning to do a better job of this as they come to broaden the work of the traditional political historians, they often need some help from anthropologists, art historians, and Black Studies, Native American Studies, and Women's Studies faculty. Efforts at internationalization, meanwhile, confront an even more massive task—trying to help students develop even broader cultural perspectives involving entire civilizations, a task requiring the talents of area specialists, historians, and language faculty who know about Chinese, Indian, Arabic, and Latin American cultures. Although institutions may legitimately vary in the urgency they sense about this task, most are giving at least some attention to multicultural and international "broadening" of the curriculum, an effort well served by, if not requiring, interdisciplinary courses.

Fourth, many professional areas are rethinking programs of preparation and in doing so are developing new configurations of subject matter that often require interdisciplinary courses. The old model for professional education, well-described as "Technical Rationality" in Donald Schön's *The Reflective Practitioner*, is being subjected to close scrutiny in some institutions.[55] Schön describes Technical Rationality as a tradition wherein students are taught a standardized body of knowledge—information, principles, theories—that they then "take out" and apply consistently to recurring professional problems. Thus most professional programs have involved a basic science phase, an applied science phase, and a professional attitudes phase. In many professions today, there is growing awareness that basic science, application, and professionalism need to be intermingled, that it is not effective to separate these efforts into distinguishable tracks (often hierarchical in their prestige), and that reserving application and professionalism for later phases (when student finally meets client) is not effective. Furthermore, professional practice is so complex today, with so many problems arising, that the old formula of theory and application simply doesn't work. More emphasis is being placed, therefore, on beginning with the problems of the field and building up knowledge about practice from the experience of the practice setting, hence, the "reflective practitioner." In an effort to prepare students for the "real world" problems of professional practice, many institutions are trying to design courses that more nearly correspond to the context of professional practice. Thus, as in the examples in the first chapter, the college of business assembles a course on "total quality management," and the law school implements a first-year course on the "lawyering process." Interdisciplinary courses serve well these efforts to develop training settings that more nearly correspond to the context of professional practice.

Finally, interdisciplinary courses better serve the students themselves in their quest for personal growth and the development of a clearer identity. Although American higher education has been deeply preoccupied with professional training and career preparation, even in its earliest years, a second theme has remained strong, the intellectual and spiritual development of the whole person. Such development was certainly the chief goal of the original liberal arts curriculum, and has continued as a theme in latter-day expressions of concern for "student development." Many students today, however, approach their studies with a grim seriousness about career preparation driven by their anxiety about getting a job. Often they forget, or we forget to remind them, that the college years are also designed for personal growth and for reflecting seriously on "what life is all about." Drawing on Victor Turner's concept of "liminal" (threshold) years, and Erickson's idea of early adulthood as a "moratorium," David Haliburton points out that the college years ought to provide a time out period for students "to get perspective on their current condition, chart plans for the future, and learn skills. The challenge is to get more life into that phase by making it possible for learners of all ages to do a little less marching and a little more dancing, as it were. The college years, at whatever stage one enters or re-enters them, form a conspicuously liminal time.[56] The disciplinary structure is perhaps at its worst as the mechanism for helping students during these liminal years develop what the Germans refer to as *Weltanschauung* (a world view), more loosely described as a "philosophy of life." It is highly unlikely, though this has long been the theory, that students develop a strong personal philosophy by taking a broad array of introductory disciplinary courses (general education), advanced disciplinary courses (the major), and any other disciplinary courses that seem attractive (electives), and integrating these into a broad philosophy through some private personal effort. This process is akin to mixing together various chemicals, presumably in the right quantities, to produce new compounds; but even chemists know that the quantities need to be exact, the temperature right, and other conditions favorable for the proper bonding to take place. In the curriculum, the "bonding process" for developing a "philosophy of life" is extremely important, and it is unlikely that it will take place if left entirely to students. What students are seeking—some more ardently than others—is to make sense of the whole, to balance what the biologist says about evolution with what the faculty in religious studies say about myth, to relate what the novelist says about human existence to what the psychologist says about human behavior. Ultimately, students need some closure—to the extent that closure can even be had—on cosmology, human nature, and the nature of society. Who are we, how did we arrive, where are we in space and time, and how are we to relate to one another, especially now that there are so many of us and we seem to be so different? It appears to some at least that this quest for answers to life's fundamental questions is better served by interdisciplinary courses than the traditional, fragmented efforts of disciplinary specialization.

Many of these ideas, presented here as a discussion of the limits of disciplinary specialization, and as a rationale for interdisciplinary courses, suggest the need for multiple perspectives and more coherence in the curriculum. This need to make more "connections" than are usually possible in disciplinary courses and traditional teaching has been well-articulated in the recent AAC report on the academic major, mentioned above.[57] That report calls for two kinds of connections: "for constructing relationships among various modes of knowledge and curricular experiences" and "for relating academic learning to a wider world, to public issues and personal experience." Although interdisciplinary, team-taught courses are not the panacea for all the excesses and short-comings of the dominant structure of disciplinary specialization, they provide at least one alternative. Together, the criticisms of disciplinary specialization and the short-comings of traditional teaching provide a reason for exploring another way. I do not suggest overthrowing the disciplinary structure, which the historical review suggests would not be easily overturned, even if that were desirable. I do suggest that interdisciplinary, team-taught courses are an important, perhaps necessary, alternative.

In the following chapters, I discuss how these courses can be elaborated and what obstacles faculty will encounter when they try to work together.

NOTES

1. Allan O. Pfnister, *The Influence of Departmental or Disciplinary Perspectives on Curricular Formation* (Toledo, OH: The Center for the Study of Higher Education, 1969), p. 7.

2. Arthur King and John Brownell, *The Curriculum and the Disciplines of Knowledge* (New York: John Wiley & Sons, 1966), pp. 67-95. The headings for each category are also direct quotations.

3. See especially "Collaboration in Research and Scholarship" in Ann Austin and Roger Baldwin, *Faculty Collaboration: Enhancing the Quality of Scholarship and Teaching.* ASHE-ERIC Higher Education Report No. 7 (Washington, DC: The George Washington University School of Education and Human Development).

4. Phillip Phenix, *Realms of Meaning* (New York: McGraw-Hill, 1964), p. 36.

5. For a more complete examination of these alternatives, see James Davis, *Better Teaching, More Learning: Strategies for Success in Postsecondary Settings* (Phoenix: American Council on Education/ Oryx Press, 1993), p. 31 ff.

6. Arthur Levine, *Handbook on Undergraduate Curriculum*, The Carnegie Foundation for the Advancement of Teaching (San Francisco: Jossey-Bass, 1978), p 492.

7. Ernest L. Boyer and Martin Kaplan, *Educating for Survival* (New Rochelle, NY: Change Magazine Press, 1977), p. 20.

8. *Ibid.*, p. 20.

9. *Ibid.*, p. 22.

10. *Ibid.*, p. 25.

11. *Ibid.*, p. 28.

12. *Charles William Elliot, Educational Reform: Essays and Addresses* (New York, 1898), pp. 125-48 quoted as "Charles William Eliot Expounds the Elective System as 'Liberty in Education'" in Richard Hofstadter and Wilson Smith, *American Higher Education: A Documentary History* (Chicago: The University of Chicago Press, 1961), pp. 705-06. Although frequent reference to "boy" would today be both sexist and demeaning, it was the accepted form of reference and the reality at the time.

13. Boyer and Kaplan, *Educating for Survival*, p. 31.

14. Burton Clark, *The Academic Life: Small Worlds, Different Worlds* (Princeton, NJ: The Carnegie Foundation for the Advancement of Teaching, 1987). See especially Chapter 2, "The Elaboration of Disciplines." Another valuable history of the development of the disciplines can be found in Wolfam Swoboda, "Disciplines and Interdisciplinarity: A Historical Perspective" in Joseph J. Kockelmans, *Interdisciplinarity and Higher Education* (University Park, PA: The Pennsylvania State University Press, 1979) pp. 49–92.

15. *Ibid.*, pp. 27-28.

16. *Ibid.*, p. 28.

17. *Ibid.*, p. 30.

18. *Ibid.*, p. 32.

19. *Ibid.*, p. 34.

20. *Ibid.*, p. 33.

21. *Ibid.*, p. 32.

22. *Ibid.*, p. 36.

23. *Ibid.*, p. 38.

24. Paul Dressel, *The Confidence of Crisis: An Analysis of University Departments* (San Francisco: Jossey-Bass, 1970).

25. Clark, *The Academic Life*, p. 36.

26. Frederick Rudolph, *The American College and University: A History* (New York: Alfred A. Knopf, 1965), pp. 339-40.

27. John Brubacher and Willis Rudy, *Higher Education in Transition: An American History—1636-1956* (New York: Harper & Row, 1958), p. 196.

20. *Ibid.*, p. 197.

29. *Ibid.*, p. 199.

30. *Ibid.*, p. 200.

31. Clark, *The Academic Life*, p. 29.

32. Brubacher and Rudy, *Higher Education in Transition*, p. 202.

33. Clark, *The Academic Life*, p. 30.

34. *Ibid.*, pp. 41-42.

35. *Ibid.*, p. 4.

36. Ernest L. Boyer, *College: The Undergraduate Experience in America*, The Carnegie Foundation for the Advancement of Teaching (New York: Harper & Row, 1987), p. 149.
37. Brubacher and Rudy, *The Higher Education in Transition*, pp. 82-83.
38. *Ibid.*, p. 80.
39. *Ibid.*, p. 80.
40. *Ibid.*, p. 81.
41. *Ibid.*, p. 84.
42. *Ibid.*, p. 85.
43. *Ibid.*, p. 86.
44. Clark, *The Academic Life*, p. 16.
45. Ernest L. Boyer, *College*, pp. 149-150.
46. *Ibid.*, p. 140.
47. Joseph Kockelmans, "Why Interdisciplinarity?" in Joseph Kockelmans, *Interdisciplinarity and Higher Education* (University Park, PA: Penn State University Press, 1979), p. 133.
48. Association of American Colleges, *The Challenge of Connecting Learning* (Washington, DC: Association of American Colleges, 1991), p. 12.
49. David Haliburton, "Interdisciplinary Studies" in Arthur Chickering and Associates, *The Modern American College* (San Francisco: Fossey-Bass, 1981), p. 454.
50. Joseph Schwab, "Problems, Topics, and Issues," Chapter I in Stanley Elam, *Education and the Structure of Knowledge* (Chicago: Rand McNally, 1964), pp. 6-11.
51. Robert Scott, "Personal and Institutional Problems Encountered in Being Interdisciplinary" in Joseph Kockelmans, *Interdisciplinarity and Higher Education* (University Park, PA: The Pennsylvania State University Press, 1979), p. 319.
52. John Naisbitt, *Megatrends* (New York: Warner Books, 1982) and John Naisbitt and Patricia Aburdene, *Megatrends 2000* (New York: William Morrow, 1990).
53. Paul Haas, Barbara Hursh, and Michael Moore, "An Interdisciplinary Model to Implement General Education," *Journal of Higher Education*, 54 (1983): pp. 42–49.
54. Wolfram W. Swoboda, "Disciplines and Interdisciplinarity" in Kockelmans, *Interdisciplinarity and Higher Education, p. 49.*
55. Donald Schön, *The Reflective Practitioner* (New York: Basic Books, 1983), pp. 3-69.
56. David Haliburton, "Interdisciplinary Studies" in Arthur Chickering, *The Modern American College,* (San Francisco: Jossey-Bass, 1981), p. 464.
57. Association of American Colleges, *The Challenge of Connecting Learning*, p. 14.

CHAPTER

Structuring and Delivering Interdisciplinary Courses: Approximating the Ideal

"A philosophy of education, like any theory, has to be stated in words and symbols. But so far as it is more than verbal it is a plan for conducting education. Like any plan, it must be framed with reference to what is to be done and how it is to be done."

—John Dewey

In the first chapter, I stated that interdisciplinary team teaching requires some degree of collaboration. Team teaching will vary in the amount of collaboration that actually takes place in general, but also specifically with regard to planning, content integration, teaching, and evaluation. The first chapter concluded with a proposition: *The greater the level of integration desired, the higher the level of collaboration required.*

Assume for purposes of discussion, that the goal of team teaching is a high level of integration and that a high level of collaboration will be required to achieve the goal. Although the definitions of team teaching presented in the first chapter accommodated many kinds and levels of collaboration, assume now that a high level of collaboration is desirable. Now call team teaching involving a high level of collaboration "the ideal." Given these assumptions, how might one proceed to approximate the "ideal" interdisciplinary, team-taught course?

GETTING THE IDEA

The ideal interdisciplinary course begins with a great idea. It is not altogether clear where these great ideas come from or how to get them. Great ideas are few and hard to come by. Often great ideas come out of the head of one individual, the solitary thinker ruminating alone in the office, or the shower for that matter. Most professors have ideas for courses they would like to teach someday. Sometimes they develop these ideas and teach "their" course. Great ideas for team-taught courses, however, are usually born of dialogue; they have their origins in discussion. The "seeds" for a team-taught course may come from one individual, but they don't begin to germinate until they are expressed, until they come out into the open for criticism, support, and elaboration. Interdisciplinary courses usually begin as the brainchild of a limited number of parents, a few fertile minds. The idea is born when these people begin to talk. The team comes into play later on to nurture the idea, elaborate it, and deliver it. Ironically, teams usually don't generate the ideas for team-taught courses. Instead, good ideas are generated by a few individuals, somehow and somewhere, with the help of the "new course muse," and then, and only then, appropriate members are sought for the team. Although this process is not an absolute rule, it appears to be a general rule: *One or two people get a good idea and then seek the appropriate team members to carry it out.*

In the examples described in the first chapter, the idea for "Evolution" came from two colleagues in the biology department who challenged themselves to think about developing a course for the core curriculum. One of those colleagues never went on to work with the course, but the other found the idea they had generated exciting and worthy of elaboration. He was the one who sought out the team and eventually, with the team, developed the idea into a course. But he is the first to admit that the course itself evolved into something different from the original idea. The idea for the "Lawyering Process" course came from another institution when a faculty member moved from one institution to another and brought the idea with him. The idea was powerful enough, and he was convincing enough, to persuade his colleagues at the new institution to assemble a team and try it. After a few years, the course was well established and the person who "had the idea" no longer needed to be associated with the it; the course had a life of its own. The idea for "Multiple Voices of America" emerged from discussions between a faculty member in history and a colleague in religious studies who were both interested in a new approach to teaching American history. The idea of multiple voices led these two white males to seek diversity in staffing the course, so that now the idea of the course is embodied in the multiple voices of the faculty who teach the course. The idea for "Quality Panorama" actually came from a planning committee that passed the idea on to another planning committee. The initial idea was altered considerably before the course was taught for the first time. For the "Making of the Modern Mind," the oldest and most well-established of the examples, faculty who have taught on the team for several years have to remind the newer members of the team who it was that had the original idea for the course and what that idea was.

What kind of participants are identified for the team? The most important criterion, of course, is expertise, faculty who have the appropriate subject expertise to express the idea of the course. What disciplines should be represented and why? But there are other considerations as well. William Newell suggests that "one needs to consider whether potential participants are open to diverse ways of thinking, wary of absolutism; able to admit that they do not know; good at listening, unconventional, flexible, willing to take risks, self-reflective, and comfortable with ambiguity.[1]

We can conclude that the ideal interdisciplinary course begins with a great idea that can come from anywhere, and that the people who have the idea don't necessarily elaborate the idea. Once the course is established the idea grows and the course takes on a life of its own, sometimes quite apart from the people who had the original idea.

INVENTING THE SUBJECT

What will be the subject of the ideal team-taught course? How will the subject be conceptualized? Most faculty members are accustomed to thinking about the subject of a course in the content of their discipline. They have been thoroughly trained in a specialization and they usually are comfortable about generating courses in that discipline. If they have a problem, it is with selecting the most appropriate content for the subject. After all, they have a lot of information, and their fields are likely exploding with new knowledge. They are often preoccupied with "coverage."

When faculty members join a team to elaborate the subject for an interdisciplinary course, they experience some initial confusion, an uneasy sense that they don't know what they are doing. They find themselves immersed in a collaborative process with other people from other disciplines, who also don't know exactly what they are doing. What they all bring to the process is *their* disciplinary perspective and very often their anxieties about coverage. Coverage becomes a problem in team-taught courses if everyone comes into the room with strong beliefs about what students need to know. Adding team members compounds the coverage problem. At first, the team may see its problem as providing more or less equal representation for the various disciplinary perspectives. The team will often devote its energies to eliminating topics, combining and recombining ideas, and paring down a multiplicity of possibilities to the essentials.

In courses with a lower level of content integration, faculty members bring their subject into the planning process and eliminate some of it so as to allow other colleagues to teach some of *their* subject. Certain trade-offs are made and a serial order of presentations is established. If higher levels of content integration are to occur, that is, if a type of content integration is to take place that more nearly approximates the ideal, a very different and more complicated process must take place. The faculty will be obliged to invent a new subject, not just present the old subject in a different form, and inventing the subject for a team-taught course is not an easy process.

In many traditional disciplinary courses, the subject is defined by the discipline. Not everyone will agree on how demographics, or organic chemistry, or music history should be taught, nor will they always agree on exactly how to define those subjects; but there is usually far more initial agreement about what the subject is in a disciplinary course than there is when faculty begin to discuss an *interdisciplinary* course. An interdisciplinary course, by its very nature, is established in order to do something that can't be done in a disciplinary course. It is in some sense "anti-disciplinary" because its creators have consciously set about to create a context for learning that does not *begin* with the discipline. Where does the interdisciplinary course begin? As William Newell states, "successful interdisciplinary courses normally focus on a topic, although the term *topic* should be construed broadly as meaning an issue, theme, problem, region, time period, institution, figure, work, or idea.[2] Interestingly enough, the great scholars, the authors of the "classics" so often recommended for study at the college level, organized their thinking around themes. As David Haliburton has noted, with a twist of humor:

> to the extent that the great writers, thinkers, and doers achieve a high degree of integration, it is at least in part because they take problems, themes, or issues as their point of departure. That is why it is so difficult to put them into pigeonholes. The only way to classify a Pascal is to say "Pascal—he is his own classification. But bring Pascal into a modern college and he would quickly be channeled into one department—mathematics or philosophy or religious studies or literature—unless, of course, he were fortunate enough to be invited to participate in a program of interdisciplinary studies.[3]

An interdisciplinary course begins with a topic and employs the disciplines in a new way to explore this topic. Thus the subject is seldom the discipline or even some aspect of the discipline, as it was learned in graduate school, but some new subject that the course faculty invents together. In the most creative interdisciplinary courses, the team members have not taken, taught, or even heard of this subject before. This subject innovation produces three enormous problems.

With few exceptions, faculty are still trained today as disciplinary specialists. They are accustomed to thinking about their disciplines first. They don't begin with themes, competencies, problems, or global concepts such as "quality" or "the modern mind" as the starting point for courses. They may occasionally think about how certain kinds of knowledge in their disciplines may apply to critical problems or relate to other fields, but they don't begin there. They begin with the discipline. To do otherwise requires some serious adjustments, venturing into uncharted waters, and abandoning the safe and familiar moorings of the disciplinary shore. It is not easy, if you are an accountant, to begin building a course around the concept of "quality." It is not easy, if you are an art historian, to begin with the concept of "the making of the modern mind." Most faculty don't have much experience with *inventing* the subject, because in traditional teaching the subject is a given. The team is initially handicapped by a lack of experience in inventing subjects.

Additionally, when faculty from different disciplinary perspectives begin to explore a theme, they find that they have differing points of view. To put the matter bluntly: They don't agree. These disagreements, initially quite rational in origin, can lead to serious power struggles. The sociologist on the team, for example, begins to assert that what people think, and the process that has shaped their thinking, is socially determined. The sociologist has a lot of data to show how persons of a particular social class or ethnic background are likely to think on a variety of subjects. In fact, sociologists can predict how people will think and act and can give data to support how accurate their predictions will be. The psychologist on the team operates with a different paradigm, involving a different set of assumptions and interests. The psychologist is interested in individual differences, how people have come to believe and behave as they do as a result of a particular developmental progression or reinforcement history. When the sociologist "elevates the importance of class differences," the psychologist is being asked to provide "secondary evidence" to explain exceptions; and when the psychologist "elevates the importance of individual developmental histories," the sociologist is being told that the "trends" are interesting but provide only general explanations of more complex phenomena. What begins as an interesting difference of opinion soon escalates into a power struggle because both faculty members believe that their explanation is superior to the other's. This disagreement should be no surprise; both have been taught that their perspective is superior and their job is teaching this to others. Soon they are not only attacking each other's ideas, but each other.

All disciplines are based on certain assumptions about what is important and about how to select and view the phenomena to be studied. In another comparison, this time of economists and sociologists, James Dusenberry has quipped, "Economics is all about how people make economic choices; sociology is all about why people have no economic choices to make."[4] These differences in perspective are not easily resolved. Odd as it may seem, many faculty have never had to confront the assumptions and limitations of their disciplinary paradigm. Faculty without experience in working on interdisciplinary teams soon find themselves involved in interdisciplinary battles; what was supposed to have been an enriching and broadening experience soon turns into an unpleasant power struggle because faculty don't agree.

In addition to inexperience with inventing a new subject and hegemonic power struggles over the superiority of their disciplinary paradigms, faculty also discover that they have important epistemological differences—real disagreements about what knowledge is and how it is generated. Again, many faculty don't have much experience with the epistemological assumptions of other disciplines and many do not recognize those of their own. Often the disagreements that arise boil down to disputes about the function of language. Most physical scientists want to use language as precisely as possible, as some would say, in a positivistic way, establishing as much correspondence as possible between the observed and measured "reality" and the words used to describe that "reality." For them, language is, and ought to be, hard and tight, nearly identical with reality. Some social scientists, on the other hand, would assert that "reality" is "socially constructed," and that what is "out there" depends largely on how the people who are having a conversation about "it" define "it." Language is soft and at best conveys only shared meanings of an interpreted reality. In the humanities, those who create and interpret artistic works— poetry, novels, paintings, films, music—often assert that the understanding of "reality," if there is such a thing, is achieved best through metaphorical uses of language and other media, creating fresh comparisons that go beyond mere description and provide insightful interpretations. For them, language is not only soft, it is intentionally slippery. These epistemological differences, which are sharp across divisional and disciplinary lines, also occur within the disciplines and professions—some psychologists study rats while others study archetypal myths—making for a rich variety of ways to define and derive knowledge within academia today. As the disciplines struggle to make room for both empirical and qualitative research perspectives, the philosophers and critical studies scholars brood over the whole mess, with their revisionist and deconstructionist programs, vying alternately for the right to point out that there is either only relative truth or no truth at all, and that the whole of the academic enterprise is either bankrupt, corrupt, or both. And what is a "mere student" to make of this display of epistemological diversity? What is a freshman to make of the babel of these authorities?

In the ideal interdisciplinary course, the power struggles over the relative importance of ideas and the epistemological differences among perspectives have been sufficiently addressed—if not necessarily resolved—to give the faculty team enough comfort with these differences to make them explicit and to convey them to students. The faculty may even have discovered some continuities and compatibilities in their fields as they invent a new subject. One of the great strengths of the interdisciplinary course, at its best, is that the faculty, who are the experts, have already wrestled with and to some extent resolved the differences in their methodological and disciplinary perspectives. Such wrestling is hard work, but most faculty teaching interdisciplinary courses recognize that it is not fair to leave this task to the students, the novices, who, running from course to course, are expected to "integrate their learning." In interdisciplinary courses, the faculty team members take on the chore of integrating their various perspectives and resolving their differences. In the ideal team-taught course, the faculty have successfully met the challenges of "connecting learning" and the students have a chance to see the relationships that they don't get to see in other courses. This is one of the great pay-offs for inventing a new subject.

From the examples presented in the first chapter, the "Making of the Modern Mind" provides an interesting illustration of efforts to develop an integrated approach to inventing the subject. Although a disciplinary "homebase" is maintained in the sections taught by disciplinary specialists, the faculty have had to come together and agree upon the integrative themes for the lectures. The subject, therefore, is not art history or music history, but the themes that describe the foundations of the "modern mind." The lectures for the first term of the course, for example, are organized according to three themes: "Faith, Reason, and the Senses in the Age of the Baroque," "The Rise of Individualism and the Road to Revolution," and "The Invention of Liberty." The faculty invented these themes, and reached enough agreement about them to use them as a means of integrating, organizing, and presenting what they know about the eighteenth century from the viewpoint of their disciplines. Thus the theme on "The Invention of Liberty" is elaborated through a series of lectures: one on Voltaire by an English professor, one on Rousseau by a philosopher, one on Watteau and David by an art historian, one on Beethoven by a pianist, and one on the ideas behind the French Revolution by a philosopher. Behind the scenes, the faculty engaged in some serious discussion to arrive at the themes and to select the artists, writers, philosophers, and the composer who could best illustrate the theme. The faculty had to address and resolve the differences they had about how to approach these key figures vis-a-vis the theme. This resolution of differences involves a great amount of "homework" on the part of the faculty, but the end result available to students is very different from what happens when a student takes a series of traditional, disciplinary courses, discovering slowly and painfully, but more likely *never*, that all these figures scattered about in all those courses had something to do with the invention of the idea of liberty, a concept which most of us, with our modern minds, take for granted. In the ideal interdisciplinary version of this course, perhaps even more disciplines, representing the physical and social sciences, would be brought together, and a new and slightly different rendition of the subject might be invented by the participants as a result of further struggle to reconcile differences and discover commonalties.

In the ideal interdisciplinary team-taught course, the subject grows out of the idea; it is invented by the faculty who participate in the course, it is more than the sum of the disciplinary parts, and it is presented to the students, as nearly as possibly, as an integrated whole. On the other hand, there is no magic number for how many disciplines to involve—the number depends on the idea for the course—but for those disciplines that are involved, the ideal to be approximated is optimal collaboration for maximal integration.

DETERMINING LEARNING OUTCOMES

Challenging as it may be for faculty teams to invent the subject of an interdisciplinary course, "subject matter," even interdisciplinary subject matter, is still something that most faculty can generate, given enough time to talk it out. The subject is what faculty feel they know best. But when faculty are asked to specify learning outcomes, they feel they are being required to enter an even more mysterious domain, one that belongs to real strangers—"educational psychologists" or "learning theorists." Not only are most faculty not on familiar ground, it is as if they are being asked to walk across hot coals.

All courses function at two levels: a content level, which I have been calling the "subject," and a process level, which has to do with the kind of learning taking place and the way that learning is occurring. Whether we are aware of it or not, both levels are operating simultaneously in every course. In some courses, the process level is hardly recognized because of the preoccupation with content; in other courses, the process level has been well conceptualized as an important component of the course, so that the planners of the course can speak in a coherent way about "desired learning outcomes." In the ideal interdisciplinary team-taught course, significant attention has been given to both levels of the course, and team members have spent time not only inventing the subject, but in settling on desired learning outcomes.

Learning outcomes are what William Newell has referred to as "subtexts," what faculty might say the course is "really about." What an interdisciplinary course is often really about is "recognizing contrasting perspectives; learning how to synthesize, think critically, and reexamine the world we take for granted, empowering students to tackle meaningful but complex issues; weaning students from dependence on experts without dismissing expertise; and teaching students to value disciplines as powerful sources of insight while becoming aware of the nature of their various limitations.[5] They are the goals that most faculty have in mind when they think about liberal education or professional competence. The problem with learning outcomes is that they are often vague and unarticulated, and seldom spelled out in relation to the subject.

A useful guide for thinking more comprehensively about learning outcomes was generated by Benjamin Bloom in 1956. Although Bloom's *Taxonomy*, as it has come to be known, is almost 40 years old, it has weathered the test of time and has not been replaced, as nearly as I know, with any better system for examining learning outcomes. In other words, it still works. A condensed summary of *Bloom's Taxonomy of Educational Objectives, Handbook I: Cognitive Domain* appears below.[6]

1:00 KNOWLEDGE
1:10 Knowledge of Specifics—
knowing terminology, such as important verbal and non-verbal symbols, and knowing specific facts, such as dates, events, persons, places, and sources of information.
1:20 Knowledge of Ways and Means of Dealing with Specifics—
knowing conventions and characteristic treatments of ideas; trends and sequences; classifications categories, sets, divisions and arrangements; criteria for judging facts, principles, and opinions; and methods of inquiry, techniques, and procedures.
1:30 Knowledge of Universals and Abstractions in a Field—
knowing principles, generalizations, theories, and structures.

2:00 COMPREHENSION
2:10 Translation—
putting concepts and ideas into other language, into other terms, or into another form of communication.
2:20 Interpretation—
going beyond the part-for-part rendering of the communication to comprehend the relationships among its various parts, to reorder, rearrange . . . to secure some total view.
2:30 Extrapolation—
seeing consequences, implications, and ramifications for other situations, predicting trends, distinguishing more probable from less probable consequences.

3:00 APPLICATION
application to new problem situations in real life, transfer of training to new environments, such as the ability to apply social science generalizations and conclusions to actual social problems, or the ability to apply science principles, postulates, theorems, or other abstractions to new situations.

4:00 ANALYSIS
4:10 Analysis of Elements—
ability to recognize the various elements in a communication, such as unstated assumptions, the difference between facts and hypoth-

eses, factual and normative statements, conclusions and supporting statements.

4:20 Analysis of Relationships—
   ability to determine the relationships among the elements, such as causal relations, the relationship of evidence to hypotheses, or the relationship of facts or assumptions to a thesis.

4:30 Analysis of Organizational Principles—
   ability to point out the structure or organization of the communication, such as form or point of view in a literary work; the relation of materials and elements in an artistic work, or the techniques used in persuasive materials.

5:00 SYNTHESIS

5:10 Production of a Unique Communication—
   getting ideas, feelings, and experiences across to others while taking into account the effect to be achieved, such as writing a creative story, essay, verse, making a speech, or creating a simple work of art.

5:20 Production of a Plan or Proposed Set of Operations—
   ability to propose a plan for testing hypotheses, to make preparations for instruction, to design a machine or building.

5:30 Derivation of a Set of Abstract Relations—
   ability to formulate and modify hypotheses, to perceive alternative ways of organizing experience in a conceptual structure, to make mathematical discoveries and generalizations.

6:00 EVALUATION

6:10 Judgment in Terms of Internal Criteria—
   ability to assess the probability of accuracy from internal evidence, such as the accuracy in reporting facts, nature of the documentation, logical fallacies of arguments.

6:20 Judgment in Terms of External Criteria—
   ability to access worth in terms of external standards, such as major theories, generalization, works of recognized excellence; skill in recognizing and weighing values in alternative courses of action; ability to use aesthetic standards in the choice and use of objects in the everyday environment.

The taxonomy is valuable not only as a list of concepts—categories for thinking about cognitive learning outcomes—but also as a theory. According to Bloom, the outcomes are hierarchical, moving from simple to complex; and (theoretically) a student must learn to do things that are lower on the list before being able to proceed to "higher order" outcomes.[7] Although one might raise questions about the theory, the taxonomy has been widely used as a useful classification scheme in the public schools in K-12 education; and many professors in postsecondary disciplinary settings have found it useful as a way of thinking about educational outcomes. The widely known Taxonomy of Cognitive Outcomes has two lesser-known cousins, *The Taxonomy of Educational Objectives, Handbook II: Affective Domain* and *A Taxonomy of the Psychomotor Domain*.[8] For certain courses, it is valuable to think about these additional categories of learning outcomes as well. Some courses involve feelings—perceptions, attitudes, beliefs, values—and some involve motor skills and physical movements. Most successful disciplinary courses have well articulated learning outcomes.

What happens when professors try to think about learning outcomes for an *interdisciplinary* course? Does the interdisciplinary context change the process of thinking about outcomes? The answer is both yes and no. No, the categories of the taxonomy need not change, but, yes, the content of the tasks that might be considered within the categories will usually be much more complex in an interdisciplinary course. The range of knowledge and the amount of integration necessary for the comprehension, application, analysis, synthesis, and evaluation of knowledge usually becomes greater. Consider, for example, the following statements of learning outcomes that might appear in interdisciplinary courses, arranged by the categories set forth in Bloom's *Taxonomy*.

Knowledge

- To know the work of selected eighteenth- and nineteenth-century artists, musicians, writers, and philosophers; the key facts of their lives; and the dates and historical context of their activity.
- To know the three primary categories of the law (case law, administrative law, and legislation) and to be able to recognize examples and place them in their proper categories.
- To know the basic principles of evolution, and to be able to describe how the theory is derived and what it attempts to explain.

Comprehension

- To be able to generate your own definition of "diversity" and to be able to put into your own words why and in what ways diversity has been important in shaping the experience of people in the United States.
- To read the texts of selected writers and philosophers, and to view and hear the works of selected artists, and to describe how the concept of "liberty" is set forth in their work.

- To see how the use of total quality management principles can increase trends in customer satisfaction, worker productivity, and net profits.

Application

- To apply your understanding of "diversity" to persistent problems in families, organizations, and local communities and at the level of international relations.

Analysis

- To identify the key elements of the types of statements being made by texts that provide "religious explanations" of the origins of life and "scientific explanations."
- To compare and contrast two case studies of organizations, one applying extensive "total quality management" principles, the other not.
- To describe the color, form, and texture of Navajo weaving, and to relate these to comparable structural elements of the Negro spiritual.

Synthesis

- To write a brief letter to your grandmother about why you think the theory of evolution makes sense, and why it does not necessarily threaten your religious beliefs, knowing well that grandmother is not likely to agree with you.
- To create a business plan for a small business (under 20 employees) that incorporates total quality principles into product development, production, management, marketing, and accounting.
- To write two briefs for a problem case, one summarizing the key points for the plaintiff, the other summarizing the likely points to be made by the defense.

Evaluation

- Given detailed descriptions of species, as represented in an extensive report on the fossil evidence, generate hypotheses about how the species should be classified, including probable dating.
- Given examples of Native American art, evaluate whether and to what extent the examples are representative of important styles and traditions, and whether they are worth the asking price of the seller.

In this list of learning outcomes, the same "levels" of Bloom's taxonomy are represented, but the tasks involve more fields and a greater number of connections across the disciplines or professional fields being represented. Although this often increases the attractiveness of the subject, and although the abilities to perform the task well are not "higher" in a hierarchical sense, they are often more complicated. It takes more skill, for example, to examine the work of writers, philosophers, artists, and musicians, than it might to examine only philosophers. Likewise, it requires more skill (and more effort) to relate total quality management principles to management, marketing, and accounting than to just one of those fields. Some of the objectives in the examples listed above are "tougher" just because they are more difficult, but some are tougher because they require an interdisciplinary perspective. An interdisciplinary course requires more disciplines and more integration for most learning outcomes. If this is the case, teams of faculty might profitably give attention to generating and selecting the *most desirable* list of learning outcomes, keeping in mind that interdisciplinary learning outcomes have the inherent potential for being more complicated.

Bloom's *Taxonomy*, with some adaptation for the interdisciplinary context, is one way of looking at outcomes. It is perhaps most useful for thinking about outcomes for courses involving several traditional disciplines. For the professions, the concept of "competencies" may be more useful. The idea of "competency-based education" goes back many years; the earliest experiments with it appeared in nursing and teacher education in the late 1960s. The idea is relatively simple: by beginning with what the professional nurse, teacher, or lawyer actually does, it is possible to identify the "competencies" one needs to perform well as a professional in that field. The outcomes of most types of professional education, therefore, can be construed as competencies, and the task of educating professionals involves providing contexts where students can cultivate these competencies.

In many professional settings, theories and skills are taught one at a time in separate courses, and application occurs, or is intended to occur, in a practicum, internship, or other field experience. Competencies may or may not be learned in individual courses; and the cumulative aspect of actually practicing and being able to perform the competency is often neglected. Interdisciplinary, team-taught courses in professional settings provide a valuable opportunity for addressing the competency as a whole, thus overcoming the deficiencies of the perceived, "one course-at-a-time" approach.

One of the learning outcomes teachers hope for in the business curriculum, for example, is that students can develop competence in using their analytical skills to identify what is going wrong or has already gone wrong in an organization, and to generate solutions or ideas about what could and should be done. Often this competency is developed through the "case method." In institutions where the curriculum is organized along departmental lines, students may encounter marketing cases, management cases, or sometimes accounting cases, but they may not engage in a comprehensive case until they take a senior capstone course or even a graduate seminar. An interdisciplinary approach to developing professional competencies provides more opportunities, early in the student's experience, to develop competencies that integrate several skills from several areas of study, as, for example, in the study of quality. Similarly, law students often gain fragments of competencies from an array of courses, but an interdisciplinary course specially designed to introduce the competencies needed to be a lawyer provides a unique opportunity to acquire and practice these skills holistically, in the way they are actually used in a typical law firm.

In thinking about the outcomes for the ideal interdisciplinary course, faculty will want to give some additional attention to those outcomes peculiar to the interdisciplinary process itself. William Newell has identified these outcomes as:

> an appreciation for perspectives other than one's own; an ability to evaluate the testimony of experts; tolerance of ambiguity; increased sensitivity to ethical issues; an ability to synthesize or integrate; enlarged perspectives or horizons; more creative, original, or unconventional thinking; increased humility or listening skills, and sensitivity to disciplinary, political or religions bias.[9]

A good question to ask is: what outcomes are we identifying that take special advantage of the interdisciplinary format?

In the ideal interdisciplinary course, learning outcomes have been discussed by the team and elaborated in sufficient detail to make clear to the faculty, and ultimately for the students, the kinds of learning intended. Learning outcomes will be specific, and will be based on some rational scheme, such as a taxonomy of cognitive objectives or a set of professional competencies. Because learning outcomes in an interdisciplinary setting can get complicated and require much of students, decisions will need to be made about which outcomes are most important, given the idea underlying the course and the definition of the subject.

ESTABLISHING SCOPE AND SEQUENCE, BREADTH AND DEPTH

As the subject is invented and learning outcomes are developed, four important additional questions need to be addressed: Where does this course begin and end? How should its content be ordered? How many topics should be included? How deeply should any one topic be explored? These issues are addressed in the careful planning of any course, but they become especially important in the development of interdisciplinary courses because more team members generate more potential answers to these questions, and, therefore, more choices are required.

Where curriculum planners speak of "scope," they are referring to the boundaries that have been set for the inclusion of material. A radar "scope," such as those used by air traffic controllers, provides information about aircraft within a particular part of the sky; the scope contains only those things that fall within the direction, vector, and distance of the radar beam. For disciplinary courses, the scope of a course is often predetermined by general understandings about where subject matter fits within the context of the discipline. In chemistry there is some general agreement about what to include and what not to include in general chemistry, organic chemistry, and physical chemistry. A course on American poetry of the nineteenth century has its boundaries set both by the nationality of the poets and the time when they wrote. Although the boundaries—the beginning and end of the subject—are clearer in some disciplinary courses than in others, there is often a prescribed domain that is fairly easy to identify, a territory that the subject fits into naturally, and is accepted across the discipline.

In interdisciplinary courses, the boundaries are not obvious; they have to be defined through dialogue about the scope of the course. For example, it is not clear, when a team of faculty sets about to create a course on "The Making of the Modern Mind," exactly where that course should begin and end. What is meant by "modern?" Does it mean that period of civilization when humans left their hunter-gather mode of existence and began to settle into agricultural communities? If so, the "modern mind" might be thought of as having its "making" in the advent of urban civilizations, such as those of ancient Greece, China, Egypt, and Mesopotamia. On the other hand, "modern" could refer to the emergence of a new way of looking at human beings that began at the time of the Renaissance; but if so, is it important to look at the Greek and Roman origins—the birth—of those things that made the Renaissance a rebirth? Where does "modern" really begin? In the course as it actually came to be taught, a consensus was reached about scope: a decision was made to focus on the eighteenth and nineteenth centuries, to begin the course there, and to deal in a less extensive way with the twentieth century. There is no *a priori* logic that the course has to be set up that way; one could as easily argue now, on the brink of the twenty-first century, that the scope of the course should be primarily twentieth-century thought. The boundaries of the course are agreed upon by the team of faculty responsible for it; they make decisions, often difficult and painful decisions, about what they want to do. The decisions are not arbitrary, they are reasoned and can be justified, but often a great amount of energy goes into making those decisions and defending them. Without clear agreements about scope, the faculty team can wander into topics that don't belong in the course; and eventually the course loses its focus, both for the faculty, and, of greater importance, for the students.

Once questions about the scope of the course have been settled, the faculty must order topics in a reasonable sequence. In disciplinary courses, the sequence of topics is often determined by an inner logic growing out of the discipline. Sometimes this process involves an ordering of skills, as in mathematics or foreign languages, that requires students to master the prerequisite skills needed to perform advanced skills. Sometimes there is a "chronological logic," as with a history course, or a "structural or conceptual logic," as with a course in astronomy. What usually happens with an interdisciplinary course, however, is that the rules for determining the sequence of topics need to be created by the team.

In the course "Multiple Voices of America," the team made a conscious choice to abandon the traditional chronological order for teaching American history. They assumed—rightly or wrongly—that students already have background from their high school social studies courses about the key chronological events of American history. Assuming, rather than abandoning, a chronological understanding, the faculty decided on a different sequencing of topics. They began with an inquiry into how the land was used, how it was settled, and how it was changed over time by the way it was used. The next set of topics, in the second term, involved the development of political structures to cope with diversity. The topics addressed in the third term of the course involved the cultural contributions of diverse peoples to the American experience. The team made a conscious decision about sequencing the content of the course around three themes, rather than teaching the course as a complete chronological coverage of political, social, and cultural events, beginning at the beginning in the first term, and ending with the present at the end of the third term. Without some sense of the logic for sequencing the topics in a course, students as well as faculty often feel lost. In interdisciplinary courses, the rules for sequencing topics usually need to be created by the team.

Members of the faculty team also need to make decisions about the breadth of topics to be included and the depth of treatment given to each topic. In a disciplinary context, this distinction is most frequently made in describing the differences between the introductory survey course and the advanced topics seminar. The survey course touches on general topics lightly, introducing students to many aspects of the subject. The seminar focuses on one or two subjects, going into significant depth. Because interdisciplinary teams usually possess a broad range of expertise, there is a natural tendency to emphasize breadth, including a broad range of topics, because the faculty know about many things. This breadth is one of the advantages of teams. On the other hand, interdisciplinary courses can also focus on a single theme, examining it in depth from several different disciplinary perspectives. In "Multiple Voices of America," the emphasis is not on providing a broad survey of American history, but on examining three themes in some depth: the land, the political process, and the personal and cultural contributions of diverse individuals. Depth is also achieved throughout the course via the Family Heritage Project, whereby students interview family members and assemble family artifacts (pictures, stories, crafts, descriptions of traditions) to explore more deeply the experience of their own family in America.

The "Lawyering Process" course, on the other hand, is consciously designed as a survey of the most important skills a student will need to function effectively as a lawyer. The skills are taught by specialists in writing, library research, and client counseling. The skills are also taken in order, beginning with the skills that a lawyer would need to talk to a client on the first encounter and continuing through the skills needed to file an appeal if the case was lost. The team has agreed to touch on all the skills lightly, but they know that they have a problem in acquainting students with all the skills they need to function well in conducting an actual trial. The whole faculty agreed with the faculty on the team that trial procedure requires a course in itself, to be presented in depth as an upper division offering. Thus the team made a conscious choice for breadth, reserving depth of treatment for certain other courses in the curriculum. As with other questions that must be answered in developing the ideal interdisciplinary course, the appropriate balance of breadth and depth needs to be struck through an informed decision reached by the team after adequate discussion.

In planning the ideal interdisciplinary course, the faculty team needs to make conscious and justifiable decisions about the scope of the course, the sequence of topics, and the appropriate balance of breadth and depth.

BUILDING THE ORGANIZATIONAL STRUCTURE

Every course has some organizational structure. Decisions need to be made about who is teaching the course, when it will be offered, how many credits to give, what texts and readings to assign, and where the course will be taught. In traditional disciplinary courses, most of these decisions are fairly uncomplicated and are usually made by one person, the teacher. In interdisciplinary team-taught courses, the organization can get complicated; the course coordinator can begin to feel like the producer/director of a Steven Spielberg film.

Many of the decisions about course structure are made in the planning phase for the course. How many students will this course enroll? Will the students always meet together as one class, or will there be some smaller groups? If so, how many? How many credit hours will be granted for the course? Given the number of credit hours, how will contact hours be arranged? Will large group sessions be interspersed with small groups or laboratories? Will the pattern of class sessions be regular (one hour of lecture followed by one hour of discussion) or will it be flexible, leaving a block of time open for various kinds of activities? Will there be field trips or other forms of experience-based learning associated with the course? All of these matters need to be decided, and, as usual, they need discussion by the team.

Once these large organizational issues have been settled, the team also needs to make decisions about the weekly and daily schedule. Exactly what will take place each time the class meets? How will these activities foster course objectives and learning outcomes? What supporting media will be used? What assignments will students be expected to complete? What materials will they read or examine? Who will find and designate these resources? How will they be made available to the students? In wrestling with these questions, the team begins to divide up team tasks, assigning lectures, groups, and responsibility for materials to various members of the team.

By far the most important organizational decision has to do with personnel: Who will actually deliver this course? In some cases, the team of faculty that plans the course coincides exactly with the team that delivers the instruction. More often, however, the faculty planners draw on several other types of personnel to help deliver the course. Teaching assistants, guest lecturers, adjunct faculty, advanced students, and other kinds of specialists can help deliver the course. If many people are involved in the course, the team must make their roles clear to them. What is it, exactly, that they are all expected to do? How are their roles different from the roles of other personnel, and how do their roles relate to the whole? On other teams, in other walks of life, team members have differentiated roles. Not everyone is expected to do the same thing. In fact, sports teams have rules about such things. In football, the quarterback can pass only to certain receivers, and penalties are given for having "an ineligible receiver down field." Team-taught courses must also have rules about who will do what. In the ideal team-taught course, a variety of personnel are used in creative ways, but all the people involved are clear about their roles and know how their efforts contribute to the whole.

One of the great advantages of teaching with a team is that roles can, in fact, be differentiated. Traditional teaching, as it has been conducted by individual professors in their own classrooms, has required that each professor do it all, without any help. The assumption is that every professor is good at everything and *needs* to be good at everything. Traditional teaching at the postsecondary level is one of the few work areas left where differentiation of function has not taken place. College teachers are specialists in their disciplines, but they have learned almost nothing about how to specialize as teachers, i.e., how to differentiate the tasks of teaching and become expert at different things. Thus, most college teachers do one thing: They go into classrooms and lecture. Team-taught courses offer an opportunity to divide up the tasks and bring different talents into play for different functions. With team-teaching, some people can specialize in large group lectures, some can specialize in facilitating case discussions, some can work with students on their writing, and others can assist students in locating and retrieving information. Students have the advantage of dealing with experts in these various roles.

The development of this specialized expertise often requires training. The participants in a team-taught course often need to learn how to play their specialized roles. One would hope, of course, that the various participants are *selected* because of their ability to play a specialized role, but often they need some additional training in that role within the context of the course. Furthermore, it is important for all the players on the team to see how their work contributes to the whole enterprise, and that achieving that perspective also requires some training.

Once the team members have been selected, their various roles differentiated, with proper training provided for them, they need to stay in good communication with each other. The personnel involved in a team-taught course also need to *function* as a team, and this means being able to work together day-by-day as the course is taught through the term. Although it is important to plan in advance for as much of the course as possible, executing a team-taught course requires much more than checking off the events on a calendar. Things *happen* in the course, and as things go well, or break down, people need to know. Sometimes things don't go as planned, and adjustments need to be made. Most team-taught courses have a "coordinator," and one of the jobs of the coordinator is to insure the smooth flow of communication. In most team-taught courses, regular meeting times are set throughout the term to insure that everyone knows what is happening, to adjust the schedule as necessary, and to deal with problems that may arise.

In making decisions about the organizational structure of the course, teams can follow usefully the old rule of architects: form follows function. The organizational structure exists to facilitate the goals and objectives of the course. The form given to the course grows naturally out of decisions made about function. Sometimes this means creating a complex organizational structure; but complexity has no value in itself, and the structure should only be as complex as needed to achieve course objectives.

Among the examples, the "Lawyering Process" course clearly has the most complicated and most interesting structure. It is a complex structure, but one that is uniquely suited to achieving the objective of the course. The overarching objective of the course is to introduce students to the components of the law and the skills that lawyers must have to perform competently. What better way to do this than to put students into simulated law firms and let them work on problem cases! The central team of faculty that planned the course made decisions about the organizational structure of the course. When the course was first offered these general decisions were also ratified by the faculty as a whole because some of the decisions had big implications. The faculty decided to offer the course to all first-year students, in both the day and evening divisions. To do this, the faculty agreed that two sets of lectures, essentially identical, would be offered, and that simulated law firms would not mix day and evening students. Beyond those differences, the course would be the same course, with the same schedule and assignments for both groups of students. The duplicate lectures are now offered twice a week and the law firms meet approximately once a week for two hours, though not every week, and not the first two weeks of the course. Some lectures are now even a part of the initial orientation week for new students. Students are divided into groups that become their firms; in the firms, they must meet their senior partners (a practicing attorney in the city), the upper division students who serve as junior partners, and their assigned writing and library consultant. Over the years, the faculty team has reordered the topics for the lectures and adjusted the work in the firms accordingly. Some assignments have been dropped and others added. Problem cases have been added, dropped, and rewritten, and the librarians have changed their methods of introducing students to the materials needed to address the problem cases. The course now involves a large cast of players. The central coordinating team, composed of faculty, does most of the lectures, except for a few guest appearances by specialists. The faculty team also divides up the responsibilities for recruiting the rest of the personnel for the course. Two faculty are responsible for recruiting the senior partners, some of whom "turn over" each year. Two other faculty are responsible for recruiting the junior partners through a time-consuming process that involves a formal application and interviews. Being a junior partner is very attractive to many upper division students, so many apply and the screening is rigorous. Some junior partners, to provide continuity, are invited to serve more than one year. The faculty member who writes the problem cases is also responsible for recruiting and supervising the writing consultants, and the librarian on the team recruits the library consultants from the library staff. Once all of the players have been recruited, separate training processes are provided for each group, as well as one large training session to coordinate the work of all of the players each summer before the course begins. During the year, the faculty team meets regularly during the term to adjust the schedule, make necessary changes, and respond to feedback from the junior partners. One faculty member serves as the team coordinator, and a full-time staff member coordinates communication and provides support materials. High standards are maintained and when it becomes evident that someone's role is not being enacted properly, taking too little or too much responsibility, and a warning has been given, replacements are made. The organization cannot accommodate a weak link; the team has to function as a team.

The ideal team-taught course has a defined structure and actually becomes a small organization. The form of the organization flows directly from its function. The team divides up its work, differentiates various roles, and recruits and trains people to perform these roles. The organizational structure of the course is important.

CHOOSING AND USING TEACHING STRATEGIES

Eventually, after extensive planning, after making many difficult decisions about the subject and learning outcomes, after selecting and training the personnel, the course must be taught. Faculty, and the other personnel who support the course, must eventually interact with students in that process we call teaching and learning. What are they to do?

I have written extensively and provided many examples in another book about this process. (See *Better Teaching, More Learning: Strategies for Success in Postsecondary Settings*. Phoenix: American Council on Education/Oryx Press, 1993.) The information in that book about teaching strategies and learning paradigms applies here; there is not enough space here to go into detail or repeat what is written there about how to select and employ teaching strategies. Instead, the focus of the discussion here is on how *teams* of teachers can best employ teaching strategies.

Assume for the moment, as I did in *Better Teaching, More Learning*, that ideas about learning can be broken into the following five paradigms:

STRATEGY	PARADIGM
Training and Coaching Developing skills by using clear objectives, breaking instruction into steps, and reinforcing progress	**Behavioral Psychology** Based on the findings of psychology, particularly operant conditioning
Lecturing and Explaining Conveying information and ideas so the can be understood understood and remembered	**Cognitive Psychology** Based on the findings of cognitive psychology about attention, information processing, and memory
Inquiry and Discovery Stimulating critical and creative thinking, problem solving, and reasoning	**Psychology of Thinking** Based on aspects of cognitive psychology and philosophy related to thinking processes
Groups and Teams Facilitating learning through group activities and team projects	**Group Communication Theory** Based on the research from speech communication on task and process behavior in groups
Experience and Reflection Drawing learning out of "real-life," out-of-the-classroom experiences	**Holistic Learning** Based on recent research on the brain and basic counseling principles

Assume also, that by thoughtful analysis of the subject, the students to be taught, and the setting where they will be taught, it is possible to select appropriate teaching strategies for the course under consideration. What can a team of teachers do with these strategies that individuals can not do? How can teaching be enhanced by a team?

Training and Coaching

In the "Training and Coaching" strategy, learning is viewed as taking place through the reinforcement of successive approximation of pre-established objectives, under conditions described as "operant conditioning." When teachers employ this strategy they have made an effort to operationalize goals, measure the present performance levels of the students, and to proceed through the gap between present abilities and the goal in small steps, reinforcing approximations of the goal along the way.

In a team-taught course, some of the teaching tasks, which correspond to different parts of the operant model tasks, can be divided up among team members. Some team members may be especially good at writing precise behavioral objectives. Others may have more skill in developing measures to assess initial (entering) and terminal (completing) performance. Still others may be good at task analysis—breaking the objective into steps and devising a plan to teach those steps. The operant model lends itself to task differentiation, and a team of teachers can attend to all parts of the model by assigning responsibility for various parts to different team members. The development of specialized learning materials—supplemental workbooks, practice exercises, audio and videotapes, and the finding or development of appropriate computer-assisted instruction (CAI)—is a job that can be spread out over the team. Ultimately, at the point when instruction takes place—whether the classroom, laboratory, the playing field, or the workstation—the behavioral paradigm cries out for the individualizing of instruction. With an instructional *team*, more hands are available to give well-timed feedback, administer reinforcement, conduct error analysis, and generally individualize the learning process. Whereas a single teacher in a traditional classroom must plan and structure the entire process and then be "everywhere at once" to provide timely feedback, a team of instructors can divide up the planning and be more widely available at the time of instruction. Obviously, the "numbers game" is very important here. Four faculty serving 240 students is really no better than one faculty member serving 60; but four faculty serving 15 students each is better than one faculty member serving 60. (The economics of team teaching is discussed in the last chapter of Part I.) Where reasonable class sizes are involved, a team of instructors and support personnel can make a big difference in implementing the "Training and Coaching" strategy.

Lecturing and Explaining

In the "Lecturing and Explaining" strategy, learning is viewed as a process whereby students attend to, process, and remember information. A great amount is known about the component parts of that process from the field of cognitive psychology. Effective lecturers know about these findings, and they design their lectures in light of that knowledge. They focus the listener's attention on a few things serially, not overloading the system, they realize that the listener is seeking general features and patterns in the information, trying to relate the unfamiliar to the familiar, and good lecturers try to provide the listener with devices for remembering the information. Any effective lecturer will try to do these things.

Team-taught courses provide interesting opportunities for some variations on this strategy. The lecturer for a particular class may want to share with the team some ideas for the forthcoming lectures in order to invite suggestions. Likewise, after a lecture, the faculty might gather to debrief—to give some reactions to the lecture and suggestions about what was effective or what students seemed to miss. If the team members know ahead of time something about the purposes of the lecture, they can enter into the question-and-answer period that often follows the lecture, or help to emphasize or clarify certain points. In other words, team members when they come to the lecture can either sit there passively, or they can serve as a kind of "extension" for the lecturer by making additional comments, or serving as a model student, asking the right questions. Sometimes it takes experience in working together for faculty to become comfortable with other faculty members in the lecture hall, and often it is necessary to establish some ground rules for participation; but once this comfort level has been achieved, the team can be effective in supporting the primary lecturer.

In addition to these more informal modes of participation by the team, it is also possible to make formal plans to share the lecture for a particular class among two or three members of the team. These plans work especially well when two or more members know the subject well, so that they both have something to contribute, or when they have different perspectives, particularly disciplinary perspectives, on the subject. Several opposing viewpoints can sometimes be brought out through a panel. Team-taught courses provide an unusual opportunity for one lecturer to comment on what another has said. The lecture can become a dialogue, sometimes among the different members of the team, but also, of course, among the students and the team members. Even a lecture, usually regarded as a solo performance, can become a team effort.

Inquiry and Discovery

Most faculty members want their students to learn to think. The "Inquiry and Discovery" strategy is used to enhance thinking skills. Teaching students how to think is difficult enough within a disciplinary framework, but teaching thinking in an interdisciplinary class, where the subject has been invented, can be a more serious challenge. Unfortunately, traditional classrooms often are not structured in such a way that students are expected to think or *can* think. Teachers are so busy telling students what others have thought, covering content, that they seldom devote a significant amount of class time to cultivating the thinking process itself. This means structuring the classroom for discussion, where students can try out new ideas in a supportive, low-risk environment. People who have studied thinking processes know that they are varied and complex, and that thinking in one area, for example, inductive reasoning in a chemistry course, is not the same as thinking in another area, for example, metaphorical thinking in a creative writing class.

In interdisciplinary courses, various modes of thinking may appear side by side in the same class. The options multiply—critical thinking, dialogical thinking, creative thinking, to name just three—and it is easy to get lost and become bogged down in confusion and controversy. On the other hand, team teaching provides some excellent opportunities for encouraging students to think more carefully and more broadly about complex subjects. Whereas one teacher in a traditional classroom is faced with how to facilitate inquiry, usually with the whole class, a team of teachers can break the class into smaller groups to inquire simultaneously about the subject. The groups may use the same methods to inquire about the same aspect of the subject, different methods to inquire about the same aspect of the subject, the same methods to inquire about different aspects of the subject, or different methods to inquire about different aspects of the subject. The subgroups may or may not report back to the entire class with their findings. These techniques are especially useful with case studies, where different groups can practice different problem-solving and decision-making strategies on the same case, on different aspects of the same case, or on different cases. This approach also works well with laboratories, where students may be working on different aspects of a problem in different labs. Whatever the format, students need a significant text to examine, an intriguing problem to solve, or a difficult decision to make; and they need a skilled facilitator to help guide their thinking. Team teaching provides more contrasting disciplinary perspectives, more good minds to select or create interesting objects of inquiry, and more facilitators skilled in more methods of inquiry.

Groups and Teams

In the "Groups and Teams" strategy, learning is viewed as a matter of feeling as well as thinking; students are encouraged to use the group process to examine their opinions, attitudes, and beliefs. There are three basic ways to use groups in classrooms. First, groups work directly under the direction of a facilitator and depend on the facilitator for guidance. Second, "leaderless" groups work independently with occasional visits from the facilitator, and may or may not designate formal leaders. Third, teams usually work together over a sustained period of time on an assigned task under the direction of an outside "manager" who works with a designated leader or a member of the team who has been given a leadership role by the team. In all three cases, the possibilities are enhanced when a team of faculty is available to work with the groups. When the facilitator plays a primary role, several faculty or other personnel are available to serve as facilitators. When "leaderless" groups are used, the faculty are more frequently available to check in on the groups and monitor their progress. When teams are used, various faculty can be responsible for direct oversight of two or three teams and can work directly with the designated leader to make sure that progress on the task is continuous by providing the support necessary to help the team function effectively. In team teaching, more people are available to find or design stimulating group instruments and to facilitate or supervise the work of the groups. Assuming that the teachers in an interdisciplinary team-taught course know how to work with groups, or can be taught to do so, the rest is simple—many hands make light work.

Experience and Reflection

In the "Experience and Reflection" strategy, learning is viewed as holistic, arising from some stimulating experience, such as work, service, or travel, and involving a process of reflection with a faculty mentor whereby the student and faculty member, working together, optimize the learning that can accrue from the experience. Although this strategy is used chiefly with more sustained forms of learning that occur outside the classroom, such as cooperative education, study abroad, or service learning, many interdisciplinary courses have an experience-based learning component. Most often this component is a field trip, service experience, or a community-based research project. A team of faculty has some advantage over a single faculty member in a traditional classroom in setting up and carrying out ancillary experience-based learning projects. Very often more faculty have more ideas and more contacts for setting up the experiences. A team of faculty can quickly generate interesting ideas for field visits, service experiences, or field research projects. Furthermore, they can share the work that goes into making the arrangements by differentiating roles and delegating tasks. The experience itself is usually enhanced when more "supervisors" are available. (What teacher has not longed for more personnel on a field visit or trip to a museum?) The reflection process, so important for seeing that meaning is extricated from the experience, can be shared by the team and done either individually or with small groups of students, formally or informally.

In the ideal team-taught course, the faculty actually teach together. They differentiate their roles and divide up responsibilities according to their talents and interests. They find, and continue to seek out, ways to work together in employing different teaching strategies. Sometimes they provide ideas and support for a colleague who has the main responsibility for a particular class; but at other times, they work together in the classroom, sharing the responsibility for the communication process with students for that day. The ideal team-taught course involves teachers actually teaching as a team.

ASSESSING LEARNING OUTCOMES AND SATISFACTIONS

All the decisions made about issues raised in the previous sections of this chapter—the idea, the subject, the learning outcomes, scope and sequence, breadth and depth, the organization, and the teaching strategies—will determine what can and ought to be done to assess student learning outcomes and satisfactions. If the team has "done its homework" on the rest of the course, the task of assessment becomes much easier. On the other hand, if the subject and desired learning outcomes are unclear, it will be difficult to develop a good assessment plan.

Most courses, discipline-based and interdisciplinary, have built into them some methods for testing students in order to determine grades. This grading process usually involves some quizzes, a mid-term and final exam, and maybe some "research" papers. Faculty often make two mistakes at this point: They usually use only this narrow range of artifacts to determine grades, and they equate the production of these artifacts, for grading purposes, with a system for assessing student learning outcomes and satisfactions. Using this narrow range of artifacts to determine grades is not wrong, just too limited given the existence of so many other options.

Furthermore, although traditional options have their merits, they are so frequently used that most students find them tedious and unchallenging. Assume, for example, that in most courses students take three quizzes, are assigned two term papers, and take a final exam. If students take four to five courses a term, two or three terms per year, averaging some 40 to 50 courses over four years, then they are likely to have taken one 120 to 150 quizzes, written 80 to 100 papers, and taken 40 to 50 final exams. Is it any wonder that so many students drop out or plod on without enthusiasm?

The traditional grading options are the ones most frequently used for a number of good reasons; long-standing traditions are no accident. They are what most college teachers experienced during their own education, they are relatively easy to use, and they measure certain things traditionally associated with learning—whether students can remember information, whether they can find and draw on sources of information, and whether they can express their ideas in writing. Within this framework, however, the traditional options for determining grades are often used in incredibly unimaginative ways by teachers and students. Is it possible to be more creative? How can assessment of student learning outcomes and satisfactions be enriched in interdisciplinary courses?

The goal, of course, is not simply to create more interesting and more diverse assessment options, although that is surely desirable; but in doing so, to measure more adequately the desired outcomes of the interdisciplinary course. The first step, therefore, in designing more creative assessment options is to return to the basic idea of the course and to the peculiar characteristics of the interdisciplinary subject that has been generated. If the underlying purpose of the interdisciplinary course is to forge creative connections, stimulate new perspectives, and explore themes and problems, then by all means, assessment should be designed to examine whether the fundamental interdisciplinary purposes of the course are being achieved. This probably means giving less priority, therefore, to the goals of traditional teaching (remembering, for quizzes and exams, and reporting, in "research papers," what others have written) and greater priority to analyzing, synthesizing, applying, and using for evaluation what has been learned in creative ways.

If Bloom's *Taxonomy* (or something comparable to it) has been used to determine and express specific learning outcomes for the course, then those outcomes can become the basis for generating creative assessment options. How is it that students might best generate outputs that demonstrate that they have achieved or can do the intellectual tasks described in the *Taxonomy*? Although appropriate assessment can be developed for learning at all levels in the *Taxonomy*, more emphasis should be placed on higher order skills involving application, analysis, synthesis, and evaluation, because those are outcomes more closely associated with the purposes of interdisciplinary courses.

With a list of well-conceived learning outcomes for the course in one hand, one might hold in the other hand a menu of assessment options that includes quizzes, exams, and "research" papers, but goes beyond these to include activities that can be especially designed to measure outcomes associated with interdisciplinary learning, such as the following:

- *Logs and Diaries:* Instruments to record systematic daily reflections and responses to ideas, issues, or experiences from various viewpoints.
- *Case Studies:* Written or oral responses to cases that test students' powers of analysis, problem-solving abilities, and skill in applying diverse perspectives.

- *Visual Representations:* Charts, tables, graphs, outlines, and models to display information, particularly the interrelationships of concepts and ideas from different disciplines.
- *Essays:* Narratives in which students must state a point of view and defend it with evidence synthesized from multiple sources.
- *Critiques:* Thoughtful discussions of the strengths and weaknesses of books, articles, films, concerts, or exhibits, using multiple criteria.
- *Proposals:* Research proposals, requests for funding, outlines of proposed programs that employ interdisciplinary perspectives.
- *Team Projects:* Reports of team projects that require the coordination of diverse individual efforts, and the synthesis of information from multiple sources.
- *Interviews:* Reports of interviews with people who have different viewpoints or perspectives on a common theme or problem.
- *Panel Discussions:* Participation on panels where issues are debated and discussed from opposing viewpoints.
- *Reflections on Experience-Based Learning:* Oral or written reflections on field trips, service learning, travel, or brief internships.
- *Creative Works*: Stories, poems, works of art, dance, dramatic sketches that portray issues, themes, or cultural patterns.
- *Role Plays and Simulations:* Acting out and then discussing or reporting on situations that can be understood best at a variety of levels or from different perspectives.

The menu can be adapted or lengthened as necessary, but these items give an indication at least of the kinds of things that students can be asked to do to demonstrate some of the desired outcomes of interdisciplinary learning. Not all of the demonstrations of learning need necessarily be graded, but there is no reason why any of the items from the above menu could not be graded, given some carefully thought-out criteria and guidelines for the process.

Much can be discovered about what students are learning from a course by examining the outputs they make for grading purposes, but it is often useful to go beyond these artifacts to gather additional information about the course from students, either formally or informally. Most of the work students produce for grades does not provide much information about whether students are satisfied with the course or not. Some "A-students" can be highly dissatisfied. Furthermore, some "A-students" may not actually get the main idea of the course.

Several things can be done to learn more about student reactions to a course. One of these is the standard course evaluation form used on many campuses with traditional courses. The problem with the traditional form, of course, is that the references are usually to "the subject" and "the teacher," so that some adaptation needs to be made to allow for the multiple subjects and the team of teachers in an interdisciplinary course. Usually, this means asking for information on various aspects of the course and the performance of individual team members. The more specific this information is, the more valuable it will be for actually making changes in the course. An overall faculty rating of "3" on a scale of 1-5 may not have much meaning when four faculty are involved in the course. Presumably, one needs to find out which parts of the team are effective or ineffective, and to find that out sooner, rather than later in the course.

One thing that is useful to know about interdisciplinary team-taught courses is what students perceive about the interdisciplinary nature of the course. In the next chapter, results are reported from a questionnaire administered to students in the five courses used as examples in this study. It is useful to examine that questionnaire briefly now. It provides for Likert-scale responses (1-5) to the following questions:

1. To what extent would you say there is evidence of collaboration (working together) by faculty in *planning* this course?
2. To what extent would you say that faculty have tried to *integrate the subject content* of this course?
3. To what extent would you say that faculty *have been successful in integrating the subject content* of this course?
4. In describing the *classroom teaching* in this course, to what extent would you say faculty were collaborating?
5. To what extent would you say faculty have collaborated in establishing and carrying out *grading and evaluation practices* for this course?

It is interesting to note that most of the questions focus on the nature of the course as an *interdisciplinary* course in order to see whether students perceive the special values peculiar to interdisciplinary team teaching. If they do not, perhaps the level of collaboration is low, or more interpretation needs to be made concerning course goals and learning outcomes. (See the chapter entitled "Faculty and Student Perceptions of Team Teaching: Satisfactions and Frustrations.") One of the most important things one might wish to find out about an interdisciplinary team taught course is whether or not, and to what degree, it is perceived as such by the students in the course. If students have no perception of this, why are the faculty going to all this trouble?

Assessment data about a course can also be gathered through informal means. It may seem odd, but faculty seldom do what is the most obvious and direct way of gathering feedback about a course: ask the students. This can be done in class, through a general discussion, after class with students who linger, at lunch or over a fruit drink with a representative group of students, or through focus groups, carefully selected to represent all backgrounds and levels of achievement. The all-important question for focus groups is: What are we trying to achieve and are we achieving it? If students can't articulate the goals of the course, or are frustrated in achieving the goals, some modifications may need to be made. If in doubt about how the course is coming across to students, ask them. If you doubt they will tell you, or it may be too painful to listen, get someone else (a qualified colleague, teaching assistant, or trusted advanced student) to ask them for you. In whatever manner the conversation with students takes place, it is important to gain feedback from them about their satisfactions as well as their overall perception of the purposes of the course and the way it is functioning.

The example courses have made some impressive efforts to develop creative assessment options. Most notable, of course, is the immediate feedback report used in the "Quality Panorama." "The Lawyering Process" uses focus groups of students to check on how the course comes across, as well as a variety of skill assessment projects associated with the work done in the simulated law firms. The faculty of "Multiple Voices" make an initial reading of exams and then get together to share good and poor examples of responses before actually putting grades on papers. Like other aspects of a good team-taught course, the whole team can get involved in assessment.

The ideal interdisciplinary team-taught course begins with a great idea. The team members face the sometimes difficult task of inventing the interdisciplinary subject and establishing learning outcomes. Teaching strategies can be identified and modified to take advantage of opportunities for collaboration. Assessment methods can be adapted to measure whether the most-valued learning outcomes are being achieved, and whether the course is meeting student expectations.

It sounds easy, but what has been described in this chapter is the "ideal" interdisciplinary team-taught course characterized by high levels of collaboration. As experienced teachers know, the ideal is not always attainable. The best ideas fall short of their potential; faculty colleagues find themselves making unhappy compromises in creating the subject and negotiating learning outcomes; team teaching often proves more difficult than teaching alone; and, unhappily, students don't always learn what we hope they will learn or want them to perceive about the course.

Moving from the ideal world back to the real world one must ask: What actually happens when faculty try to work together in teams? What communication processes are experienced and what types of human relations problems can emerge? How do faculty feel about being members of a team? How do students perceive team teaching? These are questions to be addressed in the next two chapters.

NOTES

1. William Newell, "Designing Interdisciplinary Courses," in Julie Thompson Klein and William Doty, *Interdisciplinary Studies Today* (San Francisco: Jossey-Bass, 1994), p. 37. Newell does not quote but cites as a source for the list Martin Trow, "Interdisciplinary Studies as a Counterculture: Problems of Birth, Growth, and Survival," *Issues in Integrative Studies*, 4(1984–85): pp. 1–15.

2. *Ibid.*, p. 38.

3. Richard Haliburton, "Interdisciplinary Studies" in Arthur Chickering, *The Modern American College* (San Francisco: Jossey-Bass, 1981) p. 454.

4. James Dusenberry, "Comment" in University—National Bureau of Economic Research, *Demography and Economic Change in Developed Countries* (Princeton, NJ: Princeton University Press, 1960): 233.

5. *Ibid.*, p. 43.

6. I have returned to the original text to present in the briefest, yet most useful form I can, the main ideas. Bloom provides a "Condensed Version" at the end of the text, which is still a bit too detailed for our purposes here. Without, I hope, doing an injustice to Bloom's intent, I have collapsed some subheadings in the earlier portion of the taxonomy (the 1:00 sections) to conform with the system of headings that Bloom uses in the rest of the taxonomy. I have also selected freely from his examples and paraphrased the key concepts to make the taxonomy as immediately accessible as possible for the college teacher. Bloom's *Taxonomy*, alas, appears to be widely referred to, but little read or understood, and any individual or team of teachers, wanting to know more about learning outcomes should refer directly to Benjamin Bloom, ed., *Taxonomy of Educational Objectives, The Classification of Educational Goals, Handbook I: Cognitive Domain.* (New York: David McKay, 1956). The committee of "college and university examiners" who contributed to the construction of the *Taxonomy* reads like a "Who's Who" of important educators in mid-twentieth century America.

7. Bloom, *Taxonomy*, p. 18. The intent of hierarchy is there, and the suggestion is that simpler skills are often incorporated in more complex tasks at the upper levels of the taxonomy.

8. The general classification in the affective domain include Receiving, Responding, Valuing, Organization, and Characterization by a value or value complex. See David Krathwohl, Benjamin Bloom, and Bertram Masia, *Taxonomy of Educational Objectives, The Classification of Educational Goals, Handbook II: Affective Domain* (New York: David McKay, 1964). The general classifications in the psychomotor domain are Reflex Movements, Basic-Fundamental Movements, Perceptual Abilities, Physical Abilities, Skilled Movements, and Non-Discussive Communication. See Anita J. Harrow, *A Taxonomy of the Psychomotor Domain* (New York: David McKay, 1972).

9. William Newell, "Designing Interdisciplinary Courses," p. 35.

CHAPTER 4

When Faculty Work in Teams: Learning from the Research on Groups and Teams

"It is through hearing people that I have learned all that I know about individuals, about personality, about psychotherapy, and about interpersonal relationships . . . When I really hear someone it is like listening to the music of the spheres, because beyond the immediate message of the person, no matter what that might be, there is the universal, the general."

—Carl Rogers

TEAMS IN CONTEXT

Most faculty have served on committees and the experience has not always been pleasant. For some, such service may be their only experience of working with colleagues in a team situation. On at least some occasions, faculty have had a satisfying opportunity to be a part of a committee or task force that has designed innovative programs or established new policies and procedures that have had a significant impact on the department or college. Often, however, "committee work" is filled with frustration, conflict, and the resulting sense of an enormous waste of time. One can come away from the experience wondering: Is there something inherently wrong with the structure of groups and teams? For some faculty, the sense of revulsion is so great that they prefer to stay in their office or to study at home, working quietly alone, reminding themselves that this is why they became a professor in the first place.

Unfortunately, many aspects of the life of an institution require the use of groups and teams, not the least of which is the "shared governance" and collegial management," which most faculty cherish, at least as an ideal. Like other types of organizations today, colleges and universities are increasingly turning toward groups and teams as a way of structuring their academic and administrative work; and, in doing so, they are only part of a larger movement, throughout the world of profit and non-profit organizations, toward the use of teams. As Katzenbach and Smith note in *The Wisdom of Teams*:

> Teams will play an increasingly essential part in first creating and then sustaining high performance organizations. In fact, most models of the "organization of the future" that we have heard about—"networked," "clustered," "nonhierarchical," "horizontal," and so forth—are premised on *teams surpassing individuals as the primary performance unit in the company*.[1]

Whatever one might think about the relative value of the contributions of individuals and teams, it appears, at least for the near future, that teams will be used to achieve a variety of types of outcomes in almost every kind of organization. The issue today is not whether to use teams, but how to use them effectively. The use of teams for teaching in colleges and universities is part, therefore, of a broader context in which team collaboration is coming to be valued highly.

If teams are valued, and if team teaching has many of the specific advantages outlined previously, what guidance can be given to faculty when they work in teams? How can the typically "bad experience" of working on committees be avoided when faculty collaborate in their teaching? Is it possible to learn something from the literature on groups and teams, and to put that knowledge into practice when faculty collaborate in developing and delivering interdisciplinary, team-taught courses?

DEFINING GROUPS AND TEAMS

All teams are groups, but not all groups are teams. Teams are a specialized kind of group. In a stimulating recent study of teams by Carl Larson and Frank LaFasto entitled *Teamwork: What Must Go Right/What Can Go Wrong*,[2] teams are defined as two or more people with a "specific performance objective or recognizable goal to be attained; and (wherein) coordination of activity among the members of the team is required for the attainment of the team goal or objective." The distinction between a group and a team, while not always clear, appears to have much to do with the emphasis given within teams, to completing a task or fulfilling a performance objective that takes collaboration over a period of time. Thus, people who get together on Friday nights to enjoy international folk dancing might be thought of as a group, but not as a team. Teams participate, however, in the general characteristics of groups. Malcolm and Hulda Knowles offer the following helpful criteria for defining a group:

- **A Definable Membership**—collection of two or more people identifiable by name and type.
- **Consciousness of Membership**—the members think of themselves as a group, have a "collective perception of unity," and a conscious identification with each other.
- **A Sense of Shared Purpose**—the members have the same "object model" or goal or ideals.
- **Ability to Act in a Unitary Manner**—the group can behave as a single organism.[3]

Most teams have these general characteristics of groups, but the sense of purpose, the commitment to a shared task is stronger in teams. One might say a team is a group with a mission. A team needs to get something done. Because teams are a specialized kind of group, it is important to examine the literature on groups as well as the more recent writing about teams to learn about the behavior and communication that takes place within teams. In what follows, the terms "groups" and "teams" will be used more or less interchangeably, with a tendency to favor "teams," because the faculty groups that create interdisciplinary courses are called "teams" and their efforts are referred to as "team teaching."

THE FORMAL STUDY OF GROUPS AND TEAMS

Because so much stress has been placed on the importance of groups and teams in recent years, it is easy to be deceived into believing that they are a modern phenomena. But human beings have for centuries assembled themselves into groups for a variety of purposes and have given their groups special names, such as "guilds," "councils," "tribunes," "communes," "congregations," "troupes," "teams," and "companies."[4] Groups have also been used for educational purposes, from the small "bands" who followed such wandering scholars as Confucius or Plato, to the "guilds" of students in the Middle Ages who hired faculty, paid their salaries, evaluated their performance, and called them to task for not covering material they agreed to teach. How far the "student union" has strayed from its original purposes! The difference, in modern times, is that groups and teams are employed *consciously* for the explicit accomplishment of specific goals. We know when we are using a team and we know why we are using it.

The self-conscious use of groups and teams was accompanied by a parallel interest in studying them. People who consciously choose to employ groups and teams want to use them effectively; therefore, knowing how they function is important. In the words of the aforementioned subtitle of *Teamwork* by Larson and LaFasto, people who work in teams want to know "what must go right" and "what can go wrong."

The formal study of groups and teams began in employment settings. A classic set of research studies conducted by Elton Mayo and his colleagues at Western Electric in the 1930s revealed the importance of "human factors" in the productivity of workers.[5] Although the variables being studied had to do with better working conditions, such as lighting, the personal attention being given to the workers as a group by the researchers proved to be the most important consideration. Now known for the classic "Hawthorne effect" in social science research methods, the study set in motion further explorations of human factors in work environments where people work in groups.

Expanded efforts to train workers in group processes gave birth to the Human Relations Movement. The movement was advanced, somewhat by accident, in 1946, when Kurt Lewin and his associates were conducting group training for community leaders responsible for enforcing the Connecticut Fair Employment Practices Act. Lewin, a professor at MIT, was already well known for his work in group dynamics and group leadership styles.[6] The group leaders held evening meetings to discuss the processes taking place in the groups each day. Some of the workshop participants began attending evening meetings in which their behavior and its effect on the group were discussed and analyzed openly. It was discovered that when group members were confronted objectively with information about their behavior in the group and were encouraged to think about this information in a non-defensive way, meaningful learning could occur.[7] In the summer of 1947, shortly after Lewin's death, his associates gathered in Bethel, Maine, to sponsor the first formal group training programs in which trainers assisted the group in discussing its own behavior.[8] Out of these efforts by Lewin's associates came the National Training Laboratory for Group Development (NTL) established under the auspices of the National Education Association in 1949.

The other "founding fathers" of the study of group behavior are Carl Rogers, who worked with his associates at the Counseling Center of the University of Chicago, and J.L. Moreno, an Austrian immigrant known chiefly for his work with role playing and psychodrama, and to whom the term "group therapy" is attributed.[9] This pioneering research on human behavior in groups has grown into a recognized and extensive field of study, residing in the areas of human communication studies and social psychology. More recently, scholars have begun to study team behavior, and a growing body of organizational literature is emerging on how high performance teams function.

WHAT SCHOLARS KNOW ABOUT WORKING IN TEAMS

After years of research on groups and teams, scholars have developed some principles about how human beings are likely to act in groups and some theories about what practices make groups and teams productive or ineffective. These concepts, principles, and theories, drawn from the literature on groups and teams, are presented here along with a continuing commentary on their application to the work of faculty in teams that design and deliver interdisciplinary courses.

To Use or Not to Use

One might begin by asking: When should groups be used? What is known about when to use a team and when to allow individuals to work alone? One useful test of whether or not to use a group is to ask whether the task is anything more than "summative," that is, does the task require anything more than the sum of the outputs of individuals? In tasks where the output transcends the total of individual outputs, there is an "assembly effect."

> An assembly effect occurs when the group is able to achieve collectively something which could not have been achieved by any member working alone or by a combination of individual efforts. The assembly effect bonus is productivity which exceeds the potential of the most capable member and also exceeds the sum of the efforts of the group members working separately.[10]

If the team is performing a task that could be performed just as well by an individual, or as the sum of the work of individuals without an assembly effect, the team is probably not needed.[11] Faculty who collaborate on teams to plan and deliver interdisciplinary courses presumably already have agreed that they are working together as a team in order to achieve things they ordinarily would not be able to achieve alone. In particular, the integration of the subject content and the elaboration of learning outcomes should result in a product that should be "greater than the sum of the parts." On the other hand, faculty often forget that they don't *always* have to *function* as a team. Many tasks associated with a team-taught course have no assembly effect, which is to say, they could better be done alone. Some of these tasks are making preparations for class sessions, finding materials and texts, developing outside study resources, and generating exam questions. Most faculty teams will be far more productive if they make clear distinctions between the work they need to do together and the work they could do alone. Some member of the team needs to be on the alert, constantly ready to ask: Could we do this better alone? Working together is time-consuming, expensive, and, sometimes, stressful. Why not spend "high quality time together" working on those things that most require collaboration?

More Ideas

One consistent finding of the research on groups is that people working in groups generate more ideas. Not only do people bring different ideas to groups, something about the exchange of ideas in groups generates even more ideas. The level of "ideation" is 60 to 80 percent higher in groups than for individuals.[12] This increased generation of ideas is both a curse and a blessing for faculty teams. On the one hand, the team values the flow of creative ideas; this is one of the reasons the members have chosen to work as a team. On the other hand, sorting out all these ideas and deciding which ones to use can be troublesome. It is easy to become overwhelmed with possibilities. This is especially true when academics generate ideas; there is not much we can't think of, and we are trained to leave no stone unturned. Making decisions, on the other hand, may not be our strong point. Because it is seldom possible to do everything, choices must be made, and making choices can generate conflict.

A group technique known as "brainstorming" may suggest a way of resolving this problem. Although we often speak in a general way about brainstorming, it is, in its more technical sense, a specific procedure for generating and managing ideas in groups. Brainstorming has its roots in a special technique developed in 1957 by Alex F. Osborn to increase the number of ideas during a group's deliberation.[13] Osborn, a successful advertising executive with a special interest in creativity, was interested in generating more and better ideas from groups of 10 to 12 people. Osborn's rules for brainstorming are fairly simple: adverse criticism is taboo, "free-wheeling" is welcomed, quantity of ideas is desired, and combination and improvement of ideas are sought. The criticism of ideas is suspended until a later post-brainstorming session designed for the evaluation and categorizing of the ideas. The aspect of this technique that is especially valuable to faculty working in teams is the separation of the generation and evaluation phases of dealing with ideas. Faculty may find it useful to distinguish clearly between those times when they are generating ideas and those times when they are making decisions about which ideas to employ. Evaluating each idea as it is generated is time-consuming and may lead to aggression, defensiveness, and conflict in the group. Someone in the group can play a valuable leadership role by reminding the group when they are brainstorming and when they are sorting through ideas to make decisions.

Size

How big should teams be? Is there a downward or upward limit to their size or an optimal size? Most scholars in this field agree that even two people (technically a dyad) can be a group, but that when a third is added the nature of the communication changes: there is now the possibility for a network of communication, and one person can be an observer of the communication between the other two.[14] In groups, one can talk to the whole group or to certain group members, and the others can observe this interaction. There is no magic number to the upward limit of size; this depends on the purpose of the group. Some interdisciplinary courses involve more faculty than others. Usually, however, the team has a "working nucleus." A few interdisciplinary courses use a large number of personnel, including teaching assistants, adjunct faculty, or upper division students, but a distinction is usually made between the planning (decision-making) team and the implementation team. The crucial decision about size relates to the planning team. The best guideline, a conclusion drawn from the research literature, is: "A group needs to contain a number of people sufficiently small for each to be aware of and have some relation to the other."[15] The team needs to be big enough to include a sufficient number of faculty members with the important skills needed to achieve course objectives, but small enough for everyone to participate in a significant way. When team members don't feel as if they are part of the team, the team may be too big, and there may be communication problems.

Communication

Communication in groups is usually not the same as when two people talk to each other, first one speaking, then the other responding. Communication in groups bounces around among the members, not always in equally measured amounts. One thing to watch for in groups is the nature of the communication at a fairly fundamental level. Who talks? How often does each individual talk? Who do people talk to? Who do they look at when they talk—one person, the group, the floor or ceiling? Who talks after whom and who interrupts whom? And what types of statements are being made—assertions, questions, responses?[16] In general, faculty are not good at observing these behaviors unless they have had some special training in doing so; or, oddly enough, they may know how to observe these behaviors in their classes, but may not know how to transfer these skills to observing their own behavior on a team. Effective team members will be sensitive to who's doing the talking, and will learn to moderate their own participation and bring out the shy members of the group.

In addition to watching the communication within the group, effective group members practice active listening. This may or may not be a skill that the typical faculty member brings to the team. Traditional teaching stresses talking, and most faculty members are "good talkers," but listening, particularly active listening, may require a considerable amount of practice. When a person interacts with another person in a group, a "communication event" takes place that involves self-disclosure and feedback. Self-disclosure occurs when a person lets someone know something about them that the listener would not ordinarily know.[17] This need not be a deep, dark secret (although it may be), but can refer to any idea or feeling a person is expressing. The second half of the communication event occurs when someone else in the group or several members of the group make a response in return. Usually this response, if it is truly a response to what has been said, and is perceived by the sender as a response, rather than simply a new disclosure, is called "feedback."[18] In order for this transaction of self-disclosure and feedback to take place in an effective way, active listening needs to take place. People engage in many types of listening all the time—social listening, critical listening, and discriminating listening, to name a few—but members of groups can greatly enhance the communication among group members through active listening.[19] "Active listening implies that the person listens with the total self, including attitudes, beliefs, feelings, and intuitions," and on teams, active listening is essential. Active listening is sometimes further differentiated as being of two types: "deliberative listening" or "empathic listening."[20] The deliberative listener is actively engaged in trying to understand ideas, standing ready to agree or disagree, criticize, summarize, or conclude. The empathic listener is focusing on feelings, trying to understand the speaker's comments and feelings from the speaker's point of view. Most faculty, accustomed as we are to speaking, need to develop and practice active listening skills. We may be fairly good at deliberative listening—especially standing ready to criticize—but we are usually not so skilled in empathic listening, trying to see and feel what the other person is saying and understand it from their point of view.

For those who need to develop their active listening skills, there are some useful guidelines, some do's and don't's. Don't get involved prematurely with an emotional reaction to what is being said, particularly if you disagree. Try to catch yourself rehearsing a rebuttal in your head; if you are doing this, chances are you are not listening well. Notice when you are distracted, when you are responding only to certain words, when your prejudices are interfering with understanding. Try to concentrate on listening (not speaking), avoid interruptions, demonstrate interest and alertness, seek areas of agreement, search for the overall meaning, demonstrate patience, ask questions, and withhold an evaluation of the message until you are sure you understand it.[21]

Not all the communication that takes place in groups occurs at the verbal level. In recent years, new importance has been given to nonverbal communication as well. Nonverbal communication occurs in a variety of ways, and sophisticated "group-watchers" will look for the following:

- **Proxemics**—the way group members arrange themselves in space, through seating arrangements, physical distance, and general body orientation.
- **Appearance**—overall physical appearance, dress, attractiveness, style, and mood.
- **Kinesics**—body movement, postures, gestures, and movements of the head, limbs, hands, and feet.
- **Facial Expressions**—facial features, movement of eyes and mouth.[22]

Faculty members who work together will become sensitive to the way team members sit (who is in charge, who opposes whom) and will learn to read the mood of the group and the feelings of individual members by looking for clues in the body movements and facial expressions of the team members.

How does nonverbal communication relate to verbal communication? Sometimes directly, by repeating, elaborating, or extending a verbal message (pounding the table), or by accenting key points. At other times, however, a nonverbal message may contradict the verbal message, sending a visible clue to the group that what is being said is not what is being felt.[23] In a sense, then, group members are always communicating, whether they speak or not, through gestures, facial expressions, or just by occupying a particular place in the room. It is not really possible not to communicate.[24]

Faculty working on interdisciplinary teams need to work hard at developing active listening skills and at reading nonverbal cues. Inherent in the task of building interdisciplinary courses is the challenge of understanding another colleague's discipline or field of study and domain, which may be unfamiliar and may seem to operate with a strange set of assumptions and rules. Using deliberative and empathic listening skills and reading nonverbal cues will be essential if true understanding of each other's disciplines is to take place, let alone the invention (together) of a new subject.

Task and Process

Those who study groups note that the communication seems to involve two levels often simultaneously, one that has come to be called "task," the other "process." The task is the activity the group expects to perform, in this case the development and implementation of an interdisciplinary course. Team members usually direct most of their energies to thinking about and negotiating the details of the course; this is their collective task.[25] At the same time, however, and at a different level, they are dealing with the process of the group itself, the psychological and communication needs of its members. As one researcher notes, "a group is a dynamic organism, always awake, never really still; group dynamics and interpersonal dynamics and intrapersonal dynamics are operating all the time."[26] When people participate in groups, they bring with them their individual needs for identity, recognition, inclusion, status, and understanding. To put the matter bluntly, faculty bring their egos to the team, and those egos need to be fed, supported, nurtured, and soothed. Sometimes this requires "time out" from the task to deal with the personal concerns of one of the members, but more often the process work of the team is intermingled with its work on the task. It is natural, therefore, that the group is not always "on task," because sometimes the group needs to communicate, laugh, empathize, or just play. Some faculty may feel that much of the team's time is wasted—and sometimes it is—but it is important to recognize that positive process behavior is important to the team's effectiveness, and every team will divide its time to address both process and task needs.

Structure and Role

Groups and teams develop a structure to get their work done. Just as a building has a physical structure, groups develop a social structure in which different people play different roles. When teams are functioning effectively, people know what role to play, how to behave, where to be, and what to do. One of the advantages of teams is that roles can be differentiated so that not everyone on the team has to function the same way. The concept of role goes back to the classic work of the sociologist Erving Goffman who described the social system as a stage, where human beings, much like actors in a play, act out their parts in roles. Goffman believed that roles are "the basic unit of socialization" where the important "tasks in society are allocated, and arrangements are made to enforce their performance."[27] In groups, roles are the "set of expectations which group members share concerning the behavior of a person who occupies a given position in the group."[28] On teams responsible for interdisciplinary courses, faculty will quickly fall into various roles, and the astute observer will see people taking on and playing out the roles that fit them best. Someone will initiate the ideas; another will jot things down, making pictures and diagrams; still another will mediate and resolve conflict; while others will oversee the progress of the group, reminding others of the group's lack of progress toward goals. These roles are played out at both the task and process level. Exactly how and why people come to play their particular roles (usually more than one) within the group is not always clear, but it is amazing how quickly people fall into roles and how fixed the expectations become that a particular faculty member will predictably play particular roles.

Cohesiveness

When the process needs are being met in appropriate ways, the group becomes cohesive. Cohesiveness refers to the ability of the group members to get along, their loyalty, pride, and commitment to the group. Or, more simply, cohesiveness is the degree of liking that members have for each other.[29] When faculty start to bicker and make cutting remarks, when they find excuses not to come to scheduled meetings, or when they make comments outside the meetings that they won't make in the meeting, the group is beginning to lack cohesiveness. Something is "going wrong" at the process level. Interestingly, cohesiveness is an output of an effective group process, but once established, it is an input to subsequent task activities.[30] Furthermore, the outputs at the process level and task level are intertwined. If the output at the process level is called "cohesiveness" and the output at the task level may be called "productivity," clearly, there must be a relationship. As might be expected, cohesive groups are more productive, but only to a point. As cohesiveness increases, productivity increases until cohesiveness reaches such a high level that productivity falls off. When group members become too fond of each other, they spend too much time socializing and too little time on the task.[31] Members of faculty teams often discover that they have grown to like and care about each other deeply, and there is a tendency sometimes to spend more time than is really needed on the team's process. Because there is no "boss" to watch how time is being spent, and because the leader often is reluctant to cut off process communication, faculty teams are vulnerable to "time-wasting." When this happens, some team members, or perhaps the entire group, can become frustrated, and, ironically, group cohesion declines from too much process behavior. Someone in the group can play a useful role by monitoring the team's process behavior and commenting from time to time on the team's cohesion.

Stages

Most groups go through predictable stages. It takes a while for a team to begin to function as a team, to develop a structure and become productive. The life cycle of groups has been the object of much research, and although scholars who study group behavior disagree on what to call these phases, most agree that groups pass through them. One classic formulation of these stages uses four catchy rhyming words:

- **Forming**—a stage of testing and member independence, with emphasis on defining the task.
- **Storming**—a stage of intragroup conflict and emotional expression.
- **Norming**—a stage of development of group cohesion and establishing the "rules."
- **Performing**—a stage of functional role relatedness and emergence of solutions.[32]

Most faculty teams go through some stages, and patience may be necessary in the early stages while the group is finding its way. Perhaps the most important implication of this for faculty teams is the recognition that the stages are real, and when personnel changes are made—when old members leave and new members join—the team may need to "begin again" the process of finding how it is going to function as a team. A highly cohesive faculty team may be upset by the departure and addition of members, and may regress for a time to an earlier stage while the team adjusts to the changes in its composition.

Conflict

What can be worse than working with a group whose members fight all the time? What can be done to prevent or reduce conflict? It is important to realize that at least some conflict is normal and even necessary on productive teams. A useful distinction can be made, in this regard, between conflict and tension, and between primary tension and secondary tension.[33] A newly formed group almost always has an initial, low level of primary tension. Signs of primary tension are nervous laughter, long uncomfortable pauses, profuse apologies, and excessive politeness. People don't know what they are supposed to do and they are searching for their niche. The group is in the "forming" stage. Secondary tension comes where the group members have become well enough acquainted to generate true disagreement. Low levels of secondary tension are inevitable and may be regarded as healthy. It will be difficult, for example, for faculty teams to create the interdisciplinary subject without having some tension over differing disciplinary paradigms and underlying epistemological outlooks. After all, one of the main purposes of interdisciplinary courses is to engage faculty in high levels of collaboration to invent courses that are more interesting, creative, and relevant than traditional courses. The process of team-teaching will inevitably produce tension born of real differences of opinion. One would hope that intelligent people could resolve these differences in productive ways over time. Human nature being what it is, however, this is not always possible, and sometimes tension turns into open conflict. What are the signs of group conflict? Below are some of the ways "fighting behavior" is expressed in groups:

- Members are impatient with one another
- Ideas are attacked before they are completely expressed
- Members take sides and refuse to compromise
- Members disagree on plans or suggestions
- Comments or suggestions are made with a great deal of vehemence
- Members attack one another on a personal level in subtle ways
- Members insist that the group doesn't have the know-how or experience to get anywhere

- Members feel the group can't get ahead because it is too large or too small
- Members disagree with the leader's suggestions
- Members accuse one another of not understanding the real point
- Members hear distorted fragments of other members' contributions[34]

What are the sources of conflict for which this kind of behavior is the symptom? Where does conflict most frequently come from when faculty try to work together on interdisciplinary courses?

Conflict can be about goals, but it can also be about the means of reaching goals.[35] Faculty may genuinely disagree about what the purposes of the course should be, and resolving concerns about content, learning outcomes, and areas of emphasis is important in team teaching. Other disagreements relate to means—ways of presenting material and selection of appropriate readings and methods of testing and grading. When a high degree of collaboration is necessary to achieve the interdisciplinary goals of the course, it is important to find ways to resolve conflict and present to students if not a "united front," at least a workable consensus about ends and means.

Two areas of conflict deserve special mention in this context. Some conflict is personal. However much faculty may be committed to the amelioration of humanity in general, some individuals simply do not like other individuals. Personal clashes are inevitable; how they are managed is the key. One hopes to avoid longstanding power struggles, repetitive game playing, and prolonged grudge bearing. Some conflict has to do with personality.

Another source of conflict cuts deeper. Sometimes faculty hold opposing values and differing philosophies. Because of differing, fundamental value systems, some faculty may find themselves in conflict, again and again, over deep philosophical issues. One area of disagreement that often surfaces has to do with attitudes about students. Some faculty believe that students are usually intrinsically motivated, well-intentioned, and can, for the most part, be trusted to seek a challenge, work hard, and play fair in completing their assignments. Other faculty believe students are lazy and distracted, in need of constant reinforcement (or the threat of punishment), and can, for the most part, be expected to take the easy way out, cheating when necessary. Although the conditions that shape and govern student behavior vary from institution to institution, faculty differences on these matters, representing both poles and all manner of positions in between, can be found within most institutions, and sometimes on the same teaching team. When these differences are extreme, one can look for ongoing conflict.

Unfortunately, personality clashes and philosophical differences are not easily resolved; they are not a communication problem, they are a fundamental problem. Some standard mechanisms for resolving conflict include compromise, mediation, arbitration, taking a vote, and trying to reach consensus through negotiation. The key question to ask is this: When does conflict become so destructive that it interferes with the work of the team? If that begins to happen, the conflict needs to be resolved. The literature suggests that the key to the successful resolution of conflict in groups is to identify it, face it, and resolve it. Letting conflict drag on is not good for the team and eventually takes its toll on individuals. Hopefully, "the group that fights, unites!"[36]

Some conflict goes unresolved. At that point something usually needs to be done. Strong forces in the academic environment work against taking action in the face of unresolved conflict. One of these forces is itself the disinclination to take action; academics are often long on analysis and short on action. Another is the underlying belief that rational people always ought to be able to resolve their differences. Although this is a noble sentiment and a reasonable goal, there are times when it may be wise to "give up hope" of a smooth resolution, to end the endless conflict and its time-consuming efforts at resolution, and ask certain members to leave the team. If the conflict seems to revolve around one person, it may be better to terminate that person than to let him or her wreck an otherwise perfectly good team. If the conflict is always between the same two people, maybe both need to be replaced. In general, professors are probably much too timid about taking such action, and will instead suffer too long with a problem, steadfastly refusing to admit that there is a critical flaw in some member of the community of scholars, a bitter, unresolvable controversy in the ivory tower.

Apathy and Social Loafing

Sometimes group members are apathetic or don't do their share of the work. Apathy usually develops when the members are not excited about the project. With interdisciplinary courses, this can happen when a faculty member has been assigned to a course or had no real choice but to volunteer; but more likely, apathy sets in after the course has been offered several times and the team's initial enthusiasm has dropped off. Sometimes apathy also occurs when the group has not fostered a climate for risk-taking. What may be mistaken for apathy is really a reluctance to participate because it is not clear how the contribution will be received. Usually apathy—real apathy or other behavior masquerading as apathy—can be overcome if it is identified and discussed. Sometimes, when a team gets tired of a course, the members need to go back to the beginning and create the subject anew so that everyone is enthusiastic about the course in a new way. Sometimes it is necessary for the whole team to take leave from the course for a year.

More troublesome than apathy is social loafing. Research has shown that individuals, in general, tend not to work as hard in groups as they do as individuals. Known as "The Ringleman Effect" from the researcher by that name who conducted crude tug-of-war experiments in the 1880s, it has been established that two people don't pull twice as hard as one and three don't pull three times as hard as one, and so forth, as group size increases. More recent studies by social psychologists have established clearly a similar idea called "social loafing." Most social loafing occurs when it is not possible to distinguish the individual's contribution to the group output.[37] On interdisciplinary teams, some individuals will naturally contribute more than others; a problem arises, however, when certain members are perceived as not contributing their share, forgetting assignments, failing to meet deadlines, never volunteering, letting others carry the load. When this happens, resentment eventually develops. Oddly enough, two people usually get blamed, the loafer and the leader who doesn't do anything about it. Soon, group cohesion begins to diminish. Like so many other problems that groups face, the answer is simple but painful: deal with it, either directly as a group, or through the team leader.

Group Think and Efficiency

Groups tend to be unwieldy, inefficient, and slow at times. Although the outputs of team efforts may eventually be better and more creative, getting these results often takes a long time. One reason for this is that groups tend to have a short attention span. One study revealed that the average length of time used by a group to discuss a single theme was 58 seconds. Groups tend to jump quickly from topic to topic.[38] Interdisciplinary teams are often disorganized, prone to endless debate, and too focused on detail. Without a good leader to "crack the whip," they can flounder. On the other hand, sometimes groups are too efficient; they reach premature closure before they have had time to consider all the options or contemplate implications. The name given to this behavior is "groupthink." The term was coined by social psychologist Irvin Janis to apply to a mode of thinking that people engage in when they are deeply involved in a cohesive in-group, when the members' striving for unanimity overrides their motivation to appraise realistically alternative courses of action.[39] Interdisciplinary teams need to find the middle ground between glorious inefficiency, debating each decision endlessly, and groupthink, dispatching assignments prematurely before alternatives can be considered. It takes some experience to learn the difference and achieve the right balance.

HIGH PERFORMANCE TEAMS

In addition to the literature on groups, which applies equally well to the internal functioning of teams, a specialized literature on teams has emerged in recent years. Perhaps the most useful book on teams for our purposes is the work mentioned earlier by Carl Larson and Frank LaFasto entitled *Teamwork: What Must Go Right/What Can Go Wrong*.[40] Troubled by what they perceived to be a widespread inability of people in our society to collaborate effectively, the authors decided to study "high-performance teams" to see what made them effective and to discover what went wrong when they weren't effective. They identified for study, teams representative of many different types of functions from all walks of life: sports teams (Notre Dame and Navy football teams), investigative teams (the Challenger spacecraft disaster), heart surgery teams (DeBakey, Cooley), mountain climbing teams (Everest), new product teams (Chicken McNuggets, IBM/PC), epidemiology teams, management teams, and many others. Then they interviewed team members to gather data about the teams and built up a theory of "team effectiveness" from the data. They found that effective, high-performance teams consistently exhibited the following eight characteristics:

- Clear, elevating goal
- Results-driven structure
- Competent members
- Unified commitment
- Collaborative climate
- Standards of excellence
- External support and recognition
- Principled leadership

Each of these characteristics is examined below in detail and the implications for team teaching are spelled out.

Clear, Elevating Goal

Effective teams have performance objectives that are stated clearly so that everyone can tell unequivocally what the goal is and whether (or to what degree) it has been attained. The goal also needs to be "elevating" in the sense of being personally challenging to individual team members or the team as a whole, or "elevating" in the sense that achieving the goal really makes a difference to someone else, as in performing heart surgery, stopping an epidemic, or developing a new product. When teams became ineffective, their goals were ambiguous and members uncertain, or the original goal had been lost. This loss of focus or confusion of priorities usually came through organizational politics or personal power agendas of team members.

Implications. Faculty teams clearly need to be excited about their interdisciplinary course and committed to it. If they lose that excitement, the "elevating" quality of the goal is lost. Faculty need to believe that the course is important to them and to their students. Because most interdisciplinary courses involve an attempt to do something in a new way, the goal is naturally elevating. "Clear" may be another matter, because much of what the faculty is doing is creative and inventive, not lending itself to immediate clarity. "Clear," however, is just as important as "elevating" for teams, and it is important, therefore, that the learning outcomes of the course become clear at some point and remain clear. If the team is not functioning well, the first questions to ask are: Have we lost our sense of the importance of this course or are we confused about what we are doing? Or perhaps both?

Results-Driven Structure

Although the same performance objective can be reached with teams structured in different ways, the structure must always move the team toward getting results. Not all teams have the same kinds of objectives. Three basic types of teams were identified: problem-resolution teams, creative teams, and tactical teams. Each type needs a slightly different structure. Problem-solving teams need trust. All the members must work together, share everything, and sincerely trust each other. Creative teams need *autonomy*; they need to be free from organizational pressures and constraints; they need what might be called "breathing room." Tactical teams, on the other hand, need *clarity*, everyone knowing what they are supposed to do and how and when to do it. In addition, all teams, to have a results-driven structure, need clear roles, an effective communication system, methods of monitoring performance and giving feedback, and a means for recording and making fact-based judgments.

Implications. Although most high performance teams can be classified as "problem-resolution," "creative," or "tactical," faculty teams for interdisciplinary courses seem to take on the characteristics of all three types, passing in and out of phases. Sometimes they behave as creative teams to invent the subject, sometimes as tactical teams to implement the course, and sometimes as problem-solving teams when things go wrong. Sometimes trust is important, but at other times autonomy or clarity become dominant needs. Most important, perhaps, is distinguishing when the team is operating in which mode. In the design phase of the course, creativity is important; but in training the team members to carry out their respective roles, clarity is important. Team members must know how the team is functioning at any given point in time, and it is valuable to have one member of the team monitoring this and reminding the team of what they are doing and what they need.

Competent Team Members

Successful teams are composed of the right people selected for the right reasons. In general, team members need the right balance of technical skills and abilities and personal qualifications for working well with others. But not all teams need the same skills; the skills needed depend on the goal. Problem-resolution teams need members who are intelligent and analytical, but sensitive enough to interpersonal needs to build trust. Creative teams need members whose cognitive approach might appear to be a bit unusual on a day-to-day basis; these are the "what if" independent thinkers, who are tenacious and patient. Tactical teams, on the other hand, need members who are highly responsive, quick to execute, and able to work with precision within small margins for error. Tactical teams also need people who have a sense of urgency, can identify strongly with the team, and who enjoy winning or being successful. All teams need members who have the essential skills and abilities, a strong desire to contribute, and a capacity for collaboration. Teams need the right "mix" of qualified members.

Implications. An important question to ask of interdisciplinary teams is this: What mix of skills is actually needed to plan and carry out the course? What do individual faculty members bring to the team? What skills might be missing? Someone on the team might not contribute much to the planning process, but might become a brilliant lecturer once the syllabus is in place. Someone else might be an expert at leading an inquiry or facilitating groups. Interdisciplinary teams commonly reconstitute themselves from time to time. Whether composing the team initially or reconstituting it, a great opportunity exists for bringing together "just the right people" for the course. If the team is too homogeneous, some skills and viewpoints will be missing; if the team is too heterogeneous, it will have problems collaborating. The team needs the right members selected for the right reasons, and they all must have the capacity to collaborate.

Unified Commitment

Effective teams also develop a unified commitment, that elusive, hard-to-define quality of "team spirit." What is it? It is the willingness to do what needs to be done to help the team succeed. It is manifest in huge amounts of mental and physical energy to achieve the goal. It involves a strong team identity. How does it come about? It develops as a natural extension of the enthusiasm for the clear, elevating goal, but it is also nurtured by involvement, participation, and refinement of the goal and establishment of the means of getting there. Commitment involves striking a balance between giving oneself over to the group (integration) and using one's own individual talents to best help the group (differentiation). Although it is difficult to say what unified commitment is, ineffective teams clearly lack it.

Implications. Because faculty usually have multiple responsibilities—teaching, research, service, governance—as well as a never-ending obligation to be well-informed in an area of specialization, it is not always easy for them to make an unwavering commitment to a particular course. Some faculty will make this commitment with greater intensity than others. What we know about effective teams, however, suggests that faculty not only need to commit themselves to the course but to each other as a team. Eventually, faculty need to get caught up in the course, its possibilities, and the rewards that come from its effective implementation. Faculty need to develop that special sense of "we're in this together," and a strong desire to "make it work," even if this means giving up something else. Some faculty will be in a position to give more to the course at certain times, and less at others, but team members who can't make a strong overall commitment need to be replaced. It is difficult to achieve the ideal of "unified commitment," but at some point the success of the course needs to be more important than the individual agendas of the faculty who teach it.

Collaborative Climate

If the essence of teams is "teamwork," then teams need to function within a climate that fosters teamwork. The word most often used to characterize this climate was "trust," and trust was characterized as having four elements: honesty, openness, consistency, and respect. When trust exists, team members will stay focused on the goal, will communicate more effectively, will compensate for each other's shortcomings, and will be more open to criticism and risk, thus improving the overall quality of outcomes. When a collaborative climate exists, team members are more likely to share information, admit problems, help overcome obstacles, and find new ways of succeeding. Such a climate is not easy to build, but appears to be related to the involvement that team members have and the autonomy the team has to do its job.

Implications. Because most faculty are trained as specialists, they have been socialized into a profession that teaches them to work alone. Most graduate training does little to build skills in collaboration, unless, of course, a teaching assistant gets the opportunity to be part of an interdisciplinary course. Faculty should not be surprised to find, therefore, that they don't know much about collaboration, nor should they be embarrassed to seek help. It may be useful, from time to time, to seek an outside consultant to help facilitate the collaboration process. Developing a climate where faculty are willing to take risks in front of each other—for example, experimenting with a new teaching strategy—is not easy. Odd as it may seem, it sometimes takes great effort to create an open climate, where risks can be taken, mistakes made, problems acknowledged, and criticisms made. Only in such a climate will the team become truly effective.

Standards of Excellence

Standards define the expectations for performance. Pressures to perform can come from many places—from the members themselves, from the team as a whole, from the anticipation of success or risk of failure, from sources outside the team, or from the team leader. Standards have to be de-intellectualized and made concrete, so that everyone knows what they are. Standards are not achieved, however, just by setting them. Because standards are easy to ignore, teams need discipline and hard work to achieve their standards of excellence and must remain vigilant in enforcing them. Standards are only attained through performance.

Implications. Every faculty member knows that there are great courses, mediocre courses, and terrible courses. The reason we know this is that we have taken so many courses ourselves as students. Campus mythology to the contrary, most students identify the best courses as hard not easy. Behind every outstanding course stands some professor or group of professors with high standards of excellence and high expectations for both themselves and their students. Effective faculty teams need to make agreements, usually spoken as well as unspoken, about such things as researching the subject, being prepared for class, using explicit teaching strategies, returning student papers, and meeting team deadlines. If team members can agree upon and operationalize high standards for their own performance, they are in a better position to have high expectations for students. If faculty disagree on the standards, or worse yet, agree, but continually fall short, morale problems will develop. When one member continually falls below the team's expectations, either unspoken resentment or overt hostility will result. One person's poor performance drags down the reputation of the whole course, and gives students a visible excuse for putting forth less than their best effort. Faculty teams need to establish high standards and stick to them.

External Support and Recognition

The performance of teams is affected in peculiar ways by the presence or absence of external support and recognition. Such support may come in the form of praise, allocation of resources, or rewards to individual team members. Oddly enough, teams that are doing well may be able to function without it, although they believe that their achievement warrants more. Teams that are doing poorly may do even worse without it. Lack of external support, for a team that is struggling, may lead to lower morale, erosion of confidence, and feelings of frustration and futility. While external support and recognition may not be a significant factor in ensuring team success, lack thereof can contribute to failure. External support can have an especially positive effect when that support rewards the team for behaving as a team.

Implications. Because creating interdisciplinary courses is hard work and time-consuming, faculty like to know that their efforts are being appreciated. External support can take many forms for team teaching, including the following: favorable adjustment of the teaching load, financial support for planning days, a budget for guest lecturers and materials, appropriate advising and publicity, and recognition from deans and department chairs within the reward system for pay and promotion. Disincentives for participation, for example, an organizational structure that does not easily provide for teaching other than on a one course, one professor basis, will cause morale problems to develop and the team members will conclude that participation is not worth it. Interestingly enough, even small rewards, such as support for one week of planning in the summer, often carry huge symbolic value, letting the participants know that their work on the team is valued.

Principled Leadership

The leaders of effective teams see themselves as being involved in transformation, a kind of leadership that involves change. They have a vision of the future, some idea of the way things could be and should be, a desire to move beyond the status quo, and a peculiar ability to unleash the energy and talents of contributing members. Effective team leaders are "principled," in that they govern their own leadership behavior by such principles as being fair and impartial, being willing to confront and resolve issues, and being open to new ideas and information. In turn, they expect group members to be guided by principles, such as trying to collaborate effectively with others, making the team goal higher than individual goals, and standing behind team decisions. Effective team leaders create a decision-making climate that encourages members to take risks and to act, so that the goal can be achieved. Effective team leaders are able to suppress their own ego needs and create a contagion among group members that unlocks their own leadership abilities.

Implications. Some interdisciplinary courses function without a leader, but such arrangements are rare. Even if no formal leader is designated, a leader usually will emerge who plays the role of coordinator. Most team-taught courses have a coordinator, either appointed by the dean or chair, or elected by the group. Sometimes the leadership is rotated, and occasionally the leadership falls by default to the only person willing to take it on. Sometimes this person will be a talented leader, with the organizational and facilitation skills needed, but occasionally not. Like other teams, team-taught courses need strong leadership, and to ignore the importance of leadership under the presumed guise of humility or deference is to make a big mistake. Furthermore, as the research suggests, the leader needs to be "principled," exercising leadership with the authority to facilitate open communication, resolve disputes, and achieve closure, with fairness but firmness. Because faculty have a long tradition of operating as independent professionals and are often suspicious of any behavior that looks like "administration," they will often ignore the issue of leadership. What we know about high performance teams suggests that team-taught courses need principled leadership.

If these are the characteristics of effective teams, what happens when teamwork breaks down? What are the causes of malfunctioning teams? Most frequently mentioned in the study by Larson and LaFasto was lack of unified commitment, when team members, in one way or another, put their own interest above the team interest in attaining the goal. The next most frequently mentioned problem is lack of external support and recognition—the sense of not having what is needed to get the job done. With regard to leadership, the most frequent complaint is about leaders who are unwilling to confront and resolve the issue of inadequate performance of team members, i.e., letting a team member get away with poor performance. The next most frequently mentioned problem with leaders concerns those who willingly take on too many goals, thus upsetting the priorities and diluting the teams's efforts to achieve high standards in pursuing the goal.

Teamwork breaks down occasionally within faculty teams as well, and the research on teams tells us where to look. Individual agendas, either academic or personal, can get in the way of achieving a unified commitment, and some teams never achieve a desirable level of cohesion because some members are unable to commit to the larger goal of caring first and foremost about the course. Low moral can develop when outside support is perceived as lacking. Leaders who try to do too much with courses, or who fail to deal with faculty who are loafing or causing problems, unwittingly contribute to low morale.

When faculty work in teams, they behave for the most part like other people when they work on teams. What is known about group and team behavior can be applied to the settings we call "team teaching." The concepts outlined above are valuable for faculty members who are about to embark on team teaching for the first time or for seasoned experts who would like to improve their individual effectiveness or the team's overall performance. If the team is having problems, this chapter may offer clues about where to look and what to do.

What actually happens to faculty when they work in teams and how do they perceive their work with interdisciplinary courses? How do students perceive interdisciplinary courses and team teaching? These questions are answered in the next chapter.

NOTES

1. Jon R. Katzenbach, and Douglas K. Smith. *The Wisdom of Teams: Creating the High-Performance Organization*, (New York: Harper Business, 1993), pp. 18-19.

2. Carl E. Larson and Frank M.J. LaFasto, *Teamwork: What Must Go Right/What Can Go Wrong* (Newbury Park, CA: Sage Publications, 1989). The ideas for the rest of this section are drawn exclusively from this work and are found as would be appropriate in each chapter.

3. Malcolm Knowles and Hulda Knowles, *Introduction to Group Dynamicss*, (New York: Cambridge, 1972), pp. 39-40.

4. Alvin Zander, *The Purposes of Groups and Organizations* (San Francisco: Jossey-Bass, 1985). The examples presented in this chapter are drawn from Chapter 2, "Functions Served By Groups," p. 14ff.

5. A. Paul Hare, *Handbook of Small Group Research* (New York: Free Press, 1976), Appendix 2, "The History and Present State of Small Group Research," pp. 388, 392.

6. Robert T. Golembiewski and Arthur Blumberg, *Sensitivity Training and the Laboratory Approach* (Itasca, IL: Peacock Publishers, 1970), p. 4.

7. Alvin Goldberg and Carl Larson, *Group Communication* (Englewood Cliffs, NJ: Prentice-Hall, 1975), pp. 162-63. For more detail, see Kenneth Benne, "History of the T-Group in the Laboratory Setting" in Leland Bradford, Jack Gibb, and Kenneth Benne, *T-Group Theory and Laboratory Method* (New York: Wiley, 1964).

8. Goldberg and Larson, *Group Communication*, p. 163.

9. Thomas R. Verny, *Inside Groups* (New York: McGraw-Hill, 1974).

10. Barry E. Collins and Harold Guetzkow, *A Social Psychology of Group Processes for Decision-Making* (New York: Wiley, 1964), p. 58. Quoted in B. Aubrey Fisher, *Small Group Decision Making* (New York: McGraw-Hill, 1974), p. 65.

11. For more detail on types of group tasks (additive, conjunctive, disjunctive, complementary, etc.), see Charles Pavitt and Ellen Curtis, *Small Group Discussion* (Scottsdale, AZ: Gorsuch Scarisbrick, 1990), pp. 26-29.

12. Irvin Lorge, "A Survey of the Studies Contrasting the Quality of Group Performance and Individual Performance, 1920-1957," *Psychological Bulletin*, 55 (1958): pp. 337–72.

13. Alex F. Osborn, *Applied Imagination* (New York: Scribner's 1957). Cited in Alvin Zander, *Making Groups Effective* (San Francisco: Jossey-Bass, 1982), p. 21. The exposition of Osborn's ideas is drawn from Arthur M. Coon, "Brainstorming—A Creative Problem-Solving Technique" in Robert Cathcart and Larry Samovar, *Small Group Communications* (Dubuque, IA: W. C. Brown, 1988), p. 135ff.

14. Fisher, *Small Group Decision Making*, pp. 24-26 for information on group size.

15. John K. Brilhart, *Effective Group Discussion* (Dubuque, IA: W. C. Brown, 1982), pp. 20-21.

16. Golembiewski and Blumberg, *Sensitivity Training*, p. 87. The questions are borrowed from a larger checklist for observing group communication.

17. Fisher, *Small Group Decision Making*, p. 29.

18. *Ibid.*, p. 70.

19. Larry Barker, et. al., *Groups in Process* (Englewood Cliffs, NJ: Prentice-Hall, 1983), p. 83.

20. Charles M. Kelley, "Empathic Listening" in Cathcart and Samovar, *Small Group Communication*, pp. 350-51.

21. Barker, Wahlers, Watson, and Kibler, *Groups in Process*, pp. 82-87. The list above is found on p. 87.

22. John E. Baird, Jr., and Sanford Weinberg, "Elements of Group Communication" in Cathcart and Samovar, *Small Group Communication*, p. 296. The list is shortened, adapted, and paraphrased.
23. *Ibid.*, p. 297.
24. Lawrence Rosenfeld, "Nonverbal Communication in the Small Group" in Cathcart and Samovar, *Small Group Communication*, p. 306.
25. Barber, Wahlers, Watson, and Kibler, *Groups in Process*, p. 37.
26. Patrick R. Penland and Sara Fine, "Group Dynamics" in Cathcart and Samovar, *Small Group Communication*, p. 26.
27. Erving Goffman, *Encounters* (New York: Bobbs-Merrill, 1961), p. 87. Quoted in Fisher, *Small Group Decision Making*, p. 167.
28. Hare, *Handbook of Small Group Research*, p. 131.
29. *Ibid.*, pp. 39-43.
30. Pavitt and Curtis, *Small Group Discussion*, p. 64.
31. Fisher, *Small Group Decision Making*, p. 42.
32. Bruce W. Tuckman, "Development Sequence in Small Groups," *Psychological Bulletin*, 63, 1965, pp. 384-99. Described in Fisher, *Small Group Decision Making*, p. 140.
33. Fisher, *Small Group Decision Making*, pp. 50-55.
34. Leland Bradford, Dorothy Stock, and Murray Horowitz, "How to Diagnose Group Problems" in Golembiewski and Blumberg, *Sensitivity Training*, p. 142. Quoted directly.
35. Pavitt and Curtis, *Sensitivity Training*, pp. 100-01.
36. Fisher, *Small Group Decision Making*, pp. 57-59.
37. Pavitt and Curtis, *Small Group Discussion*, pp. 38-40.
38. Fisher, *Small Group Decision Making*, p. 63. The study referred to is David M. Berg, "A Descriptive Analysis of the Distribution and Duration of Themes Discussed by Task-Oriented Small Groups," *Speech Monographs*, 34, 1967j, pp. 172-75.
39. Irving Janis, *Victims of Groupthink: A Psychological Study of Policy Decisions and Fiascos* (Boston: Houghton Mifflin Co., 1972).
40. Larson and LaFasto, *Teamwork*. The ideas for the rest of this section are drawn exclusively from this work and are found there in the appropriate chapters by headings used.

CHAPTER 5

Faculty and Student Perceptions of Team Teaching: Satisfactions and Frustrations

"An assemblage of learned (persons), zealous for their own sciences, and rivals of each other, are brought, by familiar intercourse and for the sake of intellectual peace, to adjust together the claims of the respective subjects of investigation. They learn to respect, to consult, to aid each other."

—John Henry Cardinal Newman

How do faculty perceive their involvements in team teaching? How did they get involved? In what ways do they describe the types and levels of collaboration that take place? What roles do they play on the team? What are the satisfactions and dissatisfactions that are associated with team teaching? Do students perceive and appreciate faculty collaboration? Do students believe that interdisciplinary team-taught courses are any different from other courses they take?

METHODS

To address these questions, selected faculty, three each from the five courses used as examples, were interviewed to probe their perceptions of team teaching. A semi-structured, hour-long interview was conducted using the list of questions appearing on the adjoining page as an interview guide. Faculty were cooperative, eager to talk, and articulate in describing their experience on teams. Although these 15 faculty are all from one institution, thus producing a certain homogeneity with regard to environmental factors that may influence their experience, they represent a wide range of backgrounds with regard to disciplinary home, specialization, rank, highest degree and field earned, years of teaching experience, and length of involvement with team teaching. The table on page 103 summarizes their diverse background and experience. Particularly noteworthy are the long years of teaching experience, the diversity of fields and specialized interests, and the preponderance of faculty in upper ranks. In drawing a sample in any interview study where the goal is to gain an in-depth understanding of a small but representative number of subjects, one might ask: Would the results be different if more people and different people had been interviewed? Would the trends that appeared with these subjects be changed significantly, would they be further elaborated, or would the results become redundant if more subjects were interviewed? In this case, it may be necessary to concede that the results might be somewhat different at other campuses, depending on the arrangements of the courses and the type of institutional support for team teaching, and some warning may be necessary about making generalizations from these faculty to campuses with a rather different mission. On the other hand, the patterns that began to emerge from these interviews were so striking and so consistent, that it seems unlikely that additional interviews would add much to what was discovered through these conversations. Faculty from diverse disciplinary backgrounds working in rather different types of courses had fairly consistent views on what participation in interdisciplinary, team-taught courses is like. In other words, there were easily-identifiable trends.

To understand student perceptions of interdisciplinary, team-taught courses, another approach was used. In each of the courses used as examples in this study, a questionnaire was given toward the end of the course to students enrolled in the course. The questionnaire was designed to elicit student perceptions of the types and amount of collaboration in the course and perceptions about how this course compared to courses taught by one instructor. Although students were free not to participate, and although the questionnaire reached only those who attended class the day it was administered, participation was high, and an average return of well over 60 percent of the total enrollment was obtained for each class. Thus the information gathered from students through this survey was broad rather than deep, and it tells us only about the average perceptions of large numbers of students. The data are useful, however, as a one-point-in-time snapshot of how students perceive the interdisciplinary nature of the courses in which they were enrolled.

SEMI-STRUCTURED INTERVIEW GUIDE FOR FACULTY

1. As nearly as you can recall, how did you first become associated with this course?
2. What do you know about the origins of this course? Who had the idea for this course?
3. How would you characterize faculty collaboration (or lack of collaboration) in:
   a) planning this course
   b) integration of the subject content of this course
   c) classroom teaching for this course
   d) grading and evaluation practices in this course?
4. How would you describe the process of collaboration (working together)? Has it been easy or difficult?
5. What has been satisfying about working together, if anything? What has been frustrating, if anything?
6. Is it more time consuming or less time consuming working as a team member than working as an individual on a course you teach by yourself?
7. What do you think you gain through team teaching? What do you give up?
8. What have you learned from participating as a team member in this course?
9. What do you think has been your greatest contribution to this course?
10. What would you like to tell me about your participation in this course that I haven't asked you about? Is there anything you want to elaborate further?

FACULTY INVOLVEMENT IN TEAM TEACHING

Not all faculty get involved in team teaching in quite the same way, but most exhibit a genuine openness to the idea, and even a clear attraction to such arrangements. Occasionally, a faculty member originates a course idea, but as noted in the chapter on structure, this is rare. Of the 15 faculty interviewed, only three, one from "Making of the Modern Mind," one from "Multiple Voices of America", and one from the "Origin and Evolution of Life," were actually the originators of the course idea. As the founder of "Making of the Modern Mind" notes, "I had a great experience with a colleague teaching in the old Coordinated Humanities Program, and then came the edict, the template for CORE. We were furious at first, but then we said, here's the structure for doing something we had been talking about anyway. I found the team and persuaded them to do it. Come on, I told them, there's no revenge like success."

CHARACTERISTICS OF FACULTY INTERVIEWED (N=15)

Departments Represented: 10; accounting, anthropology (2), art (2), biological sciences (2), law (3), management, marketing, music, philosophy, religious studies

Highest Degree:

    Ph.D. _11_   M.S. _1_   J.D. _3_

Disciplines Represented in Graduate Studies: 11; accounting, art history (2), anthropology (2), comparative endocrinology, law (3), management, marketing, musicology, philosophy, religion, zoology

Sub-specialization Represented in Graduate Studies: 12; accounting/economics, American art and architecture, American religious history, archaeology, administrative and constitutional law, consumer behavior, cultural history, European art (18th-20th century), legal writing, law librarianship, musicology

Current Specialized Interest Area: European cultural history and modern continental philosophy; historical constructions of race; 20th century orchestra literature, aesthetics and criticism; surrealism and art nouveau, Dutch art, and women's studies; cultural contact and change, North American anthropology; management accounting, not-for-profit accounting, quality; measurement and multi-variate methods; comparative endocrinology, critical thinking; avian and wetland ecology, archaeology, biological anthropology; general management, quality; administrative and constitutional law; legal research and writing; law school administration.

Rank:

    Assistant Professor _2_, Associate Professor _6_, Professor _4_,
    Lecturer _2_, Director _1_

Tenure:

    yes _10_   no _2_   nontenure track _3_

Years of Service at University of Denver:

    Range =   3 to over 20

    Mean of 20 or under = 9.9

    Over 20 =   3 faculty

Total Years of Teaching:

    Range =   2 to over 20

    Mean of 20 or under = 9.75

    Over 20 =   7 faculty

Years of Team-Teaching at University of Denver:

    Range =   2 to over 20

    Mean of 20 or under = 5.9

    Over 20 =   2 faculty

Most faculty were invited to join the course they teach in now. Someone knew about them or heard about them from a colleague and they were approached, explored, and invited. "The biologists heard about me from the coordinator of the core curriculum, so we got together to talk," notes the anthropologist from "Origin and Evolution of Life." "I was specifically invited by the guy who had the idea for the course," notes the Southwest studies specialist from "Multiple Voices of America." Some were even invited at the time they were hired. "I was replacing someone who was on the Modern Mind team, so they hired me with the idea that I would be in that spot. They even flew me in the first summer before I arrived to participate in the planning. I felt like I was joining a community and we were getting lavish attention." Another faculty member from the team for "Multiple Voices" notes, "They were waiting for someone with a background in American art history to make this course work. When they hired me they told me about the idea for this course and hoped I would be interested. I was. So I participated in the planning from the very beginning." Other faculty volunteered. "I know that our Director wanted to get more people from the School of Music into the core curriculum. I was looking for something different, so I volunteered for Modern Mind." One faculty member volunteered for "Quality Panorama" but only after some urging from colleagues and thoughtful consideration about his interests. "I taught some material on quality in my other courses, so I knew something about it. I also believed that this material was important, and I didn't want to see it lost. I knew that the course I was teaching was going to disappear, but I didn't want the ideas to disappear, so I volunteered to be in the quality course."

Some faculty ended up on the team because they were in the right place at the right time and it was obvious that they were the one to do the job. "I inherited the job as law librarian, and one of the things the law librarian did was to coordinate the legal research component of Lawyering Process." Another team member from "Lawyering Process" notes, "I was on the curriculum committee that approved the course, and I was also the obvious choice for doing the lectures on case law, administrative law, and legislation, because I taught that material in the course that was being combined with the other two to make 'Lawyering Process'." Another faculty member notes, "I was the one with real-world experience about quality in the business world, so I was a natural for that team."

Some faculty worked their way in gradually. One of the biologists in "Origin and Evolution of Life" notes that he was "pulled in for a three-week lecture segment and ended up doing a whole term the following year." He never intended to be involved but liked it and took on an expanded role that included the planning process as well.

For some, the entry was not perceived as completely voluntary. "I laughed when this course was proposed. It will never go, I thought. But a colleague asked me to do something they really needed, so I agreed to try." Another faculty member noted some subtle pressures. "They asked me which course I was going to be in. I told them that I hoped NONE, because it really looks like a mess to me. They persisted in asking me which one, and they made me feel like I had a bad attitude, so I volunteered, you might say."

Although the patterns are diverse, the trend is clear. With only a few exceptions, faculty wanted to get involved in team teaching. It held out the appeal of a new experience and the opportunity to do something in a different way. In recruiting faculty to participate in an interdisciplinary course, therefore, it makes sense, first, to seek the person who has "the right stuff" to add to the subject being created, but it is also important to seek open and eager partners. Most faculty who get involved in team teaching appear to have a predisposition toward collaboration, a willingness to take the risk, and, for some, a genuine interest in doing something creative. Others are not quite sure what they are getting into, but they are willing to try. Perhaps the most important quality, after academic qualifications, is an openness to the experience.

PERCEPTIONS OF COLLABORATION IN PLANNING

If team teaching involves high levels of collaboration in planning, content integration, teaching, and evaluation, how do faculty perceive that collaboration across these dimensions? Most of the faculty interviewed identified planning as the area in which they experienced the highest levels of collaboration. Most of the teams met for extended periods of time, usually in the summer, to plan for the course; and most had ongoing meetings, some more frequent than others, during the academic year when the course was being taught. Among the examples, "Making of the Modern Mind" had the longest history and the most established structure. In the beginning, four faculty who knew each other well and were excited about the idea planned the course in detail. "We had one each from art, music, literature, and philosophy, and we were eager to achieve an equal balance, with no second-class partners." Now that the course has its structure, planning focuses more around logistics, or who will do what at what times this year. "Everyone who teaches one of the seminars is on the planning committee, and we all meet to be sure that we are agreed on schedule and policies." Much of the planning for the "Origin and Evolution of Life" was done by one person initially, but not so much out of choice as necessity. "When he got a grant to support our work in the summer, that's when we began to plan more as a team. We got into a much more serious discussion of our central focus, what topics to include, and what's left out."

Some courses appear to settle into a stable pattern fairly quickly; other courses seem always to be in the planning phase, and things never quite get "nailed down." The faculty for "Multiple Voices of America" engaged in a full year of planning before the course was offered for the first time, but it has been changing every year and this year has been no exception. "We decided to revamp the course in major ways because it wasn't taking advantage of the talents of the faculty. It was also too negative, too tragic." These flaws sent the faculty back to the drawing board for more planning. "Planning for this course is still the most collaborative thing we do. We have to teach each other about our subject, and that's what takes time." As the faculty on the team learn more about each other's subjects, they generate new ideas about how to change the course, so planning has become an ongoing process.

For some courses, the planning process changes depending on who is in charge. Planning can be very different, depending on who is on the team and who is leading the team. The first coordinator of the "Lawyering Process" saw it as his course, and he was constantly changing things around almost at random. "Apparently, without consulting anyone, he had hired some first year students for the coming year," notes one of the faculty. "Soon after, he left the course, the students were dismissed, and three legal writing consultants were hired. I had to coordinate the writing of the problem cases and get it done in a few months." Then a new coordinator took over, and he wanted to be democratic, but he had his own ideas about how he wanted the course to go and really wasn't comfortable with real collaboration. When he stepped down and still another coordinator came on board, the team process changed again. The current coordinator thinks of himself as a facilitator and operates with what he calls "an empowerment model." He wants high levels of collaboration in planning. "Everyone on the team is participating now," he says, "and they do it in the meetings; there are no outside deals. I want to recognize their expertise and acknowledge their different approaches. We delegate some things and expect people to play their roles, doing what they want to do, but we also seek loyalty and commitment." Although the team had some prob-lems, and one person eventually left, the others agree that now there is true collaboration in the planning process.

With some courses, planning occurs at more than one level. An original design team designed the broad outlines for "Quality Panorama" and another implementation team worked on the delivery of the course. "I served on both," notes the current course coordinator, "and that has worked well, so that the course wasn't just handed off from one team to another. Planning by the implementation team is now ongoing. "I would say," notes a colleague on the implementation team, "that we have our highest levels of collaboration in planning, maybe a four on a scale of one to five."

It seems clear from these perceptions, that faculty seek, find, and enjoy a collaborative process in planning interdisciplinary courses, and that fairly high levels of collaboration are reached without great difficulty. Faculty need time for planning, often requiring separate time set aside in the summer months. The course coordinator clearly plays an important role in creating the atmosphere for collaboration. Effective collaboration in planning is difficult if the leader has foregone conclusions about outcomes, or if certain team members want to run off in their own direction. More planning time is needed at the beginning stages of the course, and this time tends to be used for logistics as the course matures. For most courses, planning is an ongoing process. One wonders, however, as the team becomes cohesive and the members enjoy the interpersonal interactions of the process, if too much time is spent on planning. Is there a point at which planning time turns into wasted time? How often should the course content be reworked, and do recommended changes, arrived at after hours of discussion, make a significant difference? Do other aspects of collaboration, such as classroom teaching, deserve more faculty time?

PERCEPTIONS OF COLLABORATION IN CONTENT INTEGRATION

Faculty perceptions of collaboration in content integration are mixed, but in general the level of collaboration is perceived as somewhat lower than it could be or should be. For "Making of the Modern Mind," the original intent was to maintain a disciplinary perspective in the seminars, and to coordinate what is discussed there with the topics of the lectures. This plan is perceived as generally working well, but it is not always natural. The most integration takes place in the main content themes of the lectures. When the course was originally designed, the creator of the course started the conversation with a brief handout of his concept of the course. "We all thought chronologically, and our first task was to settle on where to begin the course. We looked at our own expertise and agreed that we could not go back before 1600. Noting that we had 20 class sessions and four disciplines, we decided to take five each. At the next meeting we brought in our ideas for those five and hammered it out. Then we ordered the sessions so that there would never be back-to-back sessions by the same person." Although there is still a perception of significant overall content integration, most of it was structured in the early years of the course, and is viewed as inherited now, and not really in need of a re-examination. In addition to the logic of the structure of the themes, "we try to make connections for the students by referring to each other's lectures. Remember when professor so and so said such and such? The team is very careful about sequencing the lectures and inviting guests for the right topic on the right day. Sometimes there is a 'plop-in' that doesn't fit, and we correct that the next time the course is offered."

Content integration for the "Origin and Evolution of Life" has been more difficult to achieve. The fall quarter, on the theory of evolution, and the winter quarter, on the mechanisms of evolution, tend to stand more on their own, and are taught by different professors. "We have done something this year that's helping to integrate even those quarters: We are sitting in on each other's lectures for the whole term, and I can already see changes being made, and I know I will make some changes, too." The subject matter on human evolution in the spring term provides the best opportunities for integration and calls for more cross-disciplinary treatment. That's when the anthropologist comes in. "Where we are falling short, though," he suggests, "is in contrasting the physical scientists' ways of knowing and the social scientists' ways of knowing the material. I think those differences could be clarified better." Another member of the team wonders how much the students catch the overall conceptual integration. "They really appreciate the day-to-day references, such as, remember when we talked about this, but I'm not sure they get the broad conceptual connections we think we have in the course."

Content integration in "Multiple Voices of America" has involved high levels of collaboration in a seemingly endless process of trying to invent the subject for the course. "We wanted to take a new look at the development of America, to break out of the Euro-centric view. We wanted to hear other voices." During the first year the course was taught, the new voices of African Americans, Native Americans, and immigrant populations were heard, but the rough chronological framework remained. "It was still a history course, and we weren't sure we wanted that." The next year the focus was on conflict, the competition for the land and the social conflict. "But we felt we had created this really depressing course." It was during the planning that occurred in the following summer that the course became truly interdisciplinary and moved away from just history." The faculty introduced new topics and took better advantage of the strengths each one brought to the course. "We began to teach each other, and realized that we were going to have to learn new things." Another faculty member on the team notes, "Sometimes we tried to integrate the content in systematic ways, but at other times it was almost by accident. We'd throw out ideas, talk about them, and a new concept would emerge. What I've noticed is that some people are better conceptualizers than others. They are able to identify what the group is saying. It's important to have someone like that on the team."

The faculty team for the "Lawyering Process" has worked hard to achieve a conceptual integration of the course material, and they make frequent efforts to convey this to the students. "We use flowcharts, butterfly diagrams, the image of a wheel, anything we can get our hands on, to try to explain to the students how this material is interconnected." The idea of legal practice is the main integrative theme, what lawyers do with the client from the beginning to the end of the process. "At the intellectual level the three divisions of case law, administrative law, and legislation really unite the course, and I think we do a good job now of identifying and integrating these themes."

For "Quality Panorama," the newest of all the courses, faculty noted that content integration doesn't really happen very well until the course is offered at least once, so that everyone gets to see what everyone else is doing. "The first time this course was offered, I think the students got chunks. Now the chunks are getting stirred. We had no dress rehearsal; we just went straight to the performance." Now that the faculty has experienced the course in its entirety, they are making adjustments, reformulating content, restructuring presentations. "The first time around we each had our own bricks. Now we know the bricks and we have better mortar." One thing that helps to organize a course on quality is the nature of quality as a concept. "Quality affects everything, it really does. So quality itself can be the linchpin, the organizer." Although the faculty has moved from the "six circles" models to the Baldridge model as the central organizer, the circles are still there. "Every faculty member has a pet topic, but the topic has to relate to the quality circles or it's out," notes the course coordinator. Another member of the team notes, "We use the seven elements of the Baldridge model now, and that provides the framework, so the subject is integrated in that sense, but it's easy to fall back to the disciplines, so that when we discuss leadership we say, ok, that's manage-ment, and when we discuss customers, we say, ok, that's marketing. I think we are still struggling to integrate the disciplines."

In general, faculty express the belief that they work hard at content integration, but they often sense that they haven't achieved what they could achieve, and that they are falling short in some way. It is not easy to leave the disciplinary home (nor always necessary or desirable), and there is usually some unresolved tension between teaching "my interest and expertise" and what the invented subject really requires. Achieving the level of understand-ing required to bring about a deeper integration of the content may involve, as one faculty member put it, "teaching each other our subject." That often takes large amounts of time and a strong motivation to learn not only the colleague's subject, but ways of thinking. On the other hand, not all integration has to be earth-shaking and profound. Sometimes a common-sense theme is useful, such as "professional practice" in the "Lawyering Process", where the main thread running through the course is simply: With a client we do this first, this second, and this third. Whatever metaphors, schemes, diagrams, and struc-tures one can find to explain it all to the students (and to the team) are surely valuable. In this regard, many faculty spoke of the need to have a good conceptualizer on the team, someone to draw the diagrams and make sense of the big picture. One thing seems clear: the content gets more integrated as the course develops over time. It is very difficult to produce a highly integrated subject until the course has been taught once and the faculty all get a more concrete sense of what they are trying to achieve.

PERCEPTIONS OF COLLABORATION IN TEACHING

The level of collaboration in teaching is usually viewed as the lowest of the four areas. One wonders what standard the faculty have in mind, that they see themselves falling so short, but most of those interviewed expressed some regret that there was not more actual interaction between or among faculty in the classroom.

"The Making of the Modern Mind" was originally conceived of as a rather formal course, almost in the European tradition, with prepared lectures written out. "We have loosened up somewhat, but we don't do any dialogues or panels," notes one faculty member, who is unable to explain why. "People still do their own thing in those seminars," notes another.

The faculty in "Origin and Evolution of Life" generally agree that what they do is "serial" team teaching, "which results in little mini-courses stuck together." One faculty member points out, "we could collaborate so much more, but it isn't happening. We haven't created that environment here where faculty interact in front of the students. If it's not your day, you don't think you should participate." As another team member notes, "we are frustrated that we don't do more together, but it's difficult to break the old patterns, when you are there in a lecture hall full of students. We want to do some more creative things this spring. One thing that happens, though, is that we are sitting in and observing, and that gets us talking about our teaching."

The faculty in "Multiple Voices of America" have ventured into more collaborative teaching, but it has taken time. "In the beginning we weren't very collaborative; we inherited that formal model from the Modern Mind course, but now that we have taught each other, now that we are more comfortable with each other, we are trying some new things." Of special interest are "collaborative lectures," which two faculty design and deliver together for an assigned day. "Two of us put together a lecture on women's voices in art and literature. We picked out the examples together. I know about slides, she knew about images in text. It takes a lot of time. We met several times to get ideas, to decide what to present, to reduce it down to a manageable size, and to figure out how to make it coherent. But it's exciting. We are actually going back and forth at the same time in front of the class." Another kind of collaboration is beginning to take place in this class. "We share what we are going to do in class at our Monday meeting, before we actually do it. We are actually starting to share our teaching methods as well as the material, and we invite suggestions." Another faculty member notes, "It's hard to break away from the idea that you give a great lecture and then go break into groups to discuss it." Some collaboration took place in organizing experience-based learning events. "It was hard to organize, but we put together a museum day, when students could visit three different museums. The faculty split up so that we were at different sites to lead tours, analyze the content, make interpretations, and answer questions. Then the students rotated on to the next museum, where there were other faculty."

In the large lecture classes of the "Lawyering Process," there is still not much collaborative teaching, although some interesting experiments have begun this year. One of the faculty, a woman who is somewhat small of stature and finds it difficult to be very forceful "just talking" in a large lecture hall, has begun to stage some "demonstrations." If she is going to teach about interviewing clients, she gets one of the writing consultants, or maybe an upper division student who is working in a law office, to be a character actor for the client. Then she teaches about interviewing by doing an interview. The faculty also experimented this year with staging a video. "We called it 'Lawyering Process—The Movie' and we had a lot of fun making it and joking about it. It's about a restaurant owner who goes to a bank with a lot of money and actually gets mugged at the bank. The security guard is gone and the video cameras aren't working, so she sues the bank. It's about negligence. Last year we tried to stage it *in vivo*, and it was a flop, a real joke; but this year the video made a serious impression. It's 10 minutes, but it's really powerful."

In "Quality Panorama," faculty subgroups get together to plan a unit, what they are going to do for a sequence of classes. "But then we assign days, and people pretty much go their own way. We've at least made the classroom comfortable so that we can comment on or amplify a particular point." Another member of the team notes, "At first we all attended all the lectures, to learn what was going on. But there we were, five people in the back of the room, and we were sure the students couldn't quite figure out why we were there, and to tell the truth, neither could we. Now it is usually two faculty in the room, and we have learned how to make comments and chime in with examples. It was awkward at first, we thought—it's their class—but we are catching on now." Another member of the team ranks the collaboration in teaching as about two on a scale of one to five. "It was good to sit in for the first time, to learn what others were doing. For example, a colleague once offered a great example during my lecture, and now we know about it and I use it every time I do that lecture. But I'm not going to sit in on all those classes; I mean, really, how many times do I have to watch the instant replay."

The faculty perception that they aren't doing much collaborative teaching and should do more is, perhaps, peculiar to the campus where these faculty were interviewed; deeper forms of collaboration may be taking place in classrooms on other campuses. One suspects, however, (especially after reviewing the course descriptions for the annotations in Part II of this book), that this finding reflects a typical dilemma found on many campuses. On the one hand, faculty hold some ideal of truly collaborative interaction in the classroom and believe that more of it would be a good thing; on the other hand, long and deep traditions, lack of time, and a certain lack of imagination keep faculty from realizing their ideal.

In one sense, collaborative teaching involves breaking a long-established norm about what should take place in classrooms. Faculty have logged many hours themselves as students, and they know that the professor is royalty in the classroom, where no one but students discuss, let alone challenge, what the professor says. The reticence to interact, the confusion of faculty about what to do when they sit in, and their inability to imagine other roles are natural outcomes of years of being both a student and a teacher in single-faculty classrooms. Odd as it may seem, faculty need some support in helping them to feel that it is OK to break the norm and develop other patterns.

Exactly how to go about establishing more collaborative classroom teaching is not as clear, but the process appears to be gradual. It begins with observation, with actually going into the classroom to see what colleagues are doing, and then talking about what is observed. It continues when faculty share what they plan to do when they teach, and when they get feedback and suggestions about their plans. It begins to grow more elaborate when faculty actually plan for and try some experiments, some initial attempts at collaborative lectures, conducting a simulated interview, making a video, or cooperating in carrying out field trips. Collaborative teaching takes some "getting used to."

It also takes time and imagination. Lack of time, of course, could be an excuse for lack of imagination, but collaborative teaching may take more time. Or, the more critical factor may be lack of imagination. Because most faculty have not themselves experienced much collaborative teaching, they lack concrete models of what they could do. Faculty might profitably revisit the models presented in this book in the chapter on the ideal team-taught course to think more creatively about the many options they could employ *together* as they select classroom teaching strategies. Collaborative teaching is probably the weakest link in otherwise creative efforts to develop team-taught interdisciplinary courses.

One could ask, of course, whether collaborative teaching is really necessary, that is, whether the values of interdisciplinary, team-taught courses are not sufficiently realized without collaborative teaching. The best answer to that question, it seems, is: It depends. Some good interdisciplinary courses don't involve collaborative teaching; in fact, serial presentation appears to be the most frequently used form of delivery in many good courses. The question of necessity might best be answered with another question: Are some learning outcomes *best* achieved through collaborative teaching? Is there an interdisciplinary connection that could be made most pointedly, and which might otherwise be lost, through collaborative teaching? The anthropologist and biologist in "Origin and Evolution of Life" might find a dialogue, rather than two separate lectures, to be the best way to portray to students the key points at which their sciences have contributed to the study of human origins, as well as the limits to those contributions. If the faculty in "Multiple Voices of America" want students to gain an appreciation of how ethnic family histories can be strikingly different, then perhaps a panel of faculty, telling their own histories and sharing their reactions, will make that point more vividly than a lecture on family histories delivered by one faculty member. It is not so much that serial teaching is wrong—one teacher lecturing on one topic may be perfectly appropriate for certain learning outcomes—it is that the failure to consider alternatives results in unrealized potential, perhaps the loss of a great opportunity for students to experience a different kind of learning. Given the fact that most interdisciplinary courses are developed to build connections across disciplines and enlarge perspectives on an invented subject, something important is being lost when faculty do not capitalize on opportunities to collaborate in their classroom teaching at least some of the time.

PERCEPTIONS OF COLLABORATION IN GRADING AND EVALUATION

Although evaluation methods tend to be somewhat traditional, with heavy reliance on exams and term papers, many of the faculty interviewed could identify some interesting forms of collaboration in making and evaluating student assignments.

In "The Making of the Modern Mind," each section leader makes exam questions for his or her own section, but the questions are shared so that everyone can see everyone else's questions. There is also a uniform agreement about the general form of exams, the amount of emphasis to be placed on certain areas, and the points to be awarded. "We collaborate to set the ground rules, and we stick together on this, but then we design and grade our own exams."

A similar pattern is followed in "Origin and Evolution of Life," preparing individual exams and sharing them. More important, perhaps, has been the hammering out of a shared philosophy of evaluation. "We've really become involved in the Reflective Judgment Model of Karen Kitchener and Pat King in emphasizing, much more than we did at first, critical thinking skills. We do more with essays, short answers, and in-class writing assignments, and we have almost eliminated multiple choice questions." This shift was a conscious process and grew out of NSF support for faculty to attend conferences and try new approaches to evaluation. "We have made a definite shift toward trying to test thinking processes as opposed to content." Although the professors make their own tests and do their own grading, there is a perception of shared philosophy.

For "Multiple Voices of America," the grading and evaluation process has become highly collaborative. Not only do faculty confer on exam questions and develop an exam used across all sections, but they have also developed a technique for collaborating in grading. "We read the exams (over the weekend) and then we meet to discuss them before we assign a grade. We compare our expectations with what we got, and we read examples to each other. Here's a good example of a thesis statement, we say, or this is one that is not sufficient. This way we can develop common criteria for what is A, B, or C." The faculty also have developed a computer record of all student work, so that it is possible at a glance to compare a student's current work with previous work. The team also has in place an appeals process, a small sub-team to deal with student challenges. "We meet weekly, every Tuesday, to discuss assignments and hammer out grading policies. We put a lot of time and effort into this."

Exam making for the "Lawyering Process" course has become highly collaborative. The person who writes the problem cases for the simulated law firms also writes a fact problem, usually an entertaining scenario of events culminating in a law suit, which serves as the basis for cleverly devised multiple choice questions generated by other team members on the topic areas they presented in the course. The faculty bring in their questions, already unified around the fact problem, to check them out with each other for content, overlap, and wording. An essay component of the exam is graded separately. "We communicate a lot about the evaluation process and we spend time reviewing the exams before we give them."

For "Quality Panorama," team members generate questions, and when the exam has been completed, each professor grades his or her own question. Then the course coordinator pulls the whole exam together and assigns a grade. "This can be a little frustrating for students, particularly when we are grading cases, because someone will give a high grade and someone else gives a low one." More recently, the team has been trying to apply quality principles to the grading and evaluation process. "One of the quality principles is that you are supposed to have zero defects. Well, if that's the case, shouldn't we let students work at it until they get it right? We've instituted a rework option, like the old mastery learning idea. Some students will go through three rewrites. Our target is for more students, if possible all students, to earn an A. Isn't that what we want, a defect-free product? So, we say our goal is an A. Some of our colleagues think we are weird, we are deviant, but we think the goal in a quality course should be A." Interestingly enough, grading practices for this course have emerged from a team effort to apply the concept of quality to grading and evaluation.

In general, faculty agree that they engage in relatively high levels of collaboration to settle on a philosophy of evaluation and to carry out examination processes. There are probably more collaborative efforts in establishing questions than in grading them, but at least some promising practices are emerging in collaborative grading. However, this same collaboration seems to generate little creativity in seeking unique outputs from students as demonstrations of learning. In fact, collaboration seems to reinforce traditional practices rather than produce new methods. No doubt most faculty could profit from spending more time on generating more options, such as those listed in the chapter in this book on the ideal interdisciplinary course, and less time on evaluating traditional exam questions.

Do faculty need to collaborate on testing and evaluation in team teaching? Perhaps not. Traditional methods carried out by individual faculty members may be adequate; but as in the case of collaborative teaching, some potential may be lost in not working together. The availability of a team of faculty provides an opportunity to set certain evaluation tasks that might be richer and more appropriate for evaluating interdisciplinary outcomes than individual professors constructing, giving, and grading their own tests and papers. Although collaboration in evaluation is generally perceived, with some exceptions, as fairly high, the nature of that collaboration is bounded for the most part by traditional ideas of giving tests and assigning papers.

PERCEPTIONS OF BEING A TEAM MEMBER

What is it like to be a team member? Does it take more time to be on a team? Is it a relatively difficult process, relating to other colleagues, or do the human interactions work fairly smoothly? What is the role of the leader in helping the team function collaboratively? Do some teams become dysfunctional?

With few exceptions, the faculty identified their participation on a team as more time-consuming than teaching a course alone. A lot of time is spent in planning. "Another thing that affects the time factor is that you often do a lot of reading outside your field," notes one faculty member. "Things can pile up," notes another. "It could be a nightmare. So you have to build calendars and plan to use your time wisely." As one faculty member stated, "I have a love/hate thing about the time. I love being involved, but I wonder if I should spend my time this way. I cram the meeting into my busy schedule and sometimes we just sit there chewing on old things, covering the same ground." Another faculty member says, "Sometimes it's a struggle just to get everyone together, but I could also see that in some ways it can be more efficient than working alone because the product is better." Says another, "It's not only the planning; the collaborative presentations really take time." Although most faculty agree that team teaching takes significantly more time, some realize that time is simply one of the costs of an interdisciplinary course. "I'd surely have trouble doing *this* course as one person. I couldn't." Another concurs, "My personal time is less than if I were to try to do this course by myself." On the other hand, another faculty member notes, "What's lost, costs; you just don't have that time to do something else."

Faculty had mixed views about whether the experience of being on a team was stressful, although generally faculty didn't find participation on a team to be a difficult thing, full of stresses and strains. "Our team has 12 people, so you might expect some stress, but we have great cohesion and I think the students sense this. It's very positive. Everyone is working together. But selection is the key. Not everyone will plop into a course and fit like a car cylinder. You need to have common interests and teaching goals." With a large team, such as the faculty for "The Making of the Modern Mind," turnover can be a problem. "When a new person comes in, there is a need for orientation, and adjuncts are almost always a problem, being busy with other things; sometimes they just don't show up." As one faculty member notes, "There isn't much stress because there isn't much for us to interact on that we would disagree about." On the other hand, a team member in the same course notes, "I would enjoy more fruitful arguments." Getting along, at a superficial level appears not to be a problem, but changing behavior can be. "I know one faculty member who has changed, and it has not been easy." Some faculty see interpersonal stress to be a function of size. "It was not easy the first few years; so when they turned to me to be the coordinator, I said that the only way I would consider it would be with a model of 100 students and five faculty. They agreed, and I think it runs more smoothly now." Sometimes the subject contributes to the interpersonal stress of the group, as in "Multiple Voices of America." "In dealing with diversity we are studying something that the society has trouble trying to do. You can't do this diversity stuff and call it easy." Others note that the challenge is more intellectual than interpersonal. "It takes time and energy to get inside the approach that another person represents." One faculty member, who taught for a while in both "Making of the Modern Mind" and "Multiple Voices," notes, "A lot depends on whether you are clear about what you are trying to do. In Modern Mind we settled things early and we knew what we wanted. They still don't know what they want to do in Multiple Voices, so naturally the meetings are interminable."

A lot depends on the personnel and the leadership. Of the five courses studied, the "Lawyering Process" has had the most interpersonal stress, partly because of the leadership but also because of the strong personalities of one or two members. "People had different expectations of collaboration. I was frustrated because I wanted a lot. It took me a long time to accept that it's going to be hierarchies. When we changed leaders the first time, I had my hopes up, but it was like changing one fascist for another. Then another member comes in and she wants a lot of collaboration, too. I ended up having to mediate between her and the new leader." Eventually, the team stabilized, but not until a third leader came in and the most dissatisfied faculty member left. "Now we can work as a team," notes the new leader," and some of the quieter members are much more assertive and are really beginning to make a contribution." As one team member, who has survived all of the different leaders, notes: "'Painful' is the word, not just difficult! The faculty on this team were very tough to handle: one was explosive, one surly, one impossible. There was a time when it was like the inquisition. Sometimes I would come out of the meeting and I knew I'd be knocked out for the rest of the day if I didn't find some aspirin or a Margarita. But stress has gone way down. We come out laughing now." The leader of the "Lawyering Process" said that working together was more difficult than he anticipated, and it required more effort than he thought he could give. One of his team members attributes the stress to working out the subject, not to the people. "The thing that saves it is the personalities of the players; we get along now, we actually like each other, so we are considerate."

What we learn from this group of faculty is that getting along is not an inherent problem in team teaching, so much as a function of size, subject, individual personalities, and leadership. What could be potentially frustrating is usually pleasant. Course coordinators play an important role in facilitating or disrupting the work of the team. Somewhere along the way, participants' expectations for collaboration and the actual pattern of collaboration need to become congruent. Problems need to be addressed, and sometimes that means someone should leave. In general, team members exhibit much good will and cooperation and the dysfunctional team seems to be rare and then only temporary.

FINDING A NICHE

Most faculty find their special niche on their interdisciplinary teams. The findings from the research on groups suggests that individuals take on specific roles within groups, and it is not surprising, therefore, that faculty can usually identify their special contributions to their team.

Many faculty will first identify their discipline. "I'm the art historian on the team, and I emphasize seeing, more than just words. I bring the visual images, and I think it is great stuff, so I contribute a special enthusiasm and lecture style." Another member comments, "My role, as the anthropologist on the Evolution Team, is to help put science in a social and cultural context. I've enjoyed alerting my colleagues to the fact that the social sciences have their own methods. I bring a presence from another division, but I don't know if the students get it." A faculty member on the "Multiple Voices" team says, "I bring an awareness of the complexity of Native American history, culture, and modes of expression. My discipline provides a framework for dealing with stereotypes." A member of the "Quality Panorama" team notes, "I was the only businessperson who actually had recent business experience. I think my colleagues were looking for this and treated me as more of a practitioner."

Other faculty speak of their contribution to the educational process. "I'm the only one on the team with any training in education. That, plus three years as a high school teacher, helps me to move the course away from a simple content orientation." Another faculty member notes, "My contribution is to not fear the continual reform of this course. It will always be in continual transition, and I bring that attitude to the team. I'm also the one who tries to link the course up with service learning opportunities." A member of the "Quality Panorama" team notes, "I bring a little more energy to my teaching. I like to keep it light, tell a joke, and invite participation." Several faculty commented on their leadership role as course coordinator. "I enjoy my back-stage role in giving the cues for entry and exit. I like tying it all together." Another course coordinator notes, "Someone has to be organized, to organize the task, to follow out the details, and make sudden changes or substitutions. I like to get the administration done so that we can spend more of our meeting time on teaching each other." A former coordinator notes, "I provided leadership and set standards. If someone goofed up in the seminar, I fired them. I felt it was my course and my heart and soul were in it. I also had to put out brush fires such as allegations by students of cheating, and sometimes that was very time-consuming because it involved a judgment call." The coordinator of the "Lawyering Process" team is clear about his role: "It's leadership and administration." The coordinator of the "Quality Panorama" team notes, in keeping with the course theme, "I'm the one who has to make sure that we produce according to specifications. As the only senior faculty member on a very diverse team I provide a certain stability."

Other faculty speak of a role they play in the group dynamics. A member of the "Lawyering Process" team notes, "I'm the problem solver, not the problem creator. I'm also the course memory. I've worked with a variety of teams and leaders. My main contribution to the course has been not cracking under the pressure."

Sometimes faculty speak of having a hard time in finding their niche and confess to being a little uncomfortable in their role. "I'm sandwiched in between the other two, and I'm a little inadequate. I tend to do too much with the material, and students are a little slow to warm up to me. I was surrounded by good teachers. At first I took it on the chin, but I've turned that around now. Maybe you can slide through in your own course, but in team teaching you are compared, and sometimes you need to face up to short-comings." One of the law faculty, no longer on the team, notes, "I was a thorn in their side. Now that I'm out, I'm afraid there are things that need to get done, that won't get done."

Faculty find their niche. Almost all the faculty interviewed could identify without hesitation a particular role that they played on the team, as disciplinary specialist, educator, leader, or manager of the group dynamics. One of the strengths of the team-teaching arrangement is that teams allow for role differentiation. Not everyone has to be good at everything, and few teachers, teaching alone, are. The team makes room for leaders and followers, subject specialists, and persons with special insights into educational processes. A strong team will have many niches and will draw on individual strengths in creative ways.

SATISFACTIONS AND DISSATISFACTIONS

What do faculty identify as their strongest dissatisfactions with team teaching? Are these counterbalanced with strong satisfactions? What do faculty gain or give up by being involved in team teaching? What do they learn? How does the experience contribute to their overall professional growth and general sense of productivity?

Perhaps the most surprising finding from these interviews is that the dissatisfactions are so few and the satisfactions are elaborated with such gusto. One should keep in mind, of course, that the faculty being interviewed are actually *doing* team teaching now. They are the "survivors." Those who have tried it and dropped out, and those who want nothing to do with it, are not in this sample. Nonetheless, even with this identified bias toward "participants," such a positive bottom line is surprising, especially with all the demands that team teaching makes on faculty.

Consider the dissatisfactions first. Some faculty identify a general "lack of appreciation" as being frustrating. "The institution doesn't seem to support people who do this in any special way. Maybe we get a little planning grant for a week in the summer, but that's it." Others note, "I have ideas about other things I would like to do with the course, but the resources aren't available. We could use a writing clinic for this course." Still others note their frustration with a point system for counting faculty load. "I'm splattered all over the curriculum, and they're running around checking to see how many points I've earned. It's a stupid system." Others speak of a sense of getting burned out from the relentless demands. "In a year-long course, everyone, including the students, gets alienated and you wonder what you salvage from the end of the course." Others identify frustrations that arise from the natural conflict between research and teaching. "Any teaching causes disruption of the research obligation," notes one of the biologists, "but team teaching seems to aggravate this conflict because it is so demanding. In some institutions the conflict gets resolved more easily: research is the top priority and the students get screwed.

Here, we are expected to be good at both. That's not easy when you are the coordinator of an interdisciplinary course." Others identify the nagging little details as their frustration: the worry about getting the right size enrollment, keeping track of the budget, room changes, last minute decisions. Some experience frustration over not knowing the material as well as one would as a specialist. "Sometimes I don't get enough time to make preparations with new material, so I'm a little insecure as to where I fit in with the discussion session." Others say that they don't like the effects they sometimes see with students. "Some students get very confused by all this, especially international students. Sometimes there are just too many people in the room. It's frustrating when I see the students getting frustrated." Another says quite simply, "I get frustrated when it's not as good as it could be."

When faculty are asked what they give up when they join an interdisciplinary team, they almost always reply "autonomy." One reluctant team member observes, "When I teach alone, it's my class, my grades, my disputes, and I create the atmosphere. On a team, I lose my control of those things. I can't do anything about a colleague who hands papers back late. I can't do anything about a low course evaluation. I may only contribute 20%, but I'm stuck with the whole team's evaluations." An experienced veteran of eight years of team teaching likens this to "having a strange roommate, like Felix and Oscar in the *Odd Couple*. Some people are tidy; some are slobs. It takes some adjustment, but really these are minor irritations." Others refer to giving up intellectual control. "In my upper division course, intellectual control is absolute. I teach embryology and no colleague knows whether I do or don't. Here, it's open to scrutiny." Sometimes faculty feel they are making some serious compromises. "OK, so you have to give up having your own way all the time. I can accept this, but sometimes I feel like I'm compromising my standards." Another faculty member puts it well, "You give up your own vision of what students need for a shared vision. You make big and little compromises all the time." Some of the bigger disagreements are about grading practices and students. "One person says 90 percent is an A, another says, 4 A's out of 200 just isn't right. It's not a highjump bar. So you have to adjust. But not everyone agrees." Others feel that they give up flexibility and spontaneity. "In your own class if you run over you say, well, I'll return to this tomorrow. On the team, it's someone else's turn tomorrow." Another faculty member says, "Things just get too regimented." Other faculty identify more personal losses: "I gave up Con[stitutional] Law, another course I really enjoyed, to teach in this." Others refer once again to the amount of time. "You could come in two days a week, now its four; what was eight hours of teaching is looking more like sixteen."

All these losses, frustrations, and dissatisfactions are important. This sample of faculty portrayed these complaints as fairly minor concerns—no long speeches, no intense emotion—but they serve as the beginning of a good list of what faculty are likely to find troubling about team teaching. Frustrations about time demands, decreased autonomy, and loss of flexibility are inherent problems with team teaching, and unless they are managed carefully, expressed dissatisfactions will grow stronger.

On the other hand, dissatisfactions are counterbalanced by interesting accounts of perceived satisfactions. Many faculty commented on how much new knowledge they gained from being on a team. "Well, I'm a perpetual student, so being involved in a course like this is great. I was pretty specialized in graduate school in art history, so I had to catch up on the philosophy and music, and I enjoyed that." A music professor notes, "We learn from each other; people lead you to other ideas, other readings. I was a little tired of the classical tradition in music, but I began to see it in a new way. My own subject is more interesting to me now. It was a kind of renewal for me in my discipline. Some of the things I've learned, I take back to my teaching in music." A biologist notes, "It makes me pay attention to other perspectives on the material. We realize we have different world views and that makes us realize that this goes on with the students, too." The anthropologist from "Origins and Evolution of Life" adds, "I learned so much more about evolution; it filled in some gaps in my knowledge. I come in with a constructionist perspective anyway, so I don't believe I know everything, and it just becomes a great opportunity for me to learn." A similar response came from one of the biologists on the team, "Having an anthropologist has been great. He pulled me into some real dialogue. Logical positivism makes sense if everyone else thinks that way, too. But then you realize they don't." An art historian says of the "Modern Mind" team, "It's a group of sophisticated thinkers, spurring each other on." The anthropologist on the "Multiple Voices" team points out, "I get to see how other disciplines practice their craft. The art historian helps me to see a painting in an entirely new way. And, hey, I get to read novels, and that's fun. I get to see how novels can be paired with the social science literature."

Others commented on what they learned about teaching. "There were real pedagogical benefits for me to see different teachers and how they do it." Another notes, "It's fun seeing others teach and observing their methods, learning what to do and not to do." A biologist says, "No one in my department talks about teaching. We are almost embarrassed to do this. This course gives us an excuse to talk about teaching. Others teach in their little microenvironment, and they have no excuse for looking at what they are doing." His colleague in biology concurs, "The greatest satisfaction I get from this is exchanging ideas about teaching. We go to workshops together and we have developed a real support that we feel for each other. Maybe my development as a teacher would have continued anyway, but maybe not. Maybe I would have become really burned out. This has pulled me out of my corner. When you really start thinking about the educational issues, and how little attention we pay to them, you begin to realize that college education is in bad shape." One member of the "Multiple Voices" team commented on how the team learned how to use films in the classroom. "We learned how to see, so that we could use this medium in our teaching. We learned about film review journals, the equivalent of book reviews, and showed students how to watch films. We set up second viewing opportunities and learned how to talk about clips and use clips as illustrations in our lectures. We try new things and give each other feedback."

Still others mention learning about the team process itself. "I've learned that team teaching is good, that it works, and I know how to act on a team. I was always willing to compromise, but now I know how to stick to my guns more. I've learned to listen better, to process information better, and I'm improving at coping with diversity. I'm more confident in the group now, and I'm better at stating my own position so people can understand what I'm saying." For others, the outcomes are not so positive. "I learned I don't like being on a team. I don't like giving up my autonomy and if there was a way, I'd be out of here. I learned some pretty interesting stuff about myself."

Others spoke of the social value of team teaching, the friendships gained, and the genuine good times together. "It is my only chance to interact with people from another discipline," notes a music professor. "My best friends are from that course," notes a professor from "Modern Mind." "When I was new it was a source of instant best friends. We went to each others' lectures. It was really easy. The personality mix is the key." A business professor, who has been at the institution a long time notes, "For me it involved a whole new set of friends." A colleague in business notes, "I'm a people person; I'd rather work on a team than as an individual. That's what I did in industry." For many, new friends were a surprise side-benefit.

Others found their greatest satisfaction in seeing students succeed and like the course. "Some students come back and say it was their favorite course. For many students it really works and it sticks with them. Modern Mind covers those old-style European culture topics, and they have to learn how to look and to listen. They learn a kind of etiquette that goes with this course, and they like it. That's satisfying." The coordinator of "Multiple Voices" notes, "It's a great course now. I wish it had been offered to me when I was a student. That's really satisfying to be part of something that good." A law professor notes, "At those times when something truly collaborative is born, it is very satisfying. I know that what we do now is vastly better for students than what it was before." A colleague notes, "It's been fun proving to the faculty at the College of Law that this is a valid and legitimate course. Now we are getting some quality recognition from alums, the profession, and the Bar Association." A colleague on the team notes, "I just feel good about making a contribution to the students, the school, and the profession." The leader of the "Quality

Panorama" team says that his greatest satisfactions have come from creating something new that is good. "It's leading edge, a step up in quality, and I know that our students will be able to do things that are mind-bending."

Other faculty even comment on the long-range impacts on their career. "I work in American religious history, particularly the Afro-American experience, but now I want to keep teaching in this broader multi-cultural area. I teach this course with the very earliest level of first-year college students and at the same time I teach a Ph.D. colloquium on Religion and Social Change. It's the same theme, multiculturalism, but at very different levels, and I find that challenging. I want to continue doing this." One law professor states confidently, "It is simply the best professional experience I've ever had, and I've had plenty of success previously. I turned down another offer last summer teaching business law at another institution. Tenure track, better salary, but I said no. Why? Because I feel good when I go home at night. No individually taught course could make me feel that good." A business professor remarks, "I was getting to the point where I was asking about every project whether this was my last big article, my last book. I found I was looking toward the end of my career, but now I can see this course going on for years. It has been really fun to jump into something new, to start something where you don't know exactly what you are doing." One other faculty member, with almost 20 years experience in interdisciplinary courses, notes "There is a right time for this when you are open to it and it's exciting; but right now I'm a little sick of it. I have some books I want to write, and this doesn't seem like the right time for me for collaboration. I think that there are some good reasons not to do it right now."

These interviews make obvious the important satisfactions most faculty draw from their involvement in interdisciplinary courses, and show these satisfactions to be directly related to the interactions that come from being on a team. It was not surprising to hear that faculty enjoyed the interdisciplinary conversation and the dialogue about teaching, but it was somewhat amazing to hear so many comment on their new friendships, and astounding to hear faculty comment on the influence that this experience has had in providing personal growth and renewal for their career. All in all, the balance of dissatisfaction and satisfaction, perhaps with the exception of one person, is tipped in the direction of satisfaction. These faculty believe that colleagues who are not involved in team teaching are really missing something important. In the midst of this enthusiasm one must caution, once again, that we are listening to the responses of a self-selected group from one campus who no doubt tend to be flexible and gregarious people to begin with and who might be expected to like team teaching because they are doing it. Oddly enough, however, and in support of many of these findings, the matters referred to in these interviews correspond roughly to a list of faculty concerns and satisfactions elaborated by Forrest Armstrong in his research on faculty development and interdisciplinary courses, in an article I discovered after my interview data were compiled. His list includes what he calls "opportunity costs" (giving up something to do team teaching, stress associated with content integration, the joy of getting to know new colleagues (an internal change of scenery), highly satisfying peer support, and the benefits of modeling (watching others).[1] One can conclude that the people who are attracted to team teaching usually derive deep satisfactions from it and can articulate those benefits clearly.

STUDENT REACTIONS

What are students' reactions to team teaching? How do they view the degree of faculty collaboration in team teaching? Do they experience their team-taught courses as being any more interesting or challenging than their other courses?

To address these questions, a brief survey was administered during the Spring Quarter of 1994 to the students enrolled in the courses used as examples. Except for students in "Quality Panorama," which was designed for only one quarter, students had been enrolled in the courses for three quarters (or two semesters in the case of law students), and were in a good position to express their opinions about the course. Proper procedures were followed in obtaining permission to conduct research on human subjects, and students were assured that their participation was voluntary and would in no way affect their grade. A 5-point Likert scale was used to obtain data on student perceptions of faculty collaboration and on the differences and similarities between this course and other courses taught by one instructor. A copy of the questionnaire appears on the next page.

The results are displayed at the end of this chapter in five tables, one for each course, along with demographic data about respondents. Although students were given the option of not completing the survey, the number of responses reflects actual class attendance for that day, and it can be assumed that the results express generally the opinions of each class. Given the differential in wording used to describe collaboration, it is reasonable to look for results of 3.5 to 4.0 as an indicator that students viewed collaboration as between "some" and "much". These results are indicated with an asterisk in the tables that follow. It is interesting to note that the overall results show that students in general don't perceive "very much" collaboration on any of the dimensions of planning, integration of subject content, teaching, or evaluation. The highest ratings for collaboration (between "some" and "much") were received in the "Origins and Evolution of Life," with a few high ratings also in "Multiple Voices of America," and "Making of the Modern Mind." In general, students knew that some collaborative efforts had gone into planning the course and in trying to integrate the subject matter, but in general they did not

STUDENT SURVEY
Interdisciplinary Team-Taught Courses

Please circle the number on the scale below signifying the word that best describes your response to the question.

1. To what extent would you say there is evidence of collaboration (working together) by faculty in *planning* this course?

Very Much	Much	Some	Little	Almost None	Don't Know
5	4	3	2	1	

2. To what extent would you say that faculty have tried to *integrate the subject content* of this course?

Very Much	Much	Some	Little	Almost None	Don't Know
5	4	3	2	1	

3. To what extent would you say that faculty *have been successful in integrating the subject content* of this course?

Very Much	Much	Some	Little	Almost None	Don't Know
5	4	3	2	1	

4. In describing the *classroom teaching* in this course, to what extent would you say faculty were collaborating?

Very Much	Much	Some	Little	Almost None	Don't Know
5	4	3	2	1	

5. To what extent would you say faculty have collaborated in establishing and carrying out *grading and evaluation practices* for this course?

Very Much	Much	Some	Little	Almost None	Don't Know
5	4	3	2	1	

6. *Compared to other courses* you have taken that were *taught by one faculty member* and were based in a *single discipline* (subject area), how did you like this course for

   a) capturing your interest?

Much More	More	About the Same	Less	Much Less	No Opinion
5	4	3	2	1	

b) challenging you to think?

Much More	More	About the Same	Less	Much Less	No Opinion
5	4	3	2	1	

7. About you—please check all that apply:

   _male   _female
   _undergraduate   _graduate
   _18-23 years   _24-29 years   _30 or above

see these efforts carried out in classroom teaching or evaluation practices. They almost always rated collaboration in teaching at around 3.0, indicating that they perceived only "some" collaboration. Interestingly, students often rated interest and academic challenge as between "about the same" and "higher," giving what might be thought of as a slight preference for interdisciplinary team-taught courses for interest and challenge.

How should one interpret these results? Assuming that students in a required course—all of these are either required or meet an option for a requirement—can be hypercritical, and assuming that graduate students and older students may be even more hypercritical, would it not be reasonable to conclude, even so, that students simply do not perceive high levels of collaboration in these interdisciplinary team-taught courses? In spite of faculty efforts to collaborate in significant ways in planning these courses, it appears that students don't have much grasp of or appreciation for the collaboration that has taken place behind the scenes. Nor do they seem to see how the subject content has been integrated. In spite of extensive efforts on the part of faculty to collaborate, the evidence of collaboration isn't perceived by students as "very much." In other words, although faculty may spend hours and hours in planning what they perceive as an interdisciplinary course with highly integrated subject matter, students "just don't get it." What students are looking for, and may be most able to perceive as collaboration, is what affects them more directly: classroom teaching and testing and evaluation practices. Because they don't see much team-teaching, in the form of dialogue, lectures, or panels, and because they don't see much collaborative work in grading their papers and projects, they don't rate collaboration as "very much." The hard work that faculty engage in behind the scenes to invent the subject is probably not appreciated to the extent that it should be; and because faculty, even by their own admission, don't collaborate much in the classroom delivery of instruction, their general efforts at collaboration are not fully recognized or appreciated. This is not to say that students don't perceive any efforts at collaboration, particularly in planning; it is that the levels of collaboration are not seen as very high.

One lesson in this might be that faculty may need to try to balance their collaborative efforts more equally across the functions of planning, content integration, teaching, and evaluation. Engaging in stimulating discussions about the interconnections of their disciplines is probably more fascinating for faculty than thinking out how they might best collaborate in the classroom or in designing and evaluating student projects. The natural attraction is to the intellectual work, difficult though it may be, of inventing the subject; the secondary interest is in pedagogy, where faculty have less background and tend to be more traditional and not as inventive. The failure to capitalize on opportunities for collaboration in classroom teaching, may contribute to low ratings of overall collaboration. One suspects that it may be possible to help students understand the nature of the collaboration in planning and content integration by continuing to remind them of the intellectual structure and rationale for the course; but these efforts, surely to be encouraged, are not likely to yield much unless students *see* faculty collaborating in the classroom.

On a more positive note, it is satisfying to see, at least in some of the courses, the perception of greater interest and challenge. Although the results do not suggest "much more" interest and challenge, they lean in that direction. If faculty have gone to the trouble of designing a new subject, the course should be more interesting and challenging. "Greater interest" and "more challenge" should be more consciously articulated objectives of interdisciplinary courses and team teaching. Although all courses should stimulate interest and be challenging, the potential in the interdisciplinary framework for stimulating interest and challenge for students should be more fully exploited.

It is important also to note that the qualitative data gathered through interviews with faculty capture a depth of understanding, including a range of attitudes and feelings, that are not tapped in the student survey. The incongruity may be due in part to the methods used to study faculty and students. The differences may also reflect that broader disparity between faculty purposes and student perceptions that can take place with any course or set of courses. Faculty have their agendas—to develop critical thinking skills, to challenge stereotypes, and to help students appreciate intellectual traditions, among others—and students have their agendas—to prepare for a job, to develop new skills, and to have fun, among others. These agendas don't always coincide, and interdisciplinary courses, as with all courses, are not necessarily perceived by students in the same way that they are intended by faculty. This is not to suggest to faculty that interdisciplinary teaching is a waste of time, or that institutions should give up such efforts; on the contrary, more effort and support may need to be given to interdisciplinary efforts to make them more attractive to students. What faculty may need to realize is that their general enthusiasm for the values of interdisciplinary study may need far more articulation and interpretation for students than it now gets, and their belief in the efficacy of team teaching may need far more concrete expression in the classroom than manifest at present. Although students may never come to appreciate the importance of interdisciplinary connections in the way that faculty do, there is surely much that could be done to cultivate their understanding of, and interest in, what is now becoming a widely used approach to instruction.

TABLE 1

Mean Score Questionnaire Results for "Origins and Evolution of Life"

Item	Mean
Collaborate on planning	3.8*
Tries to integrate subject	4.0*
Success in integrating subject	3.8*
Collaborating on classroom teaching	3.5*
Collaborating on evaluation	3.4
Compared to other courses:	
capturing interest	3.5+
challenging to think	3.8+
Males	37%
Females	31%
Undergraduate	98%
18-23 years	100%

*indicates score of 3.5 or higher signifying a mean between "some" and "much" collaboration
+indicates score of 3.5 or higher signifying a mean between "about the same" and "more" interesting or challenging

---

TABLE 2

Mean Score Questionnaire Results for "Multiple Voices of America"

Item	Mean
Collaborate on planning	3.7*
Tries to integrate subject	3.8*
Success in integrating subject	3.3
Collaborating on classroom teaching	3.0
Collaborating on evaluation	2.6
Compared to other courses:	
capturing interest	3.0
challenging to think	3.2
Males	42%
Females	58%
Undergraduate	100%
18-23 years	95%
24-29 years	2%
30 or above	3%

*indicates score of 3.5 or higher signifying a mean between "some" and "much" collaboration

---

TABLE 3

Mean Score Questionnaire Results for "Making of the Modern Mind"

Item	Mean
Collaborate on planning	3.5*
Tries to integrate subject	3.8*
Success in integrating subject	3.4
Collaborating on classroom teaching	2.9
Collaborating on evaluation	3.3
Compared to other courses:	
capturing interest	3.5*
challenging to think	3.3
Males	29%
Females	71%
Undergraduate	98%
Graduate	2%
18-23 years	92%
30 or above	8%

*indicates score of 3.5 or higher signifying a mean between "some" and "much" collaboration

---

TABLE 4

Mean Score Questionnaire Results for "Quality Panorama"

Item	Mean
Collaborate on planning	3.4
Tries to integrate subject	3.4
Success in integrating subject	3.1
Collaborating on classroom teaching	3.0
Collaborating on evaluation	3.1
Compared to other courses:	
capturing interest	3.8+
challenging to think	3.3
Males	48%
Females	52%
Graduate	100%
18-23 years	7%
24-29 years	67%
30 or above	26%

+indicates score of 3.5 or higher signifying a mean between "about the same" and "more" interesting or challenging

TABLE 5	
Mean Score Questionnaire Results for "Lawyering Process"	
Item	**Mean**
Collaboration in planning	3.2
Tries to integrate subject	3.4
Success in integrating subject	3.0
Collaborating on classroom teaching	2.9
Collaborating on evaluation	2.3
Compared to other courses:	
capturing interest	2.3
challenging to think	2.3
Males	52%
Females	48%
Undergraduate	8%
Graduate	93%
18-23 years	34%
24-29 years	53%
30 or above	19%

NOTE

1. Forrest Armstrong "Faculty Development through Interdisciplinarity" *The Journal of General Education*, 32:1 (Spring 1980): pp. 52–53.

CHAPTER

· · · · · · · · ·

Future Prospects for
Interdisciplinary Courses:
Issues and Problems

"A community, like the medieval communities of masters and
students, should have common interests; in the multiversity they
are quite varied, even conflicting. A community should have a
soul, a single animating principle; the multiversity has several."
—Clark Kerr

The array of examples presented in Part II of this book is impressive for
its diversity, both in the subject areas in which interdisciplinary team-
taught courses are offered, and in the institutional types where they
are found. Interdisciplinary team-taught courses are more than isolated efforts
located in a few institutions in a few subjects. If there is this much activity, one
might ask: What is the future for interdisciplinary team-taught courses? Is this
a passing phenomena, a curious fad of the decade, or is there likely to be more
of this activity? Is this a trend with a future? Answering these questions is a
descriptive and speculative task.

One might also ask the normative question: If interdisciplinary team-
taught courses are a "good-thing" for some of the reasons outlined in the
chapters on rationale and on faculty perceptions, what should be done to
support these efforts, so that this enterprise will thrive? If the courses that
appear in the extended list of examples in Part II are valuable and worthwhile,
so much so that other institutions may wish to initiate or expand their
interdisciplinary efforts, what will need to be done to support and encourage
such action?

THE FUTURE OF INTERDISCIPLINARY COURSES AND THE FATE
OF THE DISCIPLINES

One might begin by asking the following questions in a deeper and more probing way than we have up to this point: What are all these people doing with these interdisciplinary courses? Why do they take the time and put forth the effort to create these courses? What needs are they meeting for themselves, for their students, for their institutions? It has been suggested that the ideal interdisciplinary course involves bringing together faculty from different perspectives to create a "new subject." But how "new" are these new subjects? Are the new subjects only temporary arrangements for studying old subjects? Are these new arrangements for interdisciplinary learning to be viewed as isolated efforts of important but limited value in themselves, or are they part of a larger movement? Is interdisciplinary teaching to be seen as a modest attempt to provide some useful connections across the disciplines, while leaving the basic paradigm of the disciplines and professions essentially unchallenged, or is it the vanguard of a movement that will ultimately result in a paradigm shift, a new way of thinking about knowledge? These difficult questions are not easily answered, but are worthy of further exploration.

Although it would be difficult to argue at this point in time that a new curricular paradigm is emerging, ready to replace the traditional disciplinary and professional structure, some signs, at least, indicate that we have more here than just an interesting collection of courses. Although some of the courses listed among the examples can be viewed as efforts simply to connect disciplines or view professional issues from more than one disciplinary perspective, many involve genuine attempts to create a new subject involving different ways of knowing. If this is the case, to what extent do such courses represent a trend, and where is the trend going?

One way to answer these questions is to note the appearance among these exemplary courses of many topics faculty and students want to study that don't arise from, and probably never will arise from, disciplinary formats. Gender, multicultural, and international studies are prime examples of such new areas of inquiry. As these new areas develop, they are not easily "shoe-horned" into existing disciplinary structures. Just as "new subjects" broadened and eventually overcame the classical curriculum of the colonial colleges, a plethora of new subjects that no longer fit disciplinary structures could have a significant impact on the present-day curriculum. The information age is characterized by a knowledge explosion, and that vast output of new knowledge is coalescing into many new subjects. The disciplines have not lost their power to generate new knowledge, but side by side with them, other forces, assisted by new methods and technologies, are producing new subjects. As is the case with plant and animal evolution, sometimes scientists discover forms of life that can't be classified into existing species. Some new subjects don't fit into the domains of old subjects, and new scholarly domains need to be created to study them and teach about them. Over the next 50 years, many new subjects that simply don't fit the existing categories of the academic disciplines are likely to be created. Furthermore, these new subjects may not be simply new disciplines, but subjects that don't take on the characteristics of a discipline. While the disciplines continue to remain strong, new subjects of inquiry may surround and eventually overwhelm them. This may not be so much a paradigm shift as a paradigm drowning.

Another sign on the horizon is the new interest, not only in what to study, but also how to study it, a fascination with method. Whereas one could count on fairly predictable research methods in most of the disciplines over the years, recently there has been a renewed interest in approaching old subjects in new ways. For example, in the social sciences, qualitative methods, such as ethnographies and case studies, were employed rarely 15 to 20 years ago, and then only in their "home disciplines;" but now they are widely used in creative ways across all of the social sciences and in many of the humanities. Many scholars today are reaching across the disciplines to produce some fairly unusual and imaginative methodological connections. In a now famous chapter entitled "Blurred Genres: The Refiguration of Social Thought," Clifford Geertz, professor of social science at The Institute for Advanced Studies in Princeton, New Jersey, notes a recent increase in what he calls "genre mixing":

> This genre blurring is more than just a matter of Harry Houdini or Richard Nixon turning up as characters in novels or of midwestern murder sprees described as though a gothic romancer had imagined them. It is philosophical inquiries looking like literary criticism (think of Stanley Cavell on Beckett or Thoreau, Sartre on Flaubert), scientific discussions looking like belles lettres *morceaux* (Lewis Thomas, Loren Eiseley), baroque fantasies presented as deadpan empirical observations (Borges, Barthelme), histories that consist of equations and tables or law court testimony (Fogel and Engerman, LeRoi Ladurie), documentaries that read like true confessions (Mailer), parables posing as ethnographies (Castenada), theoretical treatises set out as travelogues (Levi-Strauss), ideological arguments as historiographical inquiries (Edward Said), epistemological studies constructed like political tracts (Paul Feyerabend), methodological polemics got up as personal memoirs (James Watson). Nabokov's *Pale Fire*, that impossible object made of poetry and fiction, footnotes and images from the clinic, seems very much of the time; one waits only for quantum theory in verse or biography in algebra.[1]

In reflecting on this array of examples of genre mixing, Geertz notes: "The interesting question is not how all this muddle is going to come magnificently together, but what does all this ferment mean." His suggestion is that genre mixing "has introduced a fundamental debate into the social science community concerning not just its methods but its aims."[2]

Whether this borrowing of methods is a temporary fancy or a long-term trend is hard to say, but there appears to be a significant interest not only in inventing new subjects, but also in devising new methods for studying them. If one were to bet that the "cross-fertilization" of methodologies will continue, at what point does this activity cease to be merely an enrichment of the disciplines and become an entirely new approach to gaining and transmitting knowledge? At what point do interdisciplinary courses stop being inter*disciplinary* and become a way of transmitting knowledge that no longer needs the discipline as home base? Just how much alteration has there been and will there continue to be in what Geertz calls "how we think about how we think"?[3]

One of the recent forces that has also driven a re-examination of the disciplinary structure has been the cultural studies movement. Having ignited controversy on many campuses with the startling ideas of the "deconstructionists," cultural studies advocates have inspired many disciplines to take a fresh look at the claims they make for "knowledge" in their field. Scholars are able to acknowledge now that many of the "findings" of their field seem to have been conditioned by time, culture, political outlook, gender, or power. This is not a new discovery. In fact, a well-developed subfield within sociology known as "the sociology of knowledge" addresses this problem.[4] Coined by German philosopher Max Scheler, the term "sociology of knowledge" was developed into a field through the work of sociologist Karl Mannheim, who drew heavily on the writings of Marx, Nietzsche, and the German historicists. In his famous *Ideology and Utopia,* first published in 1936, Mannheim states:

> Once we recognize that all historical knowledge is relational knowledge, and can only be formulated with reference to the position of the observer, we are faced, once more, with the task of discriminating between what is true and what is false in such knowledge. The question then arises: which social standpoint, *vis-a-vis* of history offers the best chance for reaching an optimum of truth? In any case, at this stage the vain hope of discovering truth in a form which is independent of an historically and socially determined set of meanings will have to be given up.[5]

Mannheim believes that the search for "ultimate truth" is futile, and that scholars might more profitably focus on uncovering "reciprocal interrelationships" in a given frame of thought.[6] Mannheim recommends thinking "dynamically and relationally rather than statically," and understanding that "the mode of approach to the object to be known is dependent on the nature of the knower."[7] Writing as a contemporary sociologist, Peter Berger uses the phrase "the social construction of reality," to describe this phenomena, and sees Mannheim's concept of "relationalism" not as a capitulation to relativism, "but as a sober recognition that knowledge must always be knowledge from a certain position."[8] Drawing on this heritage, cultural studies advocates have more recently focused this skepticism about "truth" on the academic disci-plines. One thing that comes from the use of interdisciplinary perspectives is an increased awareness of the "relational" nature of knowledge, and the "boundedness" of disciplinary perspectives.

Another factor that has stimulated the recent re-examination of the disci-plines is a renewed interest in the way knowledge is represented. If sociologists are concerned about the social determinants of knowledge, psychologists and linguists are interested in what happens when perceptions—whatever they may be—are expressed in some form and then reacted to by an observer. What takes place within this transaction, and to what extent is the "truth" lost or at least conditioned by the nature of this transaction? Again, the idea is not new. The problem has been explored in the work of "symbolic interactionists," such as George Herbert Mead, and has its roots in the early work of "gestalt" psychologists. The way the problem is put is to say that the meanings that scholars (and ordinary people) make of things are generated in the communication process that takes place between those who do, say, or write things, and those who perceive them. Knowledge, in its various manifestations, is constructed in charac-teristic forms or representations. Eliot Eisner, professor of education and art at Stanford University, notes that in constructing knowledge:

> we confront the formidable task of trying to represent what we have come to know through some medium. The most common medium we use is language. One feature of a medium is that it mediates and anything that mediates changes what it conveys; the map is not the territory and the text is not the event. We learn to write and to draw, to dance and to sing, in order to re-present the world as we know it. What we are able to represent depends on two key factors. First is the form of representation we wish to use. The world we are able to create in text is a different world from the one we can represent in a photograph. Second, the conceptual framework we employ directs our attention in particular ways and, therefore, what we experience is shaped by that framework. Thus, the questions we ask, the categories we employ, the theories we use, guide our inquiry; indeed, what we come to know about the world is influenced by the tools we have available.[9]

Along with a sociology of knowledge, there is a "psychology of knowledge," which can be employed to raise questions about disciplinary claims to truth. Today there is vigorous conversation within the disciplines, and across them, about how they construct knowledge. What was once clear and relatively stable, namely, the methods the disciplines employed, is now unclear and changing, perhaps even embarrassingly up for grabs. Much of this ferment is, of course, a reaction to logical positivism, and the way it has served, in one way or another, as a foundation for the methods of many of the disciplines, particu-larly the physical sciences. As the disciplines are challenged about the nature and limitations of their methods, particularly the "constructed" nature of their "representations," their overall adequacy as the sole or primary way to organize knowledge for instruction becomes dubious. The challenge today to disciplinary assumptions about their methods may be a badly needed nudge toward self-reflection that will engender greater modesty about their claims to knowledge, and more sharing of such modesty with students, or it may be the initial rumblings of something more like an intellectual earthquake.

Some argue that the disciplines are so long established—nearly one hundred years—and are so well ensconced in the structure of academia that nothing will overturn their dominance of the curriculum. Others argue that they may well drown in the information deluge or may be shaken to pieces by the earthquake caused by the re-examination of "how we think about how we think."

Still others suggest that this critique of the disciplines is not just an academic debate but one with political overtones. On the one hand (the right), some argue that the specialization of the disciplines keeps higher education from pursuing its self-expressed goals of developing well-rounded graduates able to function in society with a strong sense of moral values; on the other hand (the left), others argue that the specialization of the disciplines produces captives of the status quo who are ill-prepared to define-problems, bring about social change, and address global issues. In a provocative chapter, entitled "Being Interdisciplinary Is Very Hard to Do," Stanley Fish writes,

> if both the left and the right can lay claim to an antiprofessionalism that regards with suspicion activities tied narrowly to disciplinary pressures, there is nevertheless a difference in the ways in which the antiprofessional stance is assumed. The difference is one of sophistication and complexity of presentation: whereas the right tends to issue its call for a general, nonspecialized pedagogy in the same flag-waving mode that characterizes its celebration of the American family, the left urges its pedagogy in the context of a full-fledged epistemological argument, complete with a theory of the self, an analysis of the emergence and ontology of institutions, and a taxonomy of the various forms of pedagogical practice, from the frankly oppressive to the self-consciously liberating.[10]

In either case, the arguments are mounted against disciplinary specialization, but for different reasons, and with a different style. In both cases, though in different ways, the disciplines are attacked for an absence of social relevance. Oddly enough, interdisciplinary courses may thrive in the midst of that controversy as a promising experiment in providing greater value to society.

Although society (and students) may long for new subjects taught in new ways, academics will probably make the ultimate decisions about what we will study, how we will study it, and how we will teach it. Legislatively mandated interdisciplinary courses (in the sense that there is legislatively mandated assessment) are unlikely because the issue can't be framed that way. The use of interdisciplinary courses will wax or wane within the context of a larger set of influences that will shape the way academics think about knowledge. For now it might be best to say that "something" *is* happening to the way academics have traditionally thought about knowledge, and that this "something," as yet poorly understood, may turn out to be greater and more profound than we are able to describe at present.

Interdisciplinary courses, therefore, take their place in a larger set of developments which include, among other things, a re-examination of the disciplinary foundations of knowledge. Interdisciplinary courses are both a product of and cause of this re-examination. Thus the fate of interdisciplinary team-taught courses—whether there will be more or fewer of them and how they will eventually impact the disciplinary structure—depends on the outcomes of a much larger set of influences and an intensifying debate about the viability of the disciplines.

SUPPORTING AND ENCOURAGING INTERDISCIPLINARY EFFORTS

Moving from descriptive to normative issues, one can ask what might be done to support interdisciplinary courses, assuming that further development of these efforts is something to be valued. One way to think about this is to recall the history of the formation of the disciplines and review how the disciplines became so well established. In recounting that history, Burton Clark reminded us that the emergence of the disciplines was accompanied by the development of academic departments corresponding to the disciplines, national professional associations to serve the disciplines, and graduate education to train scholars and socialize them into the disciplines. Apparently, this mutually reinforcing set of developments worked well, for the academic disciplines are now able to celebrate approximately a century of productive existence.

Assuming, for the moment, that the disciplines found the magic formula for sustenance, it might make sense to examine interdisciplinary efforts within the context of these same three categories: institutional organizational structure, professional associations, and graduate education.

ORGANIZATIONAL AND FINANCIAL SUPPORT FOR INTERDISCIPLINARY COURSES AND TEAM TEACHING

One of the interesting trends that shows up in the courses generated through the national call for examples is that most interdisciplinary team-taught courses are embedded in some larger curricular structure. Interdisciplinary courses are usually part of a general education curriculum, a women's studies program, a concentration, or a professional sequence. They seldom stand alone. Even courses that appear to be interesting in their own right, as electives, are offered in the context of an interterm or adult education program. Some of the interdisciplinary courses described in the collection of examples in Part II are part of rather complex cluster arrangements or "learning communities." Courses are usually part of a larger curricular structure.

When the academic disciplines came into being, they were supported by the simultaneous emergence of departments. Thus, what was intrinsically valuable about the academic disciplines was further reinforced and supported by new organizational structures. This lesson should not go unnoticed by those who are interested in providing more interdisciplinary coursework. Interdisciplinary courses probably won't thrive if they are just left to float; they need to be tied to some curricular and structural mooring. Well-intended faculty with good ideas for interdisciplinary courses, who may even have assembled viable teams, won't get far with their courses unless those courses are part of some program. The courses included in the survey of examples exist, with few exceptions, within the context of some curricular program, such as general education, women's studies, a concentration, or a professional sequence.

This point is easy enough to see, but the matter doesn't end there. If colleges and universities are organized by departments, i.e., disciplines, where does an interdisciplinary course fit administratively? Through all its successes and failures, who owns it? The course may fit in the general education curriculum, and students may get credit toward meeting their general education requirements by taking it, but beyond that, where does the course fit into the academic and administrative structure of the institution? Ironically, the more diverse the disciplines represented in a course, the more difficult it becomes to answer the structural question. Everyone knows General Psychology belongs to the psychology department, but where does an interdisciplinary course fit that spans the physical sciences and the humanities? Whose course is that—the dean's? Who approves it, who staffs it, who pays for it, and under what conditions?

Naturally, the answers to those questions will vary from institution to institution. Some institutions have strong colleges, schools, centers, institutes, and divisions, as well as departments, and these become logical places to lodge an interdisciplinary course. In larger institutions, with larger departments, the focal point of much academic decision making is the department. Departments make nice homes for disciplinary courses, and large departments know how to protect their disciplinary interests, but they are probably not the logical place for interdisciplinary courses. So where is one to turn? Divisional structures are usually good for lodging interdisciplinary courses that draw upon related disciplines within the division, but they are not good for generating courses that cross divisions; in fact, they may even resist the creation of such courses. Colleges and schools provide a better home for courses that cross divisions, but they may not be the structure that encourages courses that involve collaboration across colleges, for example, between law and business. And so it goes, the more distant the collaboration, the more difficult it is to find the appropriate structure for lodging the course, including, as the metaphor implies, the proper care and feeding to nurture the well-being and satisfaction of the team of faculty who teach the course. The more distant the collaborating parties are, the higher the level of the organizational structure needed to bring them together.

Although the organizational issue has no easy answer, it may be necessary at times simply to create structures to house interdisciplinary courses and programs. These structures may take some unusual forms, such as centers, institutes, or programs, and may be given unique names by the institution as a mark of distinction. As Stanley Ikenberry notes in *Beyond Academic Departments: The Story of Institutes and Centers*, "the special ability of institutes and centers to facilitate interdisciplinary collaboration is regarded as one of the prime justifications for their existence." Sometimes the institute may even become the breeding ground for a new discipline and "may prove useful as an incubator in which the intent can be conceived, nourished, and developed."[11] Some institutions, of course, may be in a better position to create new structures than others, but experimenting with new forms may be imperative. The president of Denison University, Michelle Tolela Myers, urges liberal arts colleges to assume a special responsibility for creating organizational structures to support interdisciplinary work:

> Liberal arts colleges' focus on undergraduate education allows organizations along interdisciplinary rather than departmental lines. If we want leaders who can solve complex social, economic, and political problems which do not easily fit into neat disciplinary boxes, we surely must emphasize integration over specialization in our undergraduate curriculum. Administrative restructuring into larger interdisciplinary units would encourage faculty to talk and work across the old disciplinary boundaries, eliminate one layer of administration, and facilitate curricular change. At the administrative level, few tasks that affect the experience of our students on campus fall within clear-cut departmental lines. We need to create administrative structures that give multidisciplinary groups authority to solve problems and make decisions rather than hold on to old hierarchical structures.[12]

One promising way to create supportive administrative structures is to use what has come to be called in organizational theory "matrix management." This is a way of structuring organizations to look like a computer spreadsheet with both rows and columns. If one were to think of academic departments as columns, the vertical organization of faculty by disciplines, one can superimpose on that structure a horizontal arrangement of rows that gathers faculty into functional units that cross departmental lines. Departments are left undisturbed, while creating another set of structures that become valuable mechanisms for conversation, research ideas, sharing of literature, and perhaps, eventually, the support of interdisciplinary team-taught courses. Thus one might create clusters of faculty drawn from various disciplines composed by themes or special interests. Faculty can be drawn together from several departments, for example, an environmental cluster, a diversity cluster, an international cluster, an ethics cluster, a women's studies cluster, etc. This is what often happens in informal ways anyway; faculty with common interests somehow find each other across campus. The creation of a matrix, while leaving departments intact, provides a new mechanism for cross-disciplinary organization and communication.

Larger institutions may have more options and may be able to create a variety of alternative structures for "housing" interdisciplinary programs. Caroline Eckhardt, in a study of interdisciplinary programs and administrative structures, describes the alternative arrangements for interdisciplinary programs available at one large land-grant state university as follows:

> They exist as (1) colleges explicitly organized on interdisciplinary principles; (2) departments within conventional colleges; (3) "divisions" within colleges; (4) research units such as institutes, clinics and centers; (5) interdepartmental instructional units, with or without separate budgets; (6) intercollege instructional units, with and without separate budgets; and (7) subdepartmental units. Not surprisingly, programs perceived as interdisciplinary span the entire range of academic-administrative structures at this university.[13]

Beth Casey reports several promising examples in her chapter in *Interdisciplinary Studies Today* entitled "The Administration and Governance of Interdisciplinary Programs."[14] In some cases whole institutions have organized themselves to support interdisciplinary studies, such as The Evergreen State College (Olympia, WA), The School of Interdisciplinary Studies of Miami University (Oxford, Ohio) located on the nearby former campus of Western College for Women, and the University of Wisconsin—Green Bay. These institutions "live and breath" interdisciplinary studies and they are the main organizing principle of the curriculum. Other institutions, responding to aspects of their mission statement which call for the "integration of knowledge," "the development of the whole person," and "social relevance," have discovered ways to structure interdisciplinary studies to make them a large part of what they do and an important focus. Examples include the Human Development and Social Relations Program at Earlham College (Earlham, IN); the three Centers for Integrative Studies at Michigan State University (East Lansing, MI) housed in the three colleges of natural science, social science, and arts and letters, as well as transcollege level courses involving cooperation among eleven colleges; the Federated Learning Community of the State University of New York Stony Brook, enrolling students in discipline-based courses organized around interdisciplinary themes; and the School of Cultural Studies at Bowling Green State University (Bowling Green, OH) that brings together in one unit interdisciplinary programs in American Studies, Film Studies, Women's Studies, and Ethnic Studies. Other institutions create interdisciplinary centers, institutes, and consortia of departments, such as those at Tufts University and the University of Chicago, to encourage cross-disciplinary conversation, cooperation, and building of courses.

One good example of a college that has developed subtle but extensive organizational structures to accommodate interdisciplinary teaching and learning is The Colorado College in Colorado Springs, Colorado. Known for its Block Plan, whereby faculty teach and students take one course at a time in successive "terms" of three and one-half weeks, The Colorado College has capitalized on this distinctive format to encourage interdisciplinary courses designed around themes. Approximately one-fourth of the courses are interdisciplinary, taught by faculty who by themselves can represent more than one perspective or by faculty working in pairs. Students may select a concentration from a list of disciplinary majors or from an array of interdisciplinary majors, including Biochemistry, Classics, History, Politics, Comparative Literature, Environmental Geology, History-Philosophy, History-Political Science, Political Economy, and Neuroscience. Students may also build a more general Liberal Arts and Sciences major around one of several special interdisciplinary programs, including American Ethnic Studies, Asian-Pacific Studies, Environmental Studies, International Studies, North American Studies, Southwest Studies, Studies in War and Peace in the Nuclear Age, and Women Studies. In addition to their major, students are expected to have a thematic (as opposed to disciplinary) minor, to be selected from a list of 34 possibilities, including such areas as The Ancient World, Cinema Studies, Computers and Intelligence, Linguistics, Myth and Folklore, Renaissance Studies, and Urban Studies. As if this were not enough structure for interdisciplinary learning, The Colorado College also provides rotating Theme Houses as one form of residence life, where students of similar interests live together. In addition to a "healthy lifestyles" theme house, an Asia Center House, and a house where residents interested in writing serve as volunteers in literacy programs in the community, students can elect to live in various foreign language houses. The Colorado College also holds an Interdisciplinary Symposium where well-known guests present lectures on themes of current interest. Sometimes the Symposium is preceded by half-block courses on topics related to the Symposium theme.

The point should be clear: some institutions consciously structure academic and co-curricular life in ways that enable and support interdisciplinary studies. With appropriate curricular and organizational structures, including in some

cases requirements, interdisciplinary teaching and learning is given a significant boost. Although different institutions will need to approach the organizational issues in their own way, the future of interdisciplinary courses will
depend in part on the ability of institutions to create appropriate curricular
and administrative structures to house them.

In addition to providing the right organizational niche for interdisciplinary
courses, institutions need to provide adequate financial support for them,
particularly when team teaching is involved. In the national call for examples,
some institutions submitted several courses or entire programs of interdisciplinary courses. Other institutions, when a request was made for a specific type of
course, replied that they didn't have any. One faculty member submitted a
course with an impassioned note attached indicating that the course was team
taught last year, but that this year she was offering it alone "for financial
reasons." Clearly, some institutions have developed a workable means to
support team teaching, while for others support remains a problem. The
problem usually has two facets. One is how to think about and compute faculty
load. The other has to do with finding the additional resources often needed to
support faculty in the planning and development phases of the course or fund
special costs associated with the course. An occasional course is usually not a
problem, but a larger program involving several interdisciplinary team-taught
courses should have a well-thought-out plan for dealing with faculty load
issues and financing special needs.

One persistent problem in the support of team teaching is determining the
"teaching load" of the faculty involved in team-taught courses. (One wonders
how the word "activity" became associated with research and the word "load"
came to be used to refer to teaching.) Most institutions, for financial reasons,
as well as to achieve a degree of equity, try to establish a means of counting
faculty effort. In most institutions, this is done by assigning, usually in consultation with the department chair or dean, an agreed upon number of courses
per academic term. The number can range from one to three per term, in
institutions that emphasize research, to three to five in community colleges.
As any teacher knows, courses themselves vary in weight, so that the "heavi-
ness" in load depends also on such factors as the nature of the subject matter,
the mode of presentation, the testing and grading procedures, and the number
of students in the class. Although "equity" is hardly ever perceived by faculty
as having been achieved, either within departments or across schools and
colleges, most institutions make some efforts to regularize the means of
calculating faculty load. In some institutions (often private), this is a looser
more relaxed process, and in others (often public), more precise methods of
counting full-time equivalent loads are used. In either case, interdisciplinary
team-taught courses often become a problem for those who do the counting,
and in some cases for the counted.

If faculty teach four courses per term, but one or two of those courses are team taught, how is one to compute the faculty member's load? There are two common methods. One counting method is to hold the course constant and inquire about how many people teach the course. If four people teach one course, they are all teaching one-fourth of a course. One can credit the faculty member with teaching 1.25 or 3.5 courses and then determine whether, within the guidelines developed by the institution, the faculty member has a "fair" load. The faculty member may object to this formula, however, suggesting that in team teaching four people don't just divide up the work, each taking on one-fourth of it; but rather that the nature of team teaching requires more work. Besides, being a member of a team doesn't necessarily mean that all members put forth equal effort. What about team coordinators; shouldn't they get more "credit" for their efforts?

To address these issues some institutions develop a point system to deal with involvement in team teaching. Instead of simply dividing by the number of teachers on the team, a more rational method is used to assign points for levels of participation or extent of involvement. The points then can be applied to or converted to fractions of courses used to determine load.

Another way to compute load is to base it on enrollment. If a course enrolls 100 students and involves four faculty, that might be thought of as similar to those four faculty each teaching one course of 25 students. If the institution is willing to establish a "typical" enrollment load, then team-taught courses take their place among and are not so different from other courses. The problem with using enrollment as a criterion for determining load is that it puts a certain pressure on team-taught courses to be larger than other courses, when large size may not suit their purposes well. Furthermore, many courses taught by one faculty member in most institutions have enrollments considerably below 25. Should faculty receive credit for a half-course load for a seminar with 10 students in it? Although using enrollment as the only criterion has its problems, taking student class size and credit hours into account makes some sense in determining load.

Computing faculty load for team teaching is part of a much larger problem of counting and otherwise valuing faculty efforts generally, and team teaching should not be singled out as posing a unique problem. There are as many problems in computing faculty efforts in research, academic advising, dissertation advising (at the doctoral level), university service, and service to the community. None of these roles lends itself to formulaic methods of "counting," and most institutions, particularly those of greater size and complexity of mission, are struggling with what has come to be known nationally as "faculty roles and rewards" issues. Being a faculty member in a team-taught course is one of the differentiated roles that a faculty member may play, and finding flexible and fair ways to reward multiple roles is something that most institutions want to do. One approach to the problem is to allow faculty to play a greater role in establishing their own roles and the criteria by which they will be evaluated. In developing what Ernest Boyer has called "a mosaic of talent" within institutions and across institutions, faculty will need greater freedom to establish, in consultation with peers and superiors, how they will spend their time and how they will be evaluated.[15] Clearly, flexibility is called for in crediting faculty for their work in interdisciplinary team-taught courses. An institution that wants to encourage interdisciplinary teaching won't use faculty load issues or "expense" as an excuse, but will find ways to credit and reward faculty for doing something the institution values.

Similarly, team-taught courses can generate some additional costs for planning, materials, guest lecturers, field trips, or other special events. Although team-taught courses may generate more "associated costs" than other courses, this is not necessarily so, and does not need to become a special problem. As is the case with computing faculty load, associated costs of team-taught courses are part of a larger issue associated with courses generally today. There is a cost associated with the breakdown of the old model of traditional teaching—one person in one classroom, lecturing in front of a chalkboard. As faculty begin to approach their teaching in a new way, costs for high-tech audio-visual equipment and time for developing materials and strategies will be greater. All teaching will have higher associated costs, including team teaching, if the level of instruction is to improve. Institutions will need to anticipate, plan for, and budget these costs, just as they do other expenditures, giving them a higher priority as intrinsic rather than "extra" expenses.

Institutions that want to encourage the development of interdisciplinary team-taught courses will need to build in organizational and financial support for that activity, and not expect that new and wonderful things will happen without adequate structures and resources.

PROFESSIONAL ASSOCIATIONS TO SUPPORT INTERDISCIPLINARY STUDIES AND TEAM TEACHING

The disciplines prospered because they simultaneously developed departments at the local level and professional associations at the national level. Can interdisciplinary programs and team teaching gain visibility and support through national professional associations? In modest ways this is already happening through organizations devoted to the support and promotion of interdisciplinary studies. The most inclusive and perhaps best known of these organizations in the United States are described below.

Association for Integrative Studies (AIS)

Professor William H. Newell, Executive Director, School of Interdisciplinary Studies, Miami University, Oxford, OH 45056
Phone: (513) 529-2213
Fax: (513) 529-5849

AIS was founded in 1979 and has approximately 750 members. It serves faculty and administrators involved with integrative studies programs at the level of colleges, schools, programs, and courses. The Association brings together scholars and academic leaders interested in interdisciplinary studies in all of the arts and sciences to exchange ideas and information and to improve integrative study. AIS also provides consultants to institutions that plan to initiate or seek to modify interdisciplinary programs and offers assistance concerning instructional methodology, interdisciplinary research, and curriculum design. In addition to its annual national meeting, AIS keeps a national archive of syllabi, brochures, and other documents, and publishes the *AIS Newsletter* quarterly, *Interdisciplinary Undergraduate Programs: A Directory*, and an annual book publication, *Issues in Integrative Studies*.

Association of Graduate Liberal Studies Programs (AGLSP)

Dr. Diane Sasson, Master of Liberal Studies Programs, 138 Social Sciences Bldg., Duke University, Durham, NC 27708
Phone: (919) 684-3222
(Institutional home and presidency change every two years.
Call Duke after 1996 for forwarding information.)

AGISP is composed of member institutions with interdisciplinary graduate programs. The association has materials on program design and sample syllabi. In addition AGLSP has supported five collections of essays on graduate liberal studies.

A number of national professional associations devote attention to the undergraduate curriculum more generally, including the Association of American Colleges and Universities (AACU) and the American Association for Higher Education, and sometimes they give attention to interdisciplinary studies. For information related more directly to General Education, the following associations are useful:

National Association for Core Curriculum (NACC)

Gordon F. Vars, Executive Secretary-Treasurer, 404 White Hall, Box 5190, Kent State University, Kent, OH 44242-0001
Phone: (216) 672-0006
Fax: (216) 672-2580

NACC was founded in 1953 and has approximately 200 members. It serves teachers and professors, administrators, and curriculum directors with interests in general education programs variously known as core, common learning, unified studies, and block-time. NACC is a source of information on improving and extending core programs and teacher education for the core curriculum. NACC publishes quarterly *The Core Teacher*, a newsletter, and makes available bibliographies and information on interdisciplinary programs in schools and colleges.

Association for General and Liberal Studies (AGLS)
Dr. Bruce Busby, Executive Director, Ohio Dominican College, 1216 Subury Road, Columbus, OH 43219-2099
Phone: (614) 251-4634

AGLS was founded in 1961 and has approximately 540 members. It serves faculty and administrators associated with liberal arts and general education programs in colleges and universities. AGLS serves as a forum for issues on general education and maintains an affiliation with the American Association for Higher Education (AAHE). In addition to its annual conference, AGLS provides the *AGLS Newsletter* three times a year and publishes *Perspectives*, a semiannual journal.

National Association of Humanities Education (NAHE)
Dr. Fred Schroeder, Department of Interdisciplinary Programs, University of Minnesota at Duluth, Duluth, MN 55812
Phone: (218) 726-6370

NAHE serves middle school through adult graduate liberal studies interests, with an additional special interest in museum education. Biennial national meetings are held and consultations can be arranged. Its journal, *Interdisciplinary Humanities*, is indexed in ERIC.

In addition to these associations, numerous professional associations are devoted to particular kinds of studies that are usually thought of as employing interdisciplinary methods. Although it is not possible to list all of these, a selection of illustrations, more closely associated with the categories of interdisciplinary studies used in this book appears below:

National Council for Black Studies (NCBS)
Jacqueline E. Wade, Executive Director, 208 Mount Hall, 1050 Carmark Road, Ohio State University, Columbus, OH 43210
Phone: (614) 292-1035
Fax: (614) 292-7363

North American Association for Environmental Education
Edward McCrea, Executive Vice-President, 1255 23rd Street, NW, Ste 400, Washington, DC 20037
Phone: (202) 467-8754
Fax: (202) 862-1947

National Association for Chicano Studies (NACS)
Dr. Carlos S. Maldonado, Chicano Education Program, Monroe Hall 198, MS-170, Eastern Washington University, Cheney, WA 99004
Phone: (509) 359-2404

International Studies Association (ISA)
Dr. W. Ladd Hollist, Director, David M. Kennedy Center, 216 HRCB, Brigham Young University, Provo, UT 84602
Phone: (801) 378-5459
Fax: (801) 378-7075

National Women's Studies Association (NWSA)
Dr. Deborah Louis, University of Maryland, College Park, MD 20742-1325
Phone: (301) 405-5573

For further information, and updating of this information as time passes, please see the *Encyclopedia of Associations* (Detroit: Gale Research, Inc., current edition).

INTERDISCIPLINARY STUDIES AND GRADUATE EDUCATION .

When the disciplines emerged, graduate education was added simultaneously, as a new tier, to the American higher education system. Over the years, graduate education, through the mechanism of specialization, has added tremendous support to the disciplinary and departmental structure of American higher education. In fact, one can say that the dominance of the disciplines is due largely to the status of graduate education and the ability of graduate programs to produce disciplinary specialists. Graduate programs control their product, and for nearly one hundred years the product has been a disciplinary specialist with highly developed research skills, unhampered by any formal knowledge of teaching, students, or the institutions where graduates will work. What new teachers find, when they get to their jobs—in institutions that may vary considerably from the one where they have done their graduate studies—is that they may need to know about subjects that range far beyond their specialization, (some may not even get to teach their specialization), that knowing something about teaching could be valuable, and that understanding their students and the institution where they work might, indeed, be indispensable. Unfortunately, graduate students don't learn much about such matters in their graduate studies; on the contrary, they become strongly socialized to the cultures of their specialties through a process that may make them especially dysfunctional for interdisciplinary team teaching. As Jerry Goff and Robert Wilson have indicated "most interdisciplinary efforts must be staffed by 'cultural outcasts'; faculty who have resisted narrow cultural conditioning or have been exposed to more than one culture. Such persons are not easy to locate, and innovators should give high priority to seeking them out."[16] Although there is growing interest in changing certain aspects of the graduate experience for those seeking careers in academia today, particularly by adding courses on college teaching, little is happening to enhance the development of interdisciplinary scholars with experience and skills in team teaching.

How might aspiring college teachers cultivate their interests in team teaching? They can pursue specialties at the graduate level that are different from their undergraduate majors, although it may cost them some hours in making up prequisites. They can pursue a doctoral degree in a different area from their master's degree. They can pursue joint or dual degree or cognate studies, if permitted. For the integration of these perspectives, they are left, for the most part, on their own, with little or no guidance about how to bridge disciplines or teach on an interdisciplinary team.

The market for college teachers, although still difficult and traditional, may be changing somewhat, so that many institutions would welcome candidates more broadly prepared, both in subject areas and in teaching skills. In the faculty interviews conducted for this study, many faculty spoke of the tremendous amount of time consumed in teaching each other and learning another colleague's subject. Institutions may derive some benefit from looking for and hiring new faculty who already have an interdisciplinary orientation and are familiar with the processes associated with planning interdisciplinary courses and engaging in team teaching, although they will be hard to find. Selected graduate schools might find this an attractive approach to preparing students anticipating academic careers, and such an emphasis might give their students a "competitive advantage" to carry into the academic marketplace.

If colleges and universities want to expand their efforts in interdisciplinary course work and programs, and if they wish to become more effective with it, they will need faculty who are skilled at it and committed to it. Right now, faculty who get involved find that they have to make some big adjustments. For the most part they enjoy these transitions and the process of working together, but one has the sense that the creation and development of interdisciplinary courses would occur more rapidly and run more smoothly if these faculty had broader academic backgrounds and more understanding of the process. If there is, indeed, anything like a "movement" toward the delivery of instruction through interdisciplinary endeavors, and if that new direction is desirable, then it would be enhanced by changes in graduate education to better prepare aspiring college teachers for these new roles.

Even if a new cadre of "differently-prepared" teachers were to arrive on campuses across the land, ready to plunge into the development and delivery of interdisciplinary team-taught courses, they probably would not survive long without some changes in the way their efforts are evaluated and rewarded. Although they can at once be productive scholars and good teachers, the nature of their scholarship, and the relative value given to their teaching will need to be reconsidered at many institutions. This is a "sticky issue" because the evaluation process for promotion, tenure, and salary increases (where based on merit) is usually lodged within departments, and departments tend to assign higher value to specialized disciplinary research. Thus changes in the graduate education of college teachers need to be accompanied by changes in the "culture of evaluation" where new faculty will be employed. This may mean finding a new home for interdisciplinary faculty within the new struc-tures mentioned above, broadening the evaluation criteria and modifying the processes within existing departmental homes, or getting two or more depart-ments involved in some creative new interdisciplinary evaluation processes for faculty who teach interdisciplinary courses and conduct scholarly activities of an interdisciplinary nature. The point applies as well, of course, to continuing faculty, who like to be involved with interdisciplinary courses, but are not sure whether they are placing their careers in jeopardy by doing so. These are natural and legitimate worries for faculty at most (though not all) institutions, and in some cases the internal conflicts set up within a dedicated but divided faculty member can be serious.

If team-taught interdisciplinary courses are to prosper, those who care about them will need to learn well the lessons taught by the success of the disciplines: organizational structures within and outside the institution are important, as are the mechanisms for training and sustaining faculty.

GAINING NEW PERSPECTIVES

One thing this study has shown is that interdisciplinary course work and team teaching take a variety of forms. There is no single way to do it, and, in fact, it is difficult to settle on definitions of "interdisciplinary" and "team-taught". We know that the degree of collaboration varies considerably from course to course and within courses with regard to planning, content integration, teaching, and evaluation. The rationale for offering interdisciplinary courses varies, sometimes taking the shape of a reaction to the excesses of disciplinary specialization, but at other times wanting to respond to new directions in the social and cultural environment. Although the "ideal" team-taught course is difficult and time-consuming to create, we know certain things about this process now, and can enrich these efforts through better planning, content integration, teaching, and evaluation. We know a lot about how people behave when they work together on groups and teams, and we know how to apply this knowledge to faculty collaboration through team teaching. Faculty generally enjoy the process, finding it time-consuming but extremely satisfying in a number of ways. Students don't always understand what interdisciplinary efforts are about, and might respond better to such courses if they saw more creative collaboration in classroom teaching. The courses provided as ex-amples illustrate a multitude of subject area interests and an array of imagina-tive new arrangements for learning.

Through all this endless variety of effort to develop interdisciplinary courses and engage in team teaching, is there a constant purpose, a consistent theme? One of the questions asked at the beginning of this chapter was: What are all these people doing with these interdisciplinary courses? They are, of course, trying to achieve many different things, but if one were to seek one unifying statement that sums up what all these faculty are trying to do with all these courses, it would be this: They are trying to find and then introduce students to *new perspectives*. What is so valuable about new perspectives? Michael Polanyi, the famous philosopher and sociologist, writing in 1961, put it this way:

> At the time when flying by aeroplane was first developed, around 1914-1918, traces of prehistoric settlements were discovered from the air in fields over which many generations had walked without noticing them. Though the aerial photographs clearly revealed the outlines of the sites, the markings on the ground which constituted these outlines frequently remained unrecognizable. Such sites are comprehensive entities that are precisely traceable without mental effort from a distance, while the identification of the particulars at close quarters presents great difficulties.[17]

Surely each generation fails to notice many things in its intellectual journeys, but perhaps the faculty and at least some students of the next generation will see things no one else has seen by developing new perspectives through interdisciplinary studies.

NOTES

1. Clifford Geertz, *Local Knowledge* (New York: Basic Books, 1983), pp. 19-20.
2. *Ibid.*, p. 34.
3. *Ibid.*
4. The origins of the field and the work of Mannheim are summarized well in the Preface to Peter Berger, *The Social Construction of Reality* (Garden City, NJ: Doubleday & Co., 1966).
5. Karl Mannheim, *Ideology and Utopia* (New York: Harcourt Brace & World, 1936), pp. 79-80.
6. *Ibid.*, pp. 84-86.
7. *Ibid.*, pp. 86-87.
8. Peter Berger, *The Social Construction of Reality*, p. 10.
9. Eliot Eisner, *The Enlightened Eye* (New York: Macmillan, 1991), pp. 27-28.
10. Stanley Fish, *There's No Such Thing as Free Speech and It's A Good Thing Too* (Oxford University Press, 1994), p. 232.
11. Stanley Ikenberry, *Beyond Academic Departments: The Story of Institutes and Centers* (San Francisco: Jossey-Bass, 1972), pp. 44-45.
12. Michele Tolela Myers, "Private Liberal Arts Colleges: Lead or Die," *Liberal Education* (Summer 1994), p. 51.
13. Caroline Eckhardt, *Interdisciplinary Programs and Administrative Structures* (University Park, PA: Center for the Study of Higher Education, The Pennsylvania State University, 1978), p. 28.
14. Beth Casey, "The Administration and Governance of Interdisciplinary Programs" in Julie Thompson Klein and William Doty, *Interdisciplinary Studies Today* (San Francisco: Josey-Bass, 1994), pp. 53–67.

15. Ernest Boyer, *Scholarship Reconsidered* (Princeton, NJ: The Carnegies Commission for the Advancement of Teaching, 1990), p. 27ff.
16. Jerry Gaff and Robert Wilson, "Faculty Cultures and Interdisciplinary Studies" *Journal of Higher Education*, 43:3 (1971): pp. 198–99.
17. Michael Polanyi, *Knowing and Being* (Chicago: University of Chicago Press, 1969), p. 124.

PART

II

• • • • • • • • •

Selected Examples
of Courses

CHAPTER 7

Examples of Interdisciplinary Courses and Programs

GATHERING AND USING THE EXAMPLES

The focus of Part I of this book has been on the development and implementation of interdisciplinary, team-taught courses at the "micro" level, that is, on the types of collaboration involved in developing particular courses. Throughout the discussion, five courses from the University of Denver were used as illustrations. These courses, the faculty who taught them, and the students who took them, were used, again and again, to draw out and illustrate various principles about interdisciplinary team-teaching. Although the courses served well as examples, and the faculty were articulate in representing their experience, these courses provide a limited sample from only one campus of the vast array of arrangements that take place at other institutions. Finding a way to study and describe some of these other courses was important.

How could good examples be found and how might they be arranged, when discovered, into some coherent scheme for presentation? After some consideration and discussion with colleagues, I decided simply to construct a representative sample of institutions, to write to their presidents, and to ask for examples. Instead of asking for particular types of examples, I decided to let the institution, through its own processes, decide which course or courses to nominate.

In selecting institutions, I gave consideration to appropriate geographical distribution (a few from each state, with more drawn from more populous states), classification type (including two-year and four-year colleges and universities), control (some each of public and private), and visibility (a subjective factor having to do with the institution's being well-known and having some likelihood of offering courses that met the criteria). Using the American Council on Education directory of Accredited Institutions of Postsecondary Education, I drew up a list of 167 geographically disbursed institutions, including a few from Canada and Mexico.

The presidents of the institutions received a letter and a set of forms, and were asked to pass the request to the most appropriate person within their institutions. The call for examples requested courses that met the following criteria:

> *interdisciplinary*—a course that combines two or more disciplinary perspectives, including in the broad definition of discipline, not only traditional fields such as biology, psychology, history, etc.; but also professional fields and sub-fields, such as law, social work, and education; or occupational fields, such as graphic design, law enforcement, or computer technology.

> *team-taught*—a course that employs two or more faculty from different disciplines or fields of study in collaborative efforts, including some level of collaboration in planning the course, integrating the subject matter, teaching the course, and establishing testing and evaluation procedures for students.

> *creative*—a course that makes the cross-disciplinary connection in a creative way, employs faculty talent in an unusual way, or sets up unique arrangements for learning.

One can not be sure at this point of exactly how and why institutions did or did not respond. For some, no doubt, the request became lost or ignored as it was passed from person to person; for other institutions, we know from their response that they simply had no courses to nominate. To our pleasant surprise, we received a flood of examples, most of them usable, in a broad array of programs. In other words, for the most part, the general call for examples worked.

The question then was what to do with the examples. How could they be organized? They were studied and grouped—a thoughtful doctoral student joining in the process of review and category building—and eventually the categories that appear below were established. The process was not easy because some courses appeared to fit more than one category, and sometimes the category boundaries were not always clear. Once the categories were established, and the courses were placed within them, the courses were reviewed again, and some that were repetitive or perhaps not as "creative" or "illustrative" had to be eliminated. Once the categories were established and reviewed, a few areas appeared to be "thin," that is, lacking in depth or variety. In a few instances, then, particularly in the multi-cultural, international, and professional areas, additional specific requests for particular types of courses were made to institutions that were thought likely to have such courses. This additional, more focused, course solicitation proved to be valuable in "filling in the gaps."

The materials that were received were sufficient to begin to draft a course summary, a kind of "annotation," similar to one that might be made for a bibliography, along with information about the appropriate contact person. The contact person at each institution then received the summary descriptions for suggestions and approval. Thus the descriptions that appear below capture the essence of the course and represent well what the creators of the course believe it to be.

A brief introduction to each category provides background and orients readers to that category. Although none of these introductions is exhaustive, they provide the context for examining the examples. Within the categories, narrative commentary is sometimes provided to introduce sub-categories or lead the reader through alternative types of arrangements. Although few if any readers will examine all of the course descriptions in detail, what appears below is more than a useful reference; many of the courses make good reading, simply because they are so interesting and creative. Some readers will ask why *their* course does not appear here, knowing that it is equally interesting and creative. The answer, of course, is that it probably *should* appear here, but that the processes used in the call for national examples did not find that course, or many like them, that could also have been included. I believe the collection that appears below is at least *representative* of the creative work of many faculty in many locations at different types of institutions. The examples should be read in that spirit. For those already engaged in interdisciplinary work, there are numerous examples here for comparison and elaboration; for those just initiating interdisciplinary efforts, this is a marvelous cookbook of creative ideas. The contact persons all know that they could, in fact, be contacted, and they welcome your interest.

GENERAL EDUCATION

Interdisciplinary team-taught courses are likely to appear in the general education program. Indeed, the most frequently submitted courses in response to the national call for examples were courses that met the institution's general education requirements. What is general education and why are interdisciplinary courses often used to achieve its purposes?

General education is not easily defined because scholars don't agree on what it is, because it frequently gets confused with liberal education, and because its purposes change over time. Perhaps the clearest, most recent definition is the one provided by Arthur Levine and John Weingart:

> General education is the breadth component of the undergraduate curriculum, defined on an institution wide or college wide basis. It usually involves study in several subject areas, and frequently seeks to provide a common undergraduate experience for all students at a particular institution.[1]

Another definition sets general education over against specialization:

> General education is the term that has come to be accepted for those phases of nonspecialized and nonvocational learning which should be the common experience of all educated men and women.[2]

Although such a definition appears to focus on what general education is not, such an approach may be useful because part of the definitional problem is to make a distinction between general education and the disciplinary education usually found in concentrations or departmental majors. By definition, then, general education involves an experience for students that differs from their studies in their major.

"Liberal education," on the other hand, may best be used as a more inclusive term that stresses more the outcomes of a particular type of education and approach to learning that cultivates the general intellectual growth of the individual, and includes the connotation of "liberation," freeing the individual *from* ignorance and prejudice *for* a broader, more fully lived life. Thus liberal education, as a process, could occur throughout the baccalaureate experience, within the major, and also within professional education. Some people continue to make a sharp distinction between liberal education, with its more abstract rationalistic goals, and general education with its more instrumentalist assumptions about the development of the individual.[3] Others suggest that maintaining the distinction is probably no longer possible. As Clifton Conrad notes:

> General education goes by many names: the core curriculum, the common learning, the "required" courses. Most attempts to distinguish between general and liberal education are futile because the words have been used interchangeably by too many people for too long to lend themselves to useful distinction.[4]

Perhaps the best and briefest definition of general education is as "learning that is useful across the scope of one's life as a human being in this society."[5]

General education has, as a concept, an interesting history in American higher education. In the colonial colleges, one might say that general education was the only education there was. Only as the curriculum expanded, through the addition of many new courses in the eighteenth and nineteenth centuries, did the following question arise: What learning is most important? Is there some set of courses or some educational experience that is central? As the elective system became firmly established under the leadership of Charles

Eliot at Harvard (1869-1909), a system whereby students gained more and more control over the choice of courses they would study, the question of centrality began to be debated more vigorously. Eliot's successor, Lawrence Lowell, is credited with establishing in 1909 the "distributive model," the idea that students needed to establish some breadth in their studies and should not be free simply to choose anything. Alexander Meikeljohn, then at Amherst, is credited with establishing the first "survey course" in 1914.[6]

General education has its roots, therefore, in the idea that some things are "central" in the experience of a well-educated person. What are these things and how have they been formulated as goals? During the twentieth century, as general education developed into an important part of the undergraduate experience, coming to occupy, as it has at many institutions, one-third of the curriculum, various purposes and outcomes came to be articulated clearly as the goals of general education. One of the classic formulations of these goals came from the work of Daniel Bell, a sociologist at Columbia University, who was given a year's assignment to write about general education and make recommendations to the faculty.[7] He identified six aims of liberal (general) education: to overcome intellectual provincialism, to appreciate the centrality of method, to gain awareness of history, to show how ideas relate to social structures, to understand the way values infuse all inquiry, and to demonstrate the civilizing role of the humanities. Bell was interested in finding ways to provide a common learning, to give the student a comprehensive understanding of the Western tradition, and to combat intellectual fragmentation with interdisciplinary courses. The advocacy of interdisciplinary course work as a mechanism for delivering general education appears as early as the first edition of Bell's report in 1966, and he was able to cite historical antecedents and intellectual roots at Columbia College as far back as 1917.

Two other representative lists of goals are more recent. Ernest Boyer, on behalf of the Carnegie Foundation for the Advancement of Teaching, identifies six themes of general education:

> First, all students should come to understand the shared use of symbols. . . . Second, all students should understand their shared membership in groups and institutions. . . . Third, students should understand that everyone produces and consumes and that, through this process, we are dependent on each other. . . . Fourth, all life forms on the planet earth are inextricably interlocked, and no education is complete without an understanding of the ordered, interdependent nature of the universe. . . . Fifth, all students should understand our shared sense of time. . . . Finally, all students should explore our shared values and beliefs.[8]

The most recent elaboration of the purposes of general education is provided in a chapter by Virginia Smith in *Higher Learning in America*, 1980-2000:

1. *Heritage:* To provide a common core of great ideas or great books; to pass on a common western heritage.
2. *Counterpoint:* To expose students to a broader range of subject matter than they would find in their majors; to achieve breadth—at its best, an enriching context for the major; at its worst, simple exposure to a series of fragments.
3. *Instrumental:* To develop particular skills, such as writing, speaking, and critical thinking.
4. *Development or Empowerment:* To develop the whole learner, in contrast to emphasis on specific skills, particularly to develop the basis for becoming a lifelong learner.
5. *Social Agenda:* To infuse the general education component with some social purpose or purposes such as global awareness, environmental sensitivity, preparation for responsible citizenship in a democratic society.
6. *Valuing:* To perceive what values are operating in a situation, how values are determined, and at a few institutions even to inculcate certain values.[9]

It should be clear from this brief discussion of general education that its purposes are not always easily achieved within a disciplinary framework. One approach to general education has been to allow students to fulfill the breadth requirement of the curriculum by requiring them to distribute their studies across several disciplines by taking introductory courses. Some argue that doing so may provide some breadth, but that it falls short of many of the goals for general education listed above. Other institutions create a set of courses especially designed to address the purposes of general education, and require students to elect from the list, or in some cases where a common learning experience is desired, to take only certain designated courses. Increasingly, institutions that develop special courses to address the purposes of general education are experimenting with interdisciplinary team-taught courses. The larger, encompassing purposes of general education appear to be better addressed, at least at some institutions, through courses developed and delivered by teams of scholars from various disciplines working together.

The examples of courses that follow are presented within four categories: Developmental Studies, Humanities, Social Science, and Science.

Developmental Studies

Although there is some debate about whether developmental studies courses should be viewed as an aspect of general education, they appear to address one of the important goals of general education: the cultivation of basic academic skills necessary for further postsecondary studies. Sometimes the development of fundamental skills, such as reading text, writing orderly and coherent papers, speaking with clarity and confidence, and developing appropriate study skills and attitudes, is considered to be an integral part of many general education courses; but in other cases this task becomes the focus of a separate, often more intensive, developmental studies program. Institutions that have an "open door" admissions policy often serve students who do not demonstrate appropriate preparation in prerequisite skills for collegiate studies, and who may, for various reasons, also lack appropriate study habits and attitudes necessary for academic success. Many community colleges see this as one of their several missions and have well-developed developmental studies programs. Recently some institutions have been coordinating these efforts through cluster arrangements and interdisciplinary programs.

The program at LaGuardia Community College of the City University of New York provides an integrated approach to developing reading, writing, and speaking skills. At Cuyahoga Community College, an interdisciplinary bilingual developmental studies program addresses the special needs of Latino students. A program at the Instituto Tecnologico y de Estudios Superiores de Monterrey Campus, Estado de Mexico, in Atizapan, Mexico, provides basic skills along with physical activity, counseling, and parent involvement.

Horizontes Program

Institution: Cuyahoga Community College
Intended Audience: Puerto Rican/Latino students enrolled at the Metropolitan campus needing improvement of college entry skills
Disciplines Represented: English as a second language (ESL), Spanish, and Latino culture
Personnel: Five instructors, one in ESL, two in bilingual education, one in Spanish, and a coordinator of the mentorship program

General Description: Project Horizontes is a culturally grounded English as a Second Language (ESL) retention project developed for Latino students enrolled at the Metropolitan Campus of Cuyahoga Community College in Cleveland, Ohio. The project was developed against a backdrop of low quarter and degree completion rates on the part of Latino students. The theoretical assumption underlying the design of the project was that bilingualism needs to be treated as an expansion of expressive capabilities rather than as a barrier. Strengths in both languages and cultures need to be respected and further developed. It was anticipated that a design following these lines would reinforce self-concept. Participants would feel they were being treated with respect and appreciate the extra support. Functioning would significantly improve as reflected in grades and language tests. Retention would be markedly improved, both within and across quarters. And "positive assimilation," understood as a dynamic process rooted in students' unique historical processes and cultures, would be expedited. The project features two courses, taught concurrently; support groups;

faculty mentorship; and supplemental social activities, lectures, and luncheon forums. The two courses are a standard intermediate ESL grammar course taught in
English, with some limited reinforcement in Spanish (student composition 50%
Latino); and a team-taught ESL course featuring: a) Latino cultural awareness,
taught primarily in Spanish, b) the writing of English, taught in English with reinforcing concepts in Spanish, and c) a college survival skills component taught solely in
English (student composition 100% Latino).

Distinctive Features: An integrated program designed to address the language needs
of Latino students by conducting developmental course work in English and Spanish.
Some teaching is in English with Spanish reinforcements; some is in Spanish. Students are organized into support groups that meet every other week under faculty
facilitation and use English, Spanish, or both, as needed. In addition, social activities,
special lectures, and luncheon forums are arranged to bring together all the students
in the program. Faculty meet every two weeks to coordinate plans for classes, monitor
the program, and collaborate in assessing the progress of individual students. Realiz-
able goals for the program, relating to retention, grade point average, and English
language test scores, are being met successfully.

Contact Person: Trevor R. Guy, Dept. of English, Humanities Bldg. 223E, Cuyahoga
    Community College, 2900 Community College Avenue, Cleveland, OH 44115,
    Work Phone: (216) 987-4571, Fax: (216) 987-4404

THE NEW STUDENT HOUSE PROJECT
Institution: LaGuardia Community College, City University of New York
Intended Audience: First-year students entering college with inadequate
    preparation
Disciplines Represented: Reading, writing, speech, counseling
Personnel: Instructors in writing, speech, and reading, plus a counselor and
    project director

General Description: Under a grant from New York State Vocational Education,
the New Student House Project at LaGuardia Community College is creating, testing,
modifying, and integrating into the curriculum a thoroughgoing "coordinated studies" roster of basic skills courses in reading, writing, and speech. Modeled on successful nationwide experiments with "learning communities" and an earlier project at the
college called "Supercluster," this project purposefully restructures the curriculum to
break down traditional, often rigid barriers between disciplines and to emphasize and
utilize learning as an integrated, social process. In so doing, the project assumes that
developmental students both can handle and can profit from dealing with sophisticated learning structures. Each term of operation, the project enrolls 75 students (in
sections of 25) at several levels of competence in basic skills and creates a tailored
program of study for each. New Student House is a first-term "immersion experience"
designed to foster both a sense of intellectual community and a realization of the
importance of foundational knowledge to subsequent education. By utilizing a teach-

ing team, a collaborative approach to both planning and instruction, and a common course theme, "human relationships," the project supplies a full roster of tightly integrated courses for entering students.

Distinctive Features: Instructors collaborate to design an integrated curriculum that addresses reading, writing, and speaking as associated skills. A counselor works with all classes to help students with study skills; a project director coordinates planning, scheduling, and curriculum development. The faculty team meets weekly to coordinate class activities and review individual student progress, to revise the curriculum, and to deal with logistics. Computer-based instruction plays an important role in the reading and writing components, and collaborative learning is used for small group tasks. Various sections of classes join together several times a term for films and large group meetings, to give students a sense of being part of a larger enterprise. Innovative teaching strategies, such as improvisatory theater pedagogy, are employed to involve students in exploring the general theme about human relationships. The project is designed to help students pass the basic skills requirements and move as quickly as possible into a regular curriculum of their choice. Research has shown that students in the program have pass rates and persistence rates that are higher than a non-program control group.

Contact Person: Brian Gallagher, La Guardia Community College, CUNY, English Dept., 31-10 Thomson Avenue, Long Island City, NY 11101, Work Phone: (718) 482-5670, Fax: (718) 482-5599

Program of Academic Support

Institution: Instituto Tecnologico y de Estudios Superiores de Monterrey Campus, Estado de Mexico

Intended Audience: At-risk students to address the development of basic academic skills and attitudes

Disciplines Represented: Psychology, business administration, physical education, educational technology, quality management

Personnel: Course teachers supported by professional staff in counseling, physical education, health services, and parents

General Description: At a relatively young campus in Mexico with an explosive growth in its student population, this interdisciplinary program cultivates basic academic skills and attitudes for inadequately prepared students. Although teachers are assigned to and are responsible for particular courses in the program, they work as a team in designing and implementing the whole program and in evaluating student progress. Students take four interrelated courses in a one-semester period: Work Administration, Development of Attitudes, Academic Skills Development, and Physical Education. Instead of failing students out of the institution, the Institute provides an opportunity for students to acquire the abilities, knowledge, and attitudes necessary for successful return to their academic programs. Strong grades in the program are the only way that students can remain in the Institute and finish their studies. The goal of the program is to help students change their personal discipline habits, their way of organizing their time, their study methods, and their attitudes toward responsibility. All of these changes are directed toward the larger goal of enhancing student self-esteem. In addition, students work hard on the improvement of their oral and written communication skills. Teachers collaborate in delivering the courses and in providing feedback to each student in the program. Parents attend monthly meetings with teachers in the program to receive feedback and professional support about how to enrich their son's or daughter's development. Using total quality management principles, faculty help students to apply good management principles to their own work administration, and to apply TQM principles to their own work as a product. Students are also introduced to basic concepts of motivation and creativity. Academic skills are developed along with an understanding of learning styles and the psychological principles related to the acquisition and transmission of information.

Distinctive Features: The institute provides an interdisciplinary approach to developmental education that focuses on the whole person and addresses skills, attitudes, and physical well-being simultaneously in an intensive integrated semester-long experience. Faculty collaborate in providing consistent feedback to students in a variety of performance areas and confer with parents on how they can help. The institute is a promising model for salvaging and developing human talent, and an important development factor for Mexico.

Contact Person: Lic. Pablo Buitron Morales, Modulo de Servicio Postal, Atizapan, Mexico, 52926, Work Phone: 011-3-326-55-58, Fax: 011-3-326-57-89

College Orientation

Sometimes first-year college students have little idea of what college is or what they might study. This can be particularly true for students who are the first in their families to attend college or whose exposure to academic subjects has been, for other reasons, restricted. To address this problem, some institutions try to introduce students to the college experience through courses or other experiences designed to facilitate orientation. Although not considered "developmental" in the narrower use of that term, they serve the function of developing an openness to the college experience while cultivating awareness of what professors do in their various disciplines. A creative example of this kind of course from the University of Texas—Austin is described below.

THE IDEA OF THE LIBERAL ARTS
Institution: University of Texas—Austin
Intended Audience: First-term, first-year undergraduates
Disciplines Represented: Anthropology, economics, languages, linguistics, classics, psychology, government, history, sociology, geography
Personnel: Thirteen faculty of the College of Liberal Arts

General Description: Each week this course features a lecture by a professor in one of the departments of the College of Liberal Arts. They discuss what is means to study their disciplines, what is new in their major fields, and what career opportunities might open up to those who pursue a particular major.

Selected Topics: These follow the schedule of guest lecturers and their disciplines.

Distinctive Features: Offered for one hour of credit on a credit or no-credit basis, the course provides a quick overview and broad perspective on various liberal arts disciplines. For students with interest in probing more deeply, professors are available by appointment for further discussion. A follow-up course, "The Nature of Inquiry," involving two, one-hour lectures, on selected disciplines, is available the following term for students who want to learn more about the methodologies of different disciplines.

Contact Person: Larry Carver, College of Liberal Arts, WMB 101, F2600, University of Texas—Austin, Austin, TX 78713, Work Phone:(512) 471-4271, Fax: (512) 471-4518

Humanities

Western Civilization

One approach to the teaching of humanities for general education has been the classic Western Civilization course. Struggling with challenges from all sides—feminists, members of minority groups, critical studies theorists, and global perspectives advocates are the most vocal critics—the traditional Western Civilization course is nonetheless alive and well at many institutions and is exhibiting new life and creativity in the interdisciplinary team-taught format. Institutional mission, in some instances, justifies a traditional Western Civilization course. Good examples of creative efforts in these areas are those from Providence College and University of the South, described below.

DEVELOPMENT OF WESTERN CIVILIZATION
Institution: Providence College
Intended Audience: Required of all first- and second-year students.
Disciplines Represented: History, literature, theology, and philosophy
Personnel: 32 faculty, eight "teams" of four, one from each discipline

General Description: This course is a reaffirmation of the humanities that stemmed from an unshaken belief in the educational mission of Providence College as a Catholic liberal arts institution: to educate students to their full potential as inheritors of the great traditions, Judaeo-Christian and Graeco-Roman, that have shaped our world. Tertullian's famous question, "What has Athens to do with Jerusalem?"

remains the abiding question, but now we pose it differently. What do Socrates and Augustine, Shakespeare and Michaelangelo, Marx and Einstein, Sartre and Solzhenitsyn have to do with us, or to say to us? Students in the first year explore the major developments in Western civilization from the Greek world to the Renaissance; in the second year they explore the post-Renaissance world to the modern world. In investigating the significance of the Greek moment, for example, students are asked to consider how the concept of the *polis;* tragedies of Aeschylus, Sophocles, and Euripides; the architecture of the Parthenon; the cult of Athena; and the philosophy of Plato reflect the distinctive values and experiences of classical Greece. The students are also invited to compare the tragic vision of Sophocles with the Hebraic religious sensibility as it is embodied in the Old Testament. In a typical second-year sequence, the students examine the moral climate of the West after World War I. The effects of that conflict, so traumatic and fundamental, profoundly influenced Eliot's *Wasteland,* the rise of fascism, communist revolution, the existentialism of Sartre and Marcel, the agony of renewed war and Holocaust, the struggle of the Church in the modern world, and the renewed challenges and hopes for human freedom and dignity.

Selected Topics: Homer, Classical Greek religion, Greek society, the Persian Wars, Pre-Socratic Philosophers, the Peloponnesian War, Greek tragedy, Aeschylus, Sophists, Sophocles, Euripides, Greek art and architecture. World War I, Freud, Kafka, Russian Revolution, modern art, Eliot, Barth, Sartre, the Cold War, and Vatican II.

Distinctive Features: The course provides the historical and philosophical framework for studying the classic great texts and works of art of the West and combines younger and more experienced faculty in a course that is an interdisciplinary "common learning" experience for all undergraduates.

Contact Person: Brian Barbour, DWC Program, Moore Hall, Providence College, Providence, RI 02918, Work Phone: (401) 865-2230, Fax: (401) 865-2282 in Business Dept.

INTERDISCIPLINARY HUMANITIES PROGRAM: TRADITION AND CRITICISM IN WESTERN CULTURE

Institution: The University of the South
Intended Audience: Undergraduates meeting core curriculum
   requirements
Disciplines Represented: Literature, art, music, history, religion,
   philosophy
Personnel: Four faculty on a semester team, four different teams for four semesters

General Description: The Interdisciplinary Humanities Program is a sequence of four chronologically sequenced courses, ordinarily intended for freshmen and sophomores, which introduces the cultural history of the Western world. It focuses on major phenomena in western arts, literature, history, philosophy, and religion. In the first semester, the Ancient World, the emphasis is on representative aesthetic and philosophical achievements of Greece and Rome and the cultural roots and ideological tensions of western civilization. In the second semester, the Medieval World, the emphasis is on the evolution and complexity of medieval society, institutions, and thought. In the third semester, the Early Modern World: Renaissance to Revolution, the focus is on the period spanning 1500-1789 and the diverse and sometimes contradictory legacies of Renaissance humanism, the Protestant Reformation, and early modern science. In the fourth semester, the Modern World: Romantic to Post-Modern, the focus is on the period reaching from the latter years of the eighteenth century to the present day. The emphasis is on the philosophical and aesthetic responses to the political, industrial, economic, and scientific revolutions of modernity.

Selected Topics: Ancient world monuments and texts include the Parthenon and works by Sophocles, Plato, Virgil, and Tacitus. The Medieval semester studies selected passages of the Bible; works by Augustine, Bede, and Dante; and the Cathedral at Chartres. The Renaissance and Early Modern texts include works by More, Luther, Montaigne, Shakespeare, Descartes, Milton, and Rousseau. Music studied is by Handel and Mozart. Texts and other material for the Modern World include works by Burke, Dickens, Marx and Engels, Nietzsche, Freud, Eliot, Fitzgerald, and Lyotard, along with music by Beethoven and Wagner.

Distinctive Features: Students write four essays each semester to develop analytical and critical skills. The Humanities sequence includes an effort to incorporate the values of writing-across-the-curriculum. Essay topics are carefully selected and coordinated by the entire faculty planning group. Explicit efforts are also made to trace non-Western influences on the development of Western civilization.

Contact Person: Pamela Royston Macfie, Dept. of English, The University of the South, Sewanee, TN 37375, Work Phone: (615) 598-1138, E-Mail: pmacfie@seraph1.sewanee.edu

Eras and Themes

Some institutions find the general survey of Western Civilization to be unmanageable and have chosen, instead, to focus on a particular aspect or historical period. The course at Reed College focuses on the classical period of the flowering of Greek and Roman civilization. The same is true of the course at Brigham Young, but the focus is on the theme of war and peace. At Grinnell College, the decision was made to select for study the Medieval and Renaissance periods. At Hendrix College, the problem is addressed by selecting various time periods for more intense study, "pinnacles" of the Western intellectual tradition.

WESTERN HUMANITIES
Institution: Reed College
Intended Audience: Required of all first-year students and most transfers

Disciplines Represented: History, English literature, philosophy, art history, religious studies, political science, Spanish, and German
Personnel: 22 faculty

General Description: The first semester is devoted to a systematic examination of classical Greek culture. The second focuses on imperial Rome and its encounter with Christianity, from Augustus to Augustine. Neither a Western Civilization nor great books course, the focus is on the serious and systematic study of a culture by examining representative works considered explicitly in the light of their socio-historical setting and in the context of one another.

Selected Topics: Homer, Hesiod, the lyric poets, Aeschylus, Herodotus, Sophocles, Thucydides, Euripides, the pre-Socratic philosophers and Plato. Livy, Virgil, Ovid, Seneca, Tacitus, Pliny the Younger, Apuleius, Athanasius, Augustine, and selected readings from the Bible.

Distinctive Features: The course has been in continuous operation for nearly 50 years. The course meets for three hours per week in common lecture, three hours in seminars with individual faculty. All 22 faculty work from a common syllabus.

Contact Person: Peter J. Steinberger, Dept. of Political Science, Reed College, Portland, OR 97202, Work Phone: (503) 771-1112 x317, Fax: (503) 777-7776

THE PEN AND THE SWORD: A STUDY OF WRITING ABOUT HOW HUMAN
CIVILIZATION SEEKS PEACE AND SUFFERS WAR
Institution: Brigham Young University
Intended Audience: Honors students, undergraduates, 50-75 in number
Disciplines Represented: Ancient history, Germanic and Slavic languages
Personnel: Two faculty

General Description: Students and faculty study together an aspect of the history of civilization by focusing on literary and other artistic texts that demonstrate how humanity has always sought its ultimate potential in a peaceful society but how it has consistently fallen short, thus suffering over and over again the gross inhumanity of war. But are our ironic impulses completely chimerical? Is there no hope that humanity can find lasting peace? Must human society inevitably destroy itself in a final apocalyptic paroxysm? These are some of the questions considered in this course.

Selected Topics: Cadoux, *The Early Christian Attitude to War*, Augustine, Thucydides, Herodotus, Plato, selected readings from the Bible and the Book of Mormon, Homer, Aristophanes, a work on Alexander the Great, *The Lay of the Nibelungen*, *Henry V*, *Tale of Two Cities*, *Utopia*, *Mother Courage*, *Candide*, *All Quiet on the Western Front*, Wilfred Owen *Poems*, *Red Badge of Courage*, *Nathan the Wise*, and *Divine Comedy*.

Distinctive Features: Students work in cooperative learning group projects to prepare for and enhance discussion. The course contains some background lectures but primarily discussion.

Contact Persons: Wilfred Griggs/Alan Keele, 4012 HBLL/4096 JKHB, Brigham
   Young University, Provo, UT 84602, Work Phone: (801) 378-7714 / (801) 378-
   3153, Fax: (801) 378-4649

MEDIEVAL AND RENAISSANCE CULTURE

Institution: Grinnell College

Intended Audience: First- and second-year students seeking a general course in
   Western Civilization or third-year science students seeking a general education
   course.

Disciplines Represented: Theology, history, literature, political theory, art history,
   philosophy, natural science

Personnel: 10 faculty paired, generally one from social sciences, and one from
   humanities

General Description: The purpose of this course is to rediscover some of the basic
ideas, values, and intellectual traditions of Western Civilization from Medieval and
Renaissance culture. The chronological period under review is roughly 1100 to 1650,
and the controlling theme of the course is the impact of Graeco-Roman, Germanic,
and Christian beliefs and culture on changing conceptions of self, society, nature,
human relations, politics, aesthetics, and philosophy. The course uses these conceptions in order to highlight elements of continuity and change that occurred during the
period under review.

Selected Topics: *Song of Roland,* St. Thomas Aquinas, Dante, Machiavelli, Luther,
Montaigne, Chartres, Michelangelo, and Shakespeare, plus selected readings from a
Renaissance reader.

Distinctive Features: The course is primarily a discussion class through which
students are asked to inquire about how values change and how and why values may
conflict within a given period of history.

Contact Person: Professor Ira L. Strauber, Dept. of Political Science, Grinnell
   College, Grinnell, IA 50112, Work Phone:(515) 269-3113, Fax: (515) 269-4953

WESTERN INTELLECTUAL TRADITIONS

Institution: Hendrix College

Intended Audience: Common learning experience for first-year students

Disciplines Represented: History, literature, drama, philosophy, art, music, and
   the natural sciences

Personnel: 12 faculty from six departments lecturing in their areas of expertise and
   leading discussion sections

General Description: Not a standard survey of Western civilization, but an intense
and integrative study of four pinnacles of civilization in the history of the West. The

study includes the politics, history, social organization, economics, art, music, and architecture of classical Greece; the religious orientation of thirteenth century Europe; Europe in the seventeenth century, with attention to the emergence of science, the development of the modern nation-state, and the New World; and central Europe at the close of the nineteenth century, looking in microcosm at the springs of the twentieth century's turmoil. In all of these periods the relations of the West to non-Western cultures is addressed whether it is in the Persians, Islamic civilization, the New World and Africa, or a world of colonial empires.

Selected Topics: Classical Greece, Medieval Europe, The Origins of Modernity—Seventeenth Century, and Modernity in Crisis—Transition to the Twentieth Century.

Distinctive Features: The course is designed as a common intellectual experience for first-year undergraduates who all read and discuss the same texts. It was developed under support from a National Endowment for the Humanities challenge grant that enabled extensive planning through summer workshops. The study of Western traditions is supplemented by study of non-Western traditions and foreign language exploration in other courses. The "pinnacles" emphasis attempts to avoid the "coverage problem" of surveys.

Contact Person: John Churchill, Dean and Vice-President for Academic Affairs, Hendrix College, 1601 Harkrider, Conway, AR 72032-3080, Work Phone: (501) 329-6811, Fax: (501) 450-1200

Great Texts

Other institutions forego the sweep of historical events to focus on key texts, emphasizing a "great books" or "great texts" curriculum. Students are engaged in meaningful dialogue about selected important works. Excellent examples of interdisciplinary courses involving an emphasis on text are described below for two Canadian universities: University of King's College (in cooperation with Dalhousie University) and the University of Alberta. To enliven the discussion of texts in a humanities course at Cuyahoga Community College, two professors of opposite temperaments and political persuasions have consciously linked up to team teach a course that explores controversial themes in texts selected by each professor.

FOUNDATION YEAR PROGRAMME

Institution: The University of King's College in association with Dalhousie University

Intended Audience: Almost all first-year students at King's College proceeding to disciplinary studies in the arts and sciences at Dalhousie or to professional programs at King's College

Disciplines Represented: Literature, history, philosophy, political theory, sociology, the history of science, economics, theology, art, and music

Personnel: 28 participating faculty

General Description: Instead of a first year made up of several classes taken in separate departments of the University, students in the Foundation Year Programme are involved in a single, challenging course that looks at various subjects together. The Foundation Year is not a philosophy course or a history or English course, or a "subject" course at all. The FYP looks at those three subjects and more, giving students a chance to see how different ideas and approaches fit together without making the usual subject divisions. Beginning with the ancient Greeks and ending with texts written in the 1990s, students read a wide variety of material and study many of the major works of Western civilization. Foundation Year students, then, do not read books about (for example) the Ancient World or the Enlightenment, they read works written by people living in those periods, and so are challenged to think about who those people were, how they saw the world in which they lived, and how their thinking and writing might help us to understand our world now, at the end of the twentieth century.

Selected Topics: Representative classic authors from different periods of Western history:Homer, Sophocles, Plato, Aristotle, Vergil, Augustine, Anselm, Dante, Machiavelli, Luther, Teresa of Avila, Kepler, Shakespeare, Descartes, Hobbes, Hume, Rousseau, Kant, Mill, Darwin, Marx, Nietzsche, Dostoyevsky, Mann, Freud, Eliot, Heidegger, de Beauvoir, Sartre, Wittgenstein, Lyotard.

Distinctive Features: The "great texts" course is all that students take in their first year along with one other course. Lectures by the experts in their disciplines combined with small group tutorials, serious reading, and intensive essay writing lay a solid foundation for all further study. With a history dating to 1972, the course now has a strong reputation that attracts students from across Canada and the United States.

Contact Person: Peggy Heller, Director, Foundation Year Programme, University of King's College, Halifax, Nova Scotia, Canada B3H 2A1, Work Phone: (902) 422-1271, Fax: (902) 423-3357

LES GRANDS ECRITS (THE GREAT TEXTS)

Institution: University of Alberta, Faculte Saint-Jean

Intended Audience: Undergraduates proficient in French

Disciplines Represented: History, literature, political science, religious studies, biology

Personnel: Three historians, and one professor each from theology, biology, and literature

General Description: The course offers interdisciplinary and in-depth study of important texts related to humanistic thought, coming from different milieuxs, from the earliest civilizations in Mesopotamia through the twentieth century, and reflecting different states in the development of humanity. Emphasis is on understanding the context, content, and importance or value of each work.

Selected Topics: Selections from the I-Ching, the Bhagavad-Gita, the Bible, and works by Homer, Plato, Virgil, Dante, Voltaire, Smith, Darwin, Jung, Zola, and de Beauvoir.

Distinctive Features: Includes non-Western texts from the ancients and is offered in French, one of Canada's two main languages, with assignments to be completed in French.

Contact Person: Professor Lawrence Godbout, Faculte Saint-Jean, Edmonton, Alberta, Canada T6C 4G9, Work Phone: (403) 465-8732, Fax: (403) 465-8760

INTRODUCTION TO THE HUMANITIES
Institution: Cuyahoga Community College
Intended Audience: A three-quarter, freshmen-level course that fulfills a general humanities requirement
Disciplines Represented: Classical philosophy and American literature
Personnel: Two professors

General Description: Introduction to the Humanities is a three-quarter sequence with a shifting focus: Man as an Individual, Man and Society, and Man and the Cosmos. Each term the instructors select two major works of literature (each) as the focus for a dialogue (between the instructors) about each work.

Selected Topics: Discussions grow out of topics drawn from works by such authors as Melville, Hawthorne, Hemingway, O'Neill, Frost, Thoreau, Goethe, Conrad, Sophocles, and Ovid.

Distinctive Features: The dialogue is intentionally designed to provoke controversy and spark discussion. As the instructors themselves note: "The philosophy professor is a classicist, a political and religious conservative, and a doctrinaire cynic; the English professor is an Americanist, a moderate liberal, and a dark romantic. The students are, therefore, exposed to perceptions and attitudes that may contrast and occasionally conflict." As one professor introduces the work and presents ideas about it, the second professor serves as commentator, questioner, and devil's advocate. The course has been offered for 15 years and enrollment is seldom below 100.

Contact Person: Harvey Kassebaum, Ph.D., Dept. of English, 11000 Pleasant Valley Road, Parma, OH 44130-5199, Work Phone: (216) 987-5000, Fax: (216) 987-5114

Visual and Performing Arts

Another approach to presenting the humanities is represented by courses that focus on the visual and performing arts. The goal is not so much historical, although historical examples may be presented, but structural and aesthetic. What skills does the student need to be able to see, hear, and appreciate works from the visual arts, music, dance, theater, and film? Three interesting approaches to developing these skills through interdisciplinary team-taught courses are represented in the courses from the University of Massachusetts at Amherst, Niagara Community College, the University of Hartford, and Goshen College described below.

THE LIVELY ARTS

Institution: University of Massachusetts at Amherst

Intended Audience: Undergraduates meeting general education and writing requirement and writing program emphasis

Disciplines Represented: Western classical music, African-American music and jazz, dance, visual arts, photography, international arts

Personnel: Seven faculty, guest lecturers, part-time instructor, four teaching assistants

General Description: The principal goal in planning and teaching The Lively Arts is to help students prepare for a lifetime of understanding and enjoyment of concerts and exhibitions and gain an international view of the arts as a way to appreciate the social and cultural differences of others. The Lively Arts presents a world view of the arts, drawing upon established Fine Arts Center programs representing African-American, Asian-American, Latino, and South Asian cultures. These ongoing programs are complemented by the performing and visual arts of other cultures presented on a rotating basis. Students are asked to study the assigned readings each week before their section meeting so that they can contribute to the discussion. Selected readings are used to help students quickly learn the basic vocabulary and concepts that jazz and classical musicians, dancers and choreographers, sculptors, and photographers use daily in their work. Some of the material is familiar, some new, and provides a common ground for experiencing and discussing the arts throughout the course. Students are responsible for learning and using the appropriate language for each art form. The goal is to study the arts in historical perspective, learn what artists and musicians mean by "style" and to learn how to distinguish the style of one historical period from that of another. Several different forms of music and art are explored, each of which provides an opportunity to use the arts as a means of understanding and appreciating a different culture. The study of the work of photographers, artists, and performers often expresses their personal convictions about contemporary social conditions and political issues.

Selected Topics: Photography and Photojournalism, Documentary Photography, Listening to Music, Dance Choreography and Production, Dance Periods and Styles, Media, Styles and Functions of Art, Sculpture, Periods and Styles of Classical Music, Jazz, Periods and Styles of Jazz. In addition, a changing list of required concerts and exhibitions is offered along with alternate and extra credit concerts and optional assignments.

Distinctive Features: The course includes strong multi-cultural and experiential components, and incorporates significant amounts of writing in the form of performance and exhibition analyses, a midterm paper, and a discussion question final exam. A "process" course, intentionally innovative and unconventional, is still evolving after eight years and 3,100 students.

Contact Person: Professor John A. Jenkins, 260 Fine Arts Center, University of Massachusetts, Amherst, MA 01003, Work Phone: (413) 545-0030, Fax: (413) 545-2092

❖

Exploring the Arts

Institution: Niagara County Community College
Intended Audience: General education students
Disciplines Represented: Fine arts, music, dance, theater, poetry
Personnel: Two faculty

General Description: The course is an introductory, interdisciplinary exposure to the visual, verbal, and performing arts. The basic elements of many art forms are investigated, as well as concepts each form has in common with another. Distinctive characteristics of music, painting, sculpture, architecture, theater, dance, and photography serve as focal points organized chronologically. This course is structured on a lecture basis, with topics in the arts disciplines expanded through the expertise of professionals on the faculty. This "team" approach with shared elements enhances the ability to relate one art form to another. In addition to the lecture/demonstration format, fieldtrips and attendance at various cultural events are required.

Selected Topics: The first part of the course is used to introduce the elements of the arts: The Arts of Space (painting, sculpture, architecture, photography); The Arts of Time (music, poetry, dance); the Composite Arts (theater and film); Shaping a Work of Art; Interpreting a Work of Art. The second part of the course focuses on various genres of the arts explored in the first part of the course. For example, for architecture the genres explored are churches, theaters and civic buildings; for music, the genres are symphony concerts, sonata, song, chamber music, etc. The third and fourth sections focus on characteristics of broad historical periods and issues of appreciation and criticism. Historical periods such as Baroque, Classicism, Impressionist, Nationalist, and Twentieth Century are used as bases for comparing each art form with another.

Distinctive Features: The course is a remarkably comprehensive effort to explore most of the important forms and genres through carefully selected examples. It includes field trips and attendance at "live" performances.

Contact Person: Paul Ferington, Dean, Academic and Student Affairs, Niagara County Community College, 3111 Saunders Settlement Road, Sanborn, NY 14132-9460, Work Phone: (716) 731-6222, Fax: (716) 731-4053

ROMANTICISM IN THE ARTS

Institution: University of Hartford
Intended Audience: Meets general education requirement for students from all baccalaureate programs, may be taken during any of four years
Disciplines Represented: Music, art, and literature
Personnel: Three team-teaching in one semester, drawn from a pool of six

General Description: The decades around the year 1800 in Europe and America saw so many and such profound changes that historians have dubbed that period "the age of revolution" and "the beginning of the modern world." This course explores the cultural side of these changes in the movement called Romanticism. Romanticism united many different forms of expression, so students study a selection of artists, musicians, and writers: their lives, works, and ideas. In the process, students learn ways of analyzing and appreciating visual art, music, and literature.

Selected Topics: Revolutions in Art and Life: Jacques Louis David, Mary Wollstonecraft, William Blake, Francisco de Goya; Nature in the Heart and Mind: William Wordsworth, Ludwig van Beethoven, J.M.W. Turner, John Constable; Individualism and Its Costs: Hector Berlioz, Mary Shelley, Theodore Gericault, Georges Bizet, and selected Romantic virtuosos.

Distinctive Features: The course brings together art, music, and literature to explore common themes in Romanticism, is writing intensive, and employs a variety of means of teaching and testing, including listening assignments, museum visits, concerts, and critical essays.

Contact Person: Marcia Bundy Seabury, Director, All-University Curriculum, University of Hartford, West Hartford, CT 06117, Work Phone: (203) 768-4705, Fax: (203) 768-4070, E-mail: seabury%uhavax.dnet@ipgate.hartford.edu

THE ARTS: VISUAL AND MUSICAL

Institution: Goshen College
Intended Audience: General education requirement for all students
Disciplines Represented: Music and art appreciation
Personnel: Two faculty, one from music and one from art plus 4-6 advanced students as studio group leaders

General Description: Students are introduced to the basic elements of music and art from the European tradition for the purposes of comparing the similarities and differences of the two art forms. The study includes African and non-Western forms, music and art that serve reactionary or revolutionary purposes, and music and art that serve the purposes of religion and spirituality.

Distinctive Features: The course compares two art forms not often or easily compared, and involves the student as participant, spectator, and interpreter in various ways throughout the course. A studio component engages students in a team project that results in a class presentation. The course includes concerts and field trips to the Chicago Art Institute and Symphony.

Contact Person: Doyle C. Preheim, Dept. of Music, Goshen College, Goshen, IN 46526, Work Phone: (219) 535-7360, Fax: (219) 535-7600

Being Human

A creatively different approach to the humanities is found in a course that returns to the root meaning of the word "humanities" and asks: What does it mean to be a human person? Drawing on three familiar areas of inquiry in philosophy, the nature of the true, the good, and the beautiful, this course provides an opportunity to explore three different aspects of being human. With a clear mission as a progressive liberal arts college in the Roman Catholic tradition, Briar Cliff urges its students to explore their humanity through the course described below.

THE HUMAN PERSON (Note corresponding course under Social Science entitled "The Human Community")
Institution: Briar Cliff College
Intended Audience: First-year students
Disciplines Represented: Theology, biology, math, chemistry, philosophy, English, sociology, anthropology, theater, nursing, music, art
Personnel: 10 faculty

General Description: Among the many stated purposes of the course are the following: To explore the human species and distinguish it from the non-human universe by discovering what it means to be a person; to examine illustrations of the human quest for the true, the good, and the beautiful; to expose students to the Judeo-Christian, Western, and Franciscan traditions; and to provide a stimulating and provocative shared experience for first-year students.

Selected Topics: The Human Person, Human Origins, The Person, The Search for Truth, The Search for Goodness, The Search for Beauty. Conclusions. All students read customized text *The Accommodating Reader*, and Victor Frankl's *Man's Search for Meaning*.

Distinctive Features: The course involves lectures supplemented by faculty-led "mentor groups" for which students must present note cards detailing their preparation, questions, and responses to the material assigned for the day. A short autobiographical paper and a longer (well-researched) library paper on an important person are assigned to teach research and writing skills as well as enhance personal reflection on "being a person." The course is developmentally appropriate to entering students still asking the late-adolescent question: Who am I?

Contact Person: Ms. Deborah Lotsof, Associate Professor of Theatre and Speech Communication, Briar Cliff College, 3303 Rebecca Street, Box 2100, Sioux City, IA 51104-2100, Work Phone: (712) 279-1722, Fax: (712) 279-1698

Social Sciences

Courses designed for the social sciences in general education often focus on American history or current social issues. The intent of the interdisciplinary course is usually not to offer the typical, chronological, political history, but to explore certain themes or issues in American history. A good representative of this theme approach is the course from the State University of New York (SUNY) at Plattsburgh. An "issues" course is well represented by the one offered at the Maxwell School at Syracuse University.

LOOKING FOR AMERICA
Institution: State University of New York (SUNY), Plattsburgh
Intended Audience: First-semester students
Disciplines Represented: English, anthropology, history, communications, chemistry, sociology, library research, women's studies
Personnel: Faculty teach separate courses linked in the Looking for America cluster

General Description: A country just isn't a place; it's the collective creation of individuals, each of whom belongs to one or more groups. Group membership may be based on ethnic, social, religious, political, or gender relationships, among many others. America, then, is the sum of diverse individuals from varied traditions. What is it that we have all made? That's what Looking for America explores. Looking for America brings together different areas of study to examine, challenge, and re-think the meaning of America. In this program, students are automatically registered in a Looking for America cluster of courses related by the common focus on American culture.

Selected Topics: All students take Introduction to American Studies, which is taught collectively by the entire Looking for America faculty, and then elect other courses to total 13 hours from a cluster of integrated courses in a Looking for America learning community. Although the courses are not necessarily team taught, the program is interdisciplinary and planned and coordinated by an interdisciplinary team. The remaining courses from which students in the program may choose are Comparative Cultures, Chemistry and Society, American Civilization, 1872-Present, Introduction to Public Speaking, Composition, Visions of America, Introduction to Library Research, Introduction to Sociology, and Introduction to Women's Studies.

Distinctive Features: Not a team-taught course in the sense defined in this book, Looking for America is a cluster program involving interdisciplinary planning and integrated learning around a central topic. The course allows students to complete one-third of their general education requirements in one semester through an integrated program. Some faculty share classes, assignments, and, on occasion, team teach individual class sessions.

Contact Person: Larry Soroka, History Dept., State University of New York (SUNY), Plattsburgh, NY 12901, Work Phone: (518) 564-5211, Fax: (518) 564-7827

❖

CRITICAL CHOICES FOR AMERICA
Institution: Syracuse University
Intended Audience: Meets core requirements for general education for first- and second-year undergraduates
Disciplines Represented: Economics, geography, history, political science, sociology, writing program
Personnel: Eight faculty

General Description: The faculty has designed Critical Choices for America to raise important questions concerning the nature and meaning of "citizenship" in the United States and to encourage all members of the course community, students and faculty, to grapple with a number of "critical choices" confronting Americans today. These choices, in education, environment, and politics, require consideration of historical and contemporary issues regarding justice and injustice, the impact on the nation's economy, and concerns about "political gridlock." The course has a challenging agenda. Early in the course the course community considers the tension between the desire to foster a sense of common American identity and the desire to emphasize multicultural differences inside the national community. In a subsequent unit, the community deals with how concepts and rules of fairness are debated in America, with particular attention to education. The course community also explores the argument that some policies designed to protect the environment may exact too high a price in lost jobs and economic prosperity. A final unit is designed to assess recent political developments, considering the way in which old ideological divisions are still present along with new developments in the enduring debate over leadership and group polarization in American democracy.

Selected Topics: Human Nature and Civic Life, A Selfish or Altruistic Society?, Minority Interests and the Search for America, The Disuniting of America, Democracy and Minimal Citizens, Private or Public Citizens, The Relationship of Liberty, and Equality. Historical Perspectives on Race, Racism and the American Dilemma, Race and Public Education, Definitions of Oppression, Blaming the Victim, Affirmative Action, Is Pollution an Economic or Social Problem?, Can Government Clean Up the Environment?, Is Politics Irrelevant Today?, The Case for Limited Government, The Case for Activist Government.

Distinctive Features: The course uses workshops of 15 students on Wednesdays and Fridays to discuss course readings and debate the issues. On Mondays, the course community assembles for lectures that explore a broad range of perspectives on the issues. The goal is to challenge assumptions, deepen understanding, and eventually reach one's own conclusions.

Contact Person: Professor David H. Bennett, Dept. of History, 312 Eggers Hall, Syracuse University, Syracuse, NY 13246, Work Phone: (315) 443-5872 or (315) 443-3061, Fax: (315) 443-9085

Human Community

Another type of course, less historical, and more focused on the behavioral sciences, is one that explores the nature of human community, the various types and levels of social interaction that take place among humans. A good example is the course at Briar Cliff College described below. The course at Wittenberg University focuses on the concept of "self" in various social contexts.

THE HUMAN COMMUNITY (Note corresponding course under Humanities entitled "The Human Person")
Institution: Briar Cliff College
Intended Audience: Required of all fulltime, first-year students
Disciplines Represented: Sociology, English, theology, physical education, nursing, social work, history, education, and philosophy, varying from year to year
Personnel: Six faculty

General Description: This course raises basic questions about what it means to live in a world with other persons: What are the social, political, and economic realities of our world? How have we arrived at this state? What will the world be like in the future? How can we shape the future of humanity? In raising these questions, the course helps the students to see the value of a liberal education in understanding their role in society. Among the course goals are the following:

- to increase awareness of global conditions as we approach the twenty-first century;
- to foster respect for cultural diversity and pluralism;
- to develop informed concern for the human community and its relationship to the earth; and
- to appreciate human freedom and the opportunity it provides for choosing service and a responsible lifestyle.

Selected Topics: The Human Community Today: The Issues Facing Us; Earth Dream: Visions of the Human Community in the Future; and Moving Toward the Dream: Strategies for Realizing the Vision

Distinctive Features: Each team member serves as a mentor to a group of students for class discussions, individual conferences, and feedback on assignments. Students do research on a global issue in a foreign country and report results to two sessions of a simulated "Global Assembly." Students can fulfill one requirement of the course through a community service project and participation in a reflection group associated with the project.

Contact Person: Sr. Grace Ann Witte, Ph.D., Associate Professor of Sociology, Briar Cliff College, 3303 Rebecca Street, Box 2100, Sioux City, IA 51104-2100, Work Phone: (712) 279-5488, Fax: (712) 279-1698

The Self and Society

Institution: Wittenberg University
Intended Audience: Required of all first-year students
Disciplines Represented: Varies but usually includes sociology, psychology, political science, American literature, history
Personnel: 25 faculty annually

General Description: All new students during the first term take the same course at the same time, read the same books, and struggle with the same issues. The course is designed by a team of 25 faculty who work together to plan it, select readings, and arrange for prominent visitors nationally to serve as guest lecturers. This course uses the concept of the self in various contexts as the organizing theme for the course. A number of key issues are explored by relating them to the nature of the self and the role of self in changing contexts.

Selected Topics: The Self as an Intellectual Concept, Perspectives on the Self, The Self in Premodern Society, Self and the Physical Environment, Insiders/Outsiders and the Self, Self and Gender, Self in Urban America, Self and Race/Class, Self and the Public Sphere, Whose Reality Is It?

Distinctive Features: This "common learning" course, which is required of all incoming students, is also designated as a "writing intensive" course. The course uses the developmental task of defining the self as the theme for exploring various social science concepts and current issues. The topic for the common learning course changes from year to year.

Contact Person: William I. Buscemi, Dept. of Political Science, P.O. Box 720, Springfield, OH 45501-0720, Work Phone: (513) 327-6103, Fax: (513) 327-6340

Science

The sciences face several dilemmas in the general education curriculum. On the one hand, most science faculty want to teach "real" science (with substantive content, usually requiring proficiency in math, and laboratory work), but many nonscience majors are either frightened by, unable to handle, or uninterested in such courses. Science majors, on the other hand, usually think they are getting enough science, and often don't see why they need "general" science or why it needs to be related to the social sciences or the humanities. Much of the power of science derives from its theoretical orientation and dispassionate pursuit of "pure" research, but many students want science to be "relevant," neatly packaged into insights about environmental or health issues. These dilemmas are unlikely to be resolved in the near future, but they create a niche for interdisciplinary team-taught courses attempting to address these issues.

One approach is to create interdisciplinary science courses that make connections across the divisions to explore science in the context of larger cosmological questions: What is the earth? Where did it come from? What is life? What is human life? The courses at Oklahoma State University and University of St. Thomas attempt to address these questions.

Scientific Inquiry

Institution: Oklahoma State University
Intended Audience: Nonscience honors students
Disciplines Represented: Philosophy, history of science, astronomy, geology, biology
Personnel: Three faculty and one teaching assistant

General Description: Scientific Inquiry explores the philosophy of science and the application of the scientific method in the natural sciences. Utilizing examples from biology, geology, and astronomy, the historic development of science is explored from its earliest beginnings in mythology to contemporary issues. Lectures and discussions are supplemented by inquiry-based laboratories that emphasize observation, prediction, and problem solving.

This course interweaves the development of three areas of science from their earliest origins, to the extent that those can be identified. Science essentially begins as an interpretation, or explanation, of the natural world that people observed around them. Originally this often took the form of myth or story. Thus dinosaur bones were explained as remnants of monsters in the Navajo Monster Slayer myth or as dragon bones by the ancient Chinese.

Technology has played an integral role in the development of modern science. This too is explored in the course. Much of the information that underpins current views of the universe, the planet, and life on the planet could not be obtained earlier because the phenomena involved were too fast or too slow, too large or too small for unaided observation.

Selected Topics: History of the Universe: Aristotelian physics, Ptolemaic astronomy, Copernican astronomy, Gallilean physics, Newton, invisible universe, modern cosmology. History of the Earth: Early geology, Uniformitarian/Catastrophist debate, plate tectonics, orogeny, earthquakes, vulcanism, relative dating techniques, radio-metric dating, global climate, drying of the Mediterranean, biogeography and the fossil record. History of Life on Earth: Darwinian evolution, origin of life, early genetics, vitalism, modern biochemistry, history of life, dinosaurs, human evolution.

Distinctive Features: Team members with diverse backgrounds elaborate key scien-tific concepts as they developed in historical context. All three faculty plan together and teach in all three units of the course, attend all lectures and labs, and assign grades collaboratively. High levels of collaboration throughout produce true interdis-ciplinary integration. Three subjects of potentially great interest are used to draw students into the way scientists think and work.

Contact Person: Becky Johnson, Academic Affairs, 101 Whitehurst Hall, Stillwater, OK 74078-0004, Work Phone: (405) 744-5627, Fax: (405) 744-5495

WHAT IS LIFE? BIOLOGICAL AND PHILOSOPHICAL PERSPECTIVES
Institution: University of St. Thomas
Intended Audience: Nonscience majors in Honors Program
Disciplines Represented: Biology, philosophy
Personnel: Two faculty

General Description: This seminar addresses the question, "What is life?" In the pursuit of an answer consideration is given to other questions: How does one distinguish things that are living from those that are not? What is the relationship between nature of life and its characteristics? The first and most fundamental objective is to help students understand how and why biology and philosophy treat, and thus answer, these questions differently. By the end of this seminar, students should be able to articulate a variety of philosophical and biological accounts of life and to explain a rational basis for each of these accounts. The course is designed to help students examine critically and develop more fully their own understanding of life, while at the same time enhancing appreciation of, and respect for, the differing views and perspectives of others. It is hoped that students will come more clearly to understand that each academic discipline possesses intrinsic limitations as well as strengths, that, in their differing perspectives, they pose useful challenges to one another; and that scholars who differ in their perspectives strive most effectively for fullness of understanding when they do so in concert with one another. The course is also designed to help students recognize reasoned argument as an inherently respect-ful and productive activity and to appreciate the importance as well as the difficulty of expressing oneself precisely when writing and speaking about life and life processes.

Selected Topics: Readings include Pines, *Inside the Cell;* Nagel, *Mortal Questions;* Jonas, *The Phenomenon of Life; Scientific American: Mind* and *Brain;* Connell, *Substance and Modern Science.*

Distinctive Features: Five student teams work on term projects to explore key issues. Students learn to use scientific information to inform reasoned responses to different philosophical questions in an effort to bridge the "two cultures" of science and the humanities.

Contact Person: Ellen J. Kennedy, Ph.D., Director, Aquinas Scholars Honors Program, University of St. Thomas, Mail #4303, 2115 Summit Avenue, St. Paul, MN 55105-1096, Work Phone: (612) 962-6122, Fax: (612) 962-5093

Laboratory Experience Included

Other courses are designed to provide an authentic experience with the scientific method and laboratory experimentation on an interesting interdisciplinary topic. The courses at Tufts and the University of Hartford are good examples of general education science courses with an extensive laboratory component.

LIFE IN MOVING FLUIDS

Institution: Tufts University
Intended Audience: First-year engineering students; biology majors; liberal arts majors; pre-service teachers.
Disciplines Represented: Mechanical engineering, biology, oceanography

General Description: How do prairie dogs air-condition their burrows? How do small fish escape predator attacks by swimming close to the surface, taking advantage of wave induced drag? Why are dolphins, sand dollars, and maple samaras shaped the way they are? This course explores these and other fascinating ways that animals and plants have evolved to take advantage of air and water flow around them. The relationships between fluids and the functioning of organisms, and between fluid flow, heat transfer, and biological design are also examined. Topics include drag effects on sessile and motile organisms, life in velocity gradients and wave swept environments, lift, gliding, and thrust production effects on plants and animals. Students undertake experimental projects in the Comparative Biomechanics laboratory, which is equipped with state-of-the-art wind and liquid tunnel set-ups and fluid flow, temperature, and visual computerized data acquisition and analysis systems. This comparative biomechanics course couples concepts from engineering and biology. The main focus is an introduction to fluid mechanics in and around living organisms. In addition, the course introduces data acquisition and manipulation techniques using video cameras, video microscopes, image processing software, spreadsheets, and word processors. In an effort to help students present their work clearly, scientific writing techniques and presentation formats are also taught.

Selected Topics: Fluids, fluid flow, heat transfer, forces on bodies. Uses text: Vogel, *Life in Moving Fluids*, 2nd Edition, Princeton.

Distinctive Features: The course undertakes serious laboratory investigation of mechanical principles functioning for selected life forms to adapt them to their environment. Interesting principles, unusual species, and high technology equipment are studied and used. Projects encourage students to design lessons to teach what they are learning to primary and secondary school students.

Contact Person: Ioannis Miaoulis, Dean, College of Engineering, Anderson Hall, Tufts University, Medford, MA 02155, Work Phone: (617) 627-3237, Fax: (617) 627-3819

LIVING WITH ELECTRICITY AND ELECTRONICS
Institution: University of Hartford
Intended Audience: Nontechnical, nonscience majors for general education breadth category
Disciplines Represented: History, literature, electrical/electronic engineering technology
Personnel: Three professors

General Descriptions: Nothing has affected ordinary people the way electricity and electronics have; the intensity of the impact is far greater than that of the Industrial Revolution. Since Franklin and his kite, people have been intrigued, but often baffled and intimidated, by these phenomena. In modern society, consumers have been using electronic products all of their lives, often without understanding how these devices work, how they came into being, and how they affect human lives. This course covers the historical development of electronics technology and deals with the literature that portrays the relationship of human beings and electronic technology. The "hands on" laboratory experience enables the nontechnical student to experiment with electricity and electronics in the laboratory. The literature reflects the human struggle for a moral and ethical existence in a society increasingly dependent on technology for survival.

Selected Topics: Basics of electricity, revealing the invisible, electrical energy sources, development of electric circuits, electronic technology as beauty and function, prime movers, from 1886 onward, using technology, electronic basics, powering the machine, the transistor revolution, living with electricity and electronics.

Distinctive Features: Each unit includes technical reading and laboratory experiments coupled with appropriate poetry, fiction, and biographical sketches, carefully selected to support and explore the meaning of the scientific concepts. Strong efforts are made to integrate the subject as well as the methods: lecture, laboratory experience, discussion, teamwork, problem solving, reading, writing, and oral presentations.

Contact Person: Phyllis S. Katz, Ward College of Technology, University of Hartford, West Hartford, CT 06117, Work Phone: (203) 768-4754, Fax: (203) 768-5074

Lecture and Discussion Only

Other science courses address more directly the issue of relevance and employ lecture and discussion without a laboratory component. The intent is to attract students to the study of science through interesting topics and engaging methods. The courses at the University of Maryland at College Park and at Lansing Community College are examples of interdisciplinary courses designed with an emphasis on relevance, interest, and practicality.

ELEMENTS OF NUTRITION

Institution: University of Maryland at College Park
Intended Audience: Satisfies core life sciences nonlaboratory requirement
Disciplines Represented: Chemistry, biochemistry, psychology, social sciences, epidemiology, as well as molecular, cellular, and integrated physiology
Personnel: Three faculty

General Description: This course provides basic literacy on the fundamentals of nutrition. Because the subject can be viewed from a variety of perspectives, a team of scholars with many different areas of expertise teaches this course. Class sessions include discussions of what people eat and why, energy metabolism, community nutrition and nutrition education, and food safety. Basic concepts about how the body processes and utilizes food are presented, along with specific issues on food supplements, infant nutrition, obesity, and hunger.

Selected Topics: What You Eat and Why, Nutrition Standards and Guidelines, Food Labeling and Food Safety, The Remarkable Body, Carbohydrates, Lipids, Proteins and Amino Acids, Energy Balance and Exercise, Obesity, Minerals, Vitamins, Antioxidants/Prooxidants and Disease, Pregnancy, Infant Feeding, Nutrition and Maturation, Aging, International Nutrition, Hunger. Uses Hamilton and Whitney's, *Nutrition: Concepts and Controversies.*

Distinctive Features: The course is also highly relevant for anyone who wants to think seriously about the relationship of nutrition to wellness. It brings scientific perspectives to bear on issues that are prone to fad and multiple sources of misinformation, and urges students to think clearly and seriously about eating.

Contact Person: Coordinator—NFSC 100, Dept. of Nutrition and Food Science, Marie Mount Hall, University of Maryland at College Park, College Park, MD 20742, Work Phone: (301) 405-2139, Fax: (301) 314-9327

SCIENCE OF THE WATER PLANET AND LIVING ON THE WATER PLANET

Institution: Lansing Community College
Intended Audience: Nonscience majors
Disciplines Represented: Chemistry, physics, biology, geology, meteorology, system dynamics
Personnel: 14 faculty in four teams designed to have as many disciplines and teaching techniques represented as possible

General Description: This two-course sequence is designed to introduce students to science by exploring the natural environmental processes and the influence that human beings have on these processes. Course goals include increasing science literacy, describing the role of science in society, exploring what science is and how it works, using science content to develop critical thinking skills, team skills, and making material relevant to real life.

Selected Topics: The two courses are organized around four basic questions: What are the fundamental rules of the universe? How do energy and matter move on the earth today? How did matter and energy move on the earth in the past? How does humankind interact with the earth? Topics include forms of matter, conservation of matter and energy, lithosphere, atmosphere, hydrosphere, biosphere, history of the earth, history of life on the earth, population, energy use, land use, pollution, and sustainable futures.

Distinctive Features: Three years of development and a pilot year were used for planning by 20 faculty who used *Project 2061: Science for All Americans* (American Association for the Advancement of Science) and *Fifty Hours: A Core Curriculum for College Students* (National Endowment for the Humanities) as planning guides. The course makes serious efforts to impact faculty attitudes about teaching science and to involve students in their own learning.

Contact Person: Jerry Onofryton, 5400 Science Dept., 419 Capital Avenue, P.O. Box 40010, Lansing, MI 48901-7210, Work Phone: (517) 483-1092, Fax: (517) 483-9649

PROFESSIONAL AND TECHNICAL PROGRAMS

A profound interest in professional and technical preparation has always existed side by side with the strong theme of general and liberal studies in American higher education. An important part of the mission of Harvard University, even in the earliest years with its classical curriculum, was the preparation of clergy for the church and magistrates for public service. Although the professions, as we know them today, developed late in the nineteenth century (as described in the second chapter), the concern for professional and technical education has its origins in a movement that gave birth, more formally, to the "agricultural and mechanical" colleges, through the Morrill Act of 1862, which created in each state the opportunity to develop "land grant" colleges.[10] Although preparation for careers exists at many levels of the educational system, in what have come to be designated "vocational," "occupational," and "career education" programs, colleges and universities have played a special role in preparing students for careers that utilize highly elaborated theory and advanced levels of knowledge, and that might best be designated professional and technical.[11] Whatever one's views on the place of professional and technical programs within the postsecondary system, few would deny that this is a significant "sector" of higher education today, and that most students (the turning point was somewhere in the early 1970s) are preoccupied, some would say obsessed, with preparing themselves for the world of work.

Exactly how colleges and universities should prepare students for work is the subject of much debate, but there is clearly dissatisfaction with traditional programs and much ardent searching for new models. As described in the second chapter, most professional and technical education programs operate within a framework that Donald Schon has described as the model of Technical Rationality, whereby students are expected to learn a standardized body of knowledge—information, principles, and theories—and then go apply it in the "real world."[12] Most professional training, therefore, involves an early disciplinary or basic science phase, an applied science (skill) phase, and an applications phase. The model is being challenged at several points today. Do specialized, disciplinary studies provide the appropriate background for learning about a specific professional or technical career, or should new, interdisciplinary courses be developed that focus more directly on the issues growing up out of professional practice? How can the gap between what students are taught (in theory) and what happens in professional life (in practice) be bridged?

The courses used as illustrations below come from many different fields and use a variety of interdisciplinary mechanisms, but one can see in them serious efforts to infuse preparation for work with multidisciplinary perspectives that bring the often disparate worlds of theory and practice closer together.

Business

Although schools and colleges of business have typically organized themselves into departments, following the model of arts and sciences disciplines, with specializations in accounting, management, finance, marketing, and various career areas such as real estate and hotel and restaurant management, in recent years interest has grown in interdisciplinary courses that cut across traditional specializations. Even more interesting is the interdisciplinary work that draws in team members from engineering, or the somewhat more distant field of design. Interdisciplinary courses provide an opportunity to build certain skills, address particular themes, or undertake specific projects not easily accommodated within one of the traditional specializations. The courses described below at Carnegie Mellon University, the University of Vermont, South Dakota State University, and the University of Maryland at College Park, are representative of some of these new efforts.

DESIGN, MARKETING, AND MANUFACTURE OF NEW PRODUCTS

Institution: Carnegie Mellon University

Intended Audience: Students in industrial design, MBA candidates, electrical and mechanical engineering, and MBA candidates

Discipline Represented: Design, Marketing, Engineering

Personnel: Three faculty and guests

General Description: The Design, Manufacturing, and Marketing of New Products brings together faculty and students from the Graduate School of Industrial Administration, the Design Department in the College of Fine Arts, and the Engineering Department at Carnegie Institute of Technology. The course consists of one faculty member and eight students from each discipline. Students are assigned to four groups of six, consisting of two students from each discipline. Each group is responsible for defining a market opportunity, developing a working prototype and completing a business plan for commercializing the product. The business plan addresses marketing, design, and production issues, and forces the teams to deal with cost and engineering constraints, as well as with the market potential. The projects are supported by lectures dealing with the basic body of information relevant to product development, and demonstrations and workshops to develop specific skills, such as leading focus groups, idea generation, rapid prototyping methods, and computer-based market simulation. Time is reserved at the end of each class for group meetings and faculty/student interaction.

Selected Topics: TQM and Team Building Strategies, Product Creation Cycle: An Engineering Perspective, Marketing Overview, Product Value Analysis, Human Factors, Positioning, Product Semantics, Manufacturing Processes, User Testing, Business Planning, Pricing Strategy.

Distinctive Features: The course allows interdisciplinary teams of students to work with interdisciplinary teams of faculty to create new products. Periodic reports on team progress and final reports to present the product with a business plan are called for. The course reaches beyond business to engineering and design.

Contact Person: Dan Droz, Design Dept. MM110, Carnegie Mellon University, Pittsburgh, PA 15213, Work Phone: (412) 681-6072, Fax: (412) 765-1522

INTEGRATED PRODUCT DEVELOPMENT AND MANUFACTURING

Institution: University of Vermont

Intended Audience: Open to senior undergraduate and graduate students majoring in business, engineering and statistics

Disciplines Represented: Business administration, statistics, and electrical, mechanical, and environmental engineering

Personnel: Eight faculty

General Description: Integrated Product Development provides an overview of the challenges and opportunities of developing a product from inception to disposal. In addition to classroom lectures on topics of design, marketing, engineering, total quality management, cost analysis, and environmental issues, students work in teams to design and build a working prototype of a product. Interdisciplinary project teams include students from business, engineering, and statistics working together and benefiting from the different perspectives of each discipline. Past projects include the design of a security tote for a snowboard, a bagel slicer and, most recently, a weather measuring device.

Selected Topics: Team building, conflict resolution, project management and scheduling, need finding techniques, aesthetics, function, costing, environmental issues, materials, processes electronics, sensors, controls, specifications and logistics, rapid prototyping, human resources, business plans.

Distinctive Features: This course is similar to the one at Carnegie Mellon, but students actually design and build the prototype product. More emphasis is placed on producing the product, manufacturing specifications, and environmental impact. All eight faculty attend all classes together and work with teams of students on various aspects of the project.

Contact Person: Larry E. Shirland, Kalkin Hall, University of Vermont, Burlington, VT 05405, Work Phone: (802) 656-3177, Fax: (802) 656-8279

Rural Real Estate Appraisal

Institution: South Dakota State University
Intended Audience: Third-year and fourth-year undergraduates in agricultural business, agricultural economics, and agronomy
Disciplines Represented: Farm Business Management, Soil Science, Economics
Personnel: Two faculty, one each from economics and plant science

General Description: This course is intended for students planning careers in real estate appraisal, farm management, agricultural lending, or natural resource management. The course content combines science and resource management concepts of an academic course with an introduction to professional practice. Students are required to complete an independent appraisal project that integrates concepts and applications of economics, farm management, and soils valuation to estimating the market value of a specific farm.

Selected Topics: Land value concepts, rural appraisals, real estate legal descriptions, courthouse records, value by sale price comparison, trends in returns to farmland, soil inventory and appraisal maps, climate and soil productivity, drainage and irrigation, crop and range yields, building inventory and valuation, land values and environmental regulations, farmland financing, tax assessment.

Distinctive Features: Both instructors attend all lectures and collaborate on exams, lab assignments, field trips to farms and government agency offices, and evaluation of student appraisal projects. Students conduct an actual appraisal using knowledge gained in the course.

Contact Persons: Dr. Larry Janssen, Dept. of Economics, South Dakota State University, Brookings, SD 57007, Work Phone: (605) 688-4141, Fax: (605) 688-6386

Dr. Douglas Malo, Dept. of Plant Science, South Dakota State University, Brookings, SD 57007, Work Phone: (605) 688-4586, Fax: (605) 688-4452

JOINT PROGRAM IN TOTAL QUALITY: FOUR-COURSE SEQUENCE
Institution: University of Maryland at College Park
Intended Audience: Undergraduate students in engineering and business, taking one course in sequence during four years
Disciplines Represented: Business and engineering
Personnel: Eight faculty for four courses, two instructors each, plus staff support, program administrators, and technical assistance in multimedia theater.

General Description: The first course provides the foundational orientation to quality. The focus is to lay out the parallels between the basic concepts of quality management when implemented in different organizations. In this way, the business and engineering students see how they are in fact pursuing the same objectives, albeit in different settings. The basic theme of the second course is measurement. After setting the stage for the need for metrics and information databases in a total quality framework, the course exposes students to basic tools and techniques. There is also a strong emphasis on problem-solving aids. This second course introduces techniques and exercises directly related to quality improvement practices through innovative thinking and simulation exercises. The third course adopts an external focus by positioning the firm in the competitive arena. It is also the vehicle for exposing students to internationalization and globalization issues. The fourth course is a practicum conducted in direct collaboration with industrial partners, and is focused on a specific Total Quality Project.

Selected Topics: Introduction to Design and Quality (first course only), Introduction to Quality Strategy, Product Design and Organizational Environment, Introduction to Engineering Design, Models of Cost Estimation, Design of Experiments, Foundations of Manufacturing Excellence.

Distinctive Features: The course was developed as part of an IBM-TQM Partnership with Colleges and Universities. It uses interdisciplinary team teaching through a four-year, four-course sequence and includes innovative teaching methods, use of a multimedia theater, simulation, and off-campus experience-based learning in company settings.

Contact Person: Arjang Assad, Ph.D., Maryland Business School, Van Munching Hall, University of Maryland, College Park, MD 20742-1815, Work Phone: (301) 405-2194, Fax: (301) 314-9157

Health Sciences

The training of health professionals is still carried on primarily through discrete programs, such as medicine, dentistry, pharmacology, nursing, physical therapy, and speech pathology and audiology. Recently, awareness of the interdependence of these disciplines in health care delivery has been increasing. Patients often present needs that require attention from more than one specialist and collaboration among various health care providers is necessary. Furthermore, the issues involved in treatment, particularly ethical issues, cut across the specializations, and are best addressed through multidisciplinary perspectives. Skills needed in health care delivery, particularly in the more global area of public health and wellness education, often require communication, management, and research that are found outside of the usual domains of the health sciences. The courses presented below from the University of Alberta, Dalhousie University, Tulane University, and Vanderbilt University provide interesting examples of how multidisciplinary teams are used in the health professions.

TEAM BUILDING AND ETHICS IN HEALTH CARE
Institution: University of Alberta
Intended Audience: Students in various programs of the health sciences faculties
Disciplines Represented: Nursing, pharmacy, rehabilitation medicine, dentistry, medicine, foods and nutrition, physical education, recreation, and human ecology
Personnel: Three faculty and 12 tutors

General Description: The course is designed to bring together students from health science faculties in an interactive format to develop and enhance skills for team-centered and patient-focused health care delivery. The course goals include gaining an understanding of the training and roles of other health professions, and learning team-building and group process skills. Students also explore ethical issues and the way that ethical stances affect health care delivery. Upon completion of the course the students should be able to identify the role of other health professionals and their contributions to patient care, effectively participate as a member of a team that includes the patient in the planning of patient care, identify ways to assist other health professionals in the provision of care, and identify the ethical implications for the team.

Selected Topics: Team building exercises, patient in-take interviews, team-patient interaction, developing team care plans, and case examples of the impact of team collaboration.

Distinctive Features: The course uses problem-based learning and inquiry strategies to explore a wide array of issues. Students from various disciplines are assigned to multidisciplinary teams for discussion, sharing of information, and self-directed learning on topics of mutual interest. Students are drawn from nursing, dentistry, pharmacy, physiotherapy, speech pathology, physical education, occupational therapy, health services administration, medicine, foods and nutrition, and human ecology.

Contact Person: Cheryl Cox, BSP, MBA, Faculty of Pharmacy & Pharmaceutical Sciences, University of Alberta, 3118 Dentistry/Pharmacy Center, Edmonton, Alberta, Canada T6G 2H4, Work Phone: (403) 492-3654, Fax: (403) 492-1217

HEALTH PROMOTION: PRIMARY HEALTH CARE AND PROFESSIONAL PRACTICE

Institution: Dalhousie University
Intended Audience: Undergraduate students in a variety of health care professions and graduate students in Nursing
Disciplines Represented: Physiotherapy, occupational therapy, dental hygiene, medicine, social work, recreation, health education, physical education
Personnel: One faculty member, 10 guest lecturers, and five tutorial leaders

General Description: This course offers an opportunity for students to interact with their peers and practitioners in the health field who are pursuing studies in similar and different disciplines for the purpose of discussing how to enhance the health of our world. The concepts and theories that frame the current understanding of Primary Health Care and Health Promotion are used to guide the intellectual inquiry. Students gain from the course a working definition of individual and community health and health promotion, knowledge of the major deterrents to health in the twentieth century, acquaintance with community development theory, increased awareness of potential strategies for world health and the role of professionals and lay persons in facilitating these strategies. Students also gain skill in working in intersectorial teams. It is hoped that they will have an increased desire to contribute their unique professional perspective to a shared vision of a healthy community and a healthy world.

Selected Topics: Definitions of Health, Primary Health Care and Health Promotion, National and International Developments, Health Goal Setting, Self-Help and Mutual Aid as Health Promotion Mechanisms, Developing a Healthy Community, Educating for Healthy Behavior, Empowerment Implications, Healthy Communities as a Political Goal, Environmental Health, Future Trends and Challenges.

Distinctive Features: The course provides a unique opportunity for students to interact with prominent health professionals in lecture and in small group analytical discussions focusing on public policy issues and facilitated by tutorial leaders who have performed a health leadership function in their community. Students also prepare journal records for self-reflection on the implications of health promotion on their future practice.

Contact Person: Professor Carol Smillie, School of Nursing, 1st Floor, Forrest Bldg., Dalhousie University, 5869 University Avenue, Halifax, Nova Scotia, Canada B3H 3J5, Work Phone: (902) 494-2535, Fax: (902) 494-3487

SOCIAL MOBILIZATION FOR HEALTH

Institution: Tulane University, School of Public Health and Tropical Medicine
Intended Audience: Mid-career professionals working in developing countries in management positions in health-related programs
Disciplines Represented: Public health, communications, management science, research and evaluation, development economics, education
Personnel: 15 faculty

General Description: A highly effective development strategy pioneered by UNICEF, social mobilization (SOCMOB) aims at transforming development goals into societal action. Embracing the critical principle of community involvement, SOCMOB seeks to empower individuals for action. SOCMOB is a broad-scale development approach that calls for a continuum of activities, ranging from advocacy at the political level to information and education at the community level. It includes developing intersectoral support, bureaucratic and technocratic solidarity, and forming alliances with the nongovernmental and private sectors.

Selected Topics: Management and organizational behavior, development economics, planning and decision models, cost benefit analysis, social change and advocacy, interpersonal communication, mediated communication, community involvement, quantitative and qualitative methodologies, community education.

Distinctive Features: This three-month 18-credit intensive training program was developed with an advisory panel of leading practitioners in close collaboration with UNICEF, and with support from UNDP, WHO, USAID, and UNFPA. It provides Master's level credit for highly qualified candidates and was planned by Tulane's International Communication Enhancement Center with collaboration from Management, Communication and Education, and Research and Evaluation. Eleven institutions in developing countries are now committed to developing a similar course in their country.

Contact Person: Professor Jack C. Ling, International Communication Enhancement Center, School of Public Health/Tropical Medicine, Tulane University, 1501 Canal Street, New Orleans, LA 70112, Work Phone: (504) 584-3542, Fax: (504) 584-3653

Models of the Mind: Anthropology, Psychoanalysis, and Psychiatry

Institution: Vanderbilt University
Intended Audience: Doctoral candidates in anthropology and religion, residents in psychiatry, and other doctoral students
Disciplines Represented: Anthropology, religion, psychiatry
Personnel: Three faculty

General Description: The goal of the course is to examine a core human phenomenon: that each culture and each person deals with a part of human nature we term "the mind" (or the soul, or "anima," or "Buddha nature"). Therefore each person and each culture creates "models" of what the mind is. These models persist in myths, private fantasies, and public narratives like theologies and other official doctrinal statements and they shape societal definitions of disease, morality, deviance, and justice. Western academic culture grants to various disciplines, and their models of mind, authority to decide what "the mind" is. Therefore questions about what is "mental" and "nonmental" are typically referred to academic or other specialists (e.g., forensic psychiatry and the insanity defense.) The more specific goal of the course is to introduce students to the problem of mind, which is common to these three disciplines, and to the views of the disciplines which are unlike one another. Students are encouraged to develop a sophisticated understanding of the "problem of mind," to develop a rigorous sense of how these three disciplines—anthropology, religion, and psychiatry—speak about mind, and how they differ from one another.

Selected Topics: What is mind? Why do we find models of the mind, rather than simple definitions? How does research psychiatry approach these issues? How do persons' models of the mind and associated models of "disease" influence both their physical and psychological efforts at healing? How do social scientists understand their work in other cultures? What is the nature of truly interdisciplinary discourse about the mind?

Distinctive Features: Faculty are present at all lectures, serve as respondents, and offer friendly critiques. Students are provided interview sites and guides to discover "implicit models of mind" from diverse persons, especially those from non-European cultures. Faculty planning involves reading core texts in each other's disciplines.

Contact Person: Beth A. Conklin, Dept. of Anthropology, Vanderbilt University, Box 6050-B, Nashville, TN 37235, Work Phone: (615) 343-6125, Fax: (615)343-0230

Law

Sometimes law professors serve as part of an interdisciplinary team for courses designed for undergraduates or graduate students in other disciplines. At other times, interdisciplinary law courses are provided to serve the needs of first-year law students in building basic skills or advanced law students as they seek, to specialize. The examples described here are from University of Southern California, the Northwestern School of Law of Lewis and Clark College, and the University of Alberta.

LAW AND ECONOMICS

Institution: University of Alberta

Intended Audience: Law students and students in the arts and sciences, particularly economics

Disciplines Represented: Law and economics

Personnel: Two faculty, one each from law and economics

General Description: In this course, students learn to analyze the economic consequences and effects of property, contract, tort, and criminal law and develop an underlying economic logic for those legal subject areas. Students learn to understand the law as an economic institution, i.e., to see that the law is something that shapes and constrains the behavior of individuals as they pursue their economic interest. In order to develop an underlying economic logic, the student will be required to master critical economic concepts, such as economic efficiency (Pareto optimality), externality, public goods, and risk and risk allocation. Law, as an economic institution, comes to be understood as a social control mechanism that constrains individual behavior, usually in conformity with consensually held expectations of "the society" or "the community." The law is seen as a language of duties, rights, expectations, and entitlements. It almost never deals in economic terminology. Yet it can be understood in many instances to be promoting economic efficiency.

Selected Topics: Analysis of the economic implications of property, contract, tort, criminal, and corporate law; examination of economic logic underlying different areas of law, and illustrations of the law as an economic institution; analysis of externality, risk, deterrants, and other leading issues in economics and law.

Distinctive Features: Faculty alternate lecture topics and demonstrate the different approaches and methodologies of law and economics. The course uses an interdisciplinary textbook by Cooter and Ulen entitled *Law and Economics*. Students prep for exams on review questions distributed throughout the course by both professors.

Contact Person: Henry van Egteren, Dept. of Economics, 8-14 Tory Building, University of Alberta, Edmonton, Alberta, Canada T6G 2H4, Work Phone: (403) 492-3406, Fax: (403) 492-3300

LAW AND PSYCHIATRY SEMINAR

Institution: Northwestern School of Law of Lewis and Clark College

Intended Audience: Law Students

Disciplines Represented: Law and psychiatry
Personnel: Two professors, an attorney, and a forensic psychiatrist

General Description: This specialized topic seminar for upper division law students focuses on legal issues growing out of medical and mental health situations.

Selected Topics: Among other topics, those typically considered in the course are the insanity defense and other psychiatrically related issues in criminal law; involuntary civil commitment; the right to treatment and the right to refuse treatment; psychiatry in the civil justice system; and the interrelationship of the legal and psychiatric professions.

Distinctive Features: Team taught by faculty from each discipline as a true seminar, with students preparing and presenting papers on selected topics for discussion in the seminar sessions.

Contact Person: Stephen Kanter, NWSL of Lewis and Clark College, 10015 S.W. Terwilliger Blvd., Portland, OR 97219, Work Phone: (503) 768-6757, Fax: (503) 768-6671

LAW, LANGUAGE, AND ETHICS
Institution: University of Southern California
Intended Audience: First-year law students
Disciplines Represented: Subdisciplines of legal studies
Personnel: Three professors teaching three sections each year

General Description: This course provides an introduction to the function of legal rules and concepts in the organizing of society. Drawing on the learning from a broad variety of fields, including epistemology, ethics, semantic analysis, aesthetics, sociology, and psychoanalysis, it examines the underlying structure of legal argument and decision.

Selected Topics: Applying Rules: An Introduction; Can We Get What We Want from Legal Rules? Persons: Another Case in Applying Legal Rules; Understanding and Applying Common Law Precedent; Facts; Law's Commitments.

Distinctive Features: The course is developed by three professors who collaborate in the planning process and who draw on each other's expertise in content integration, but who present each of the three parallel sections alone.

Contact Person: Ronald R. Garet, USC Law Center, 699 Exposition Blvd., Los Angeles, CA 90089-0071, Work Phone: (213) 740-2568, Fax: (213) 740-5502

Commercial Art and Design

Another area of professional training, rather different from business, law, and the health professions, is commercial art, often referred to simply as design. Design often involves more than one medium (words and pictures, sculpture and photography) and is often applied to a particular problem or process. The courses described below from the University of Hawaii at Manoa, Rhode Island School of Design, and Niagara County Community College illustrate the use of more than one disciplinary perspective in the visual arts.

INTEGRATING EDITING AND DESIGN IN PUBLICATIONS
Institution: University of Hawaii at Manoa
Intended Audience: Students in journalism and graphic design
Disciplines Represented: Third-year and fourth-year majors in journalism and graphic design
Personnel: Journalism professor, and graphics design professor

General Description: Integrating editing and design in publications is an innovative learning community in which journalism students team up with graphic design students to produce real-world publications. This course attempts to replicate what happens in the real world. Editors and designers communicate but in different ways—one uses words and the other uses visual elements. A synergy is created when both come together to work on a communication project. Student graphic designers and editors collaborate to produce publications such as a newspaper or persuasion piece. Students meet twice each week in computer labs—once in their teams and once for class lectures, discussions, and individual hands-on work. Class sessions with themes relevant to both design and editing students are team-taught. But, as in the real world, there are sessions for editing students to concentrate on learning advanced editing skills, and sessions for design students to focus on page and graphic design and typography. Students from both fields meet to decide what text, headlines, informational graphics, maps, photos, and page design would best inform readers about an exemplary topic. Through their projects, students demonstrate the skills of their respective fields as well as problem-solving and critical thinking skills. They learn to understand each other's professional language after having gained insight and knowledge of each other's goals and problems. Working in teams gives them the added opportunity of teaching and learning from one another. The strength of individual teams will be reflected in the successful integration of text and visual elements in the student projects.

Selected Topics: History and trends in newspaper and magazine presentation, information hierarchy and news judgment, journalism for design students, graphic design for journalism students, thinking visually and working with words, designing pages, misconceptions and realities of working with editors and designers.

Distinctive Features: Faculty work as true partners, with joint lectures, role plays, and debates. Students work in collaborative teams of designers and journalists on small projects and exercises, and then eventually on two major projects—a daily newspaper and a two-page persuasion piece.

Contact Person: Professor Ann Auman, University of Hawaii at Manoa, Dept. of Journalism, 2550 Campus Road, Crawford Hall 208, Honolulu,

HI 96822, Work Phone: (808) 956-3784, Fax: (808) 956-5396, E-mail: auman@uhunix.uhcc.hawaii.edu

LOOKING AT SCULPTURE: THE PHOTOGRAPHER'S CHOICES

Institution: Rhode Island School of Design

Intended Audience: Interterm students (graduate and undergraduate), no prerequisites, attracted from sculpture, architecture, graphic design, photography, interior architecture, illustration, and industrial design

Disciplines Represented: Art history, photography, museum studies

Personnel: Museum curator of prints, drawings, and photographs; museum photographer; art historian; various guest lecturers and exhibit critic

General Description: This is a pioneering course in which students, faculty members, and museum professionals join together to explore a specific subject—the photography of art, with a special focus on the photographic documentation of sculpture. Sponsored by the Division of Liberal Arts, and conducted in the RISD Museum, the class consists of an intensive art history seminar coordinated with a relevant practicum: students integrate a study of historiography and critical theory with the studio experience of professional museum photography. The museum provides a fertile environment for many aspects of learning at the school of design: the collection promotes interaction among students, curatorial staff, and faculty members from all disciplines. Several specialists who come to the material from various points of view visit the seminar, thus feeding a natural interest in theoretical and practical issues. The jumping-off point for the course was the premise that photographs of sculpture are necessarily "representations of representations," which, even as they address complex historical constructions, define their own realities. As the seminar poured over the visions of photographers of sculpture, including Atget, Adolphe Braun, Clarence Kennedy, Robert Mapplethorpe, and Linda Connor, students became profoundly aware of the variety of documentary styles dictated by the cultural moment and the photographers' choices.

Selected Topics: "Transparency" and "Opacity," The Possibility of Documentation, The Make-Believe of Color Slides, Early Photography and the History of Art, Art Book Photography, The Postmodern Sculptor/Photographer, and Contemporary Museum Photography as a Visual Resource.

Distinctive Features: Students read and discuss significant works on sculpture, photography, and the photography of sculpture. Students select objects in the museum collection and photograph these in the natural setting of the museum or in the museum photographer's studio. Students write a final paper but also prepare an exhibit of their photographs of sculpture.

Contact Person: Mary Bergstein, Rhode Island School of Design, Two College Street, Providence, RI 02903, Work Phone: (401) 454-6267, Fax: (401) 454-6320, E-Mail: mlewis@risd.edu

Zoo and Park Design

Institution: Niagara County Community College
Intended Audience: Animal management majors
Disciplines Represented: Graphic design, Advertising design, Architectural design, Fine arts, Three-dimensional design, and some Horticulture
Personnel: One faculty member in fine arts and one faculty member in animal management

General Description: This course introduces the student to the recognition and application of good design principles and techniques particularly in relation to zoos, animal parks, and other public institutions. The topics include graphic design tools, techniques and approaches spanning typography and concept development, advertising design and the utilization of the print medium to best advantage, and environmental and architectural design strategies. Students are presented with opportunities to integrate information learned in other classes with the development of supervised projects applicable to zoological parks.

Selected Topics: Introduction to design, function and aesthetics, recognizing design problems, elements of graphic design, visitor-related design, way-finding, signage, environmental considerations, design needs of animals, specialized exhibits, zoo shops, parkland in tandem with zoos, handicapped accessibility, architectural design, advertising.

Distinctive Features: The course uses a mix of lectures, demonstrations, discussions, and visual aids to explore a variety of issues and problems related to the design of zoos and parks.

Contact Person: Professor Carol Townsend, Fine Arts Dept., Niagara County Community College, 3111 Saunders Settlement Road, Sanborn, NY 14132, Work Phone: (716) 731-3271 x487, Fax: (716) 731-4053

Natural Resource Management

Although agriculture, forestry, and wildlife management are occupations that have developed their specialized sciences and sub-fields of study, certain issues and problems bring these diverse specializations back together again. Concern for the environment, whether the land use is forestry, agriculture, or mining, is a common theme for many of these specialties, and is often taught through interdisciplinary courses that draw on the talents and perspectives of several of these areas at once. Similarly, the problem-solving processes used in real world land-use planning and management often utilize interdisciplinary teams; and it makes sense, therefore, to give students experience in working on these teams. The courses described below from Oklahoma State University, South Dakota State University, the University of Alberta, and the

University of Waterloo assemble interdisciplinary faculties and sometimes groups of students to address problems or gain experience in planning.

AGROECOSYSTEMS: A BASIS FOR LIFE
Institution: Oklahoma State University
Intended Audience: Various agriculture majors, but also nonmajors interested in agriculture policy
Disciplines Represented: Animal science, agronomy, range science, and forestry
Personnel: Four faculty

General Description: The course is designed to provide an understanding of ecosystems and selected natural processes affecting agriculture and the environment. The goal of the course is to help students relate to the ideas and thought processes involved in resolution of critical natural and renewable resource policy issues. Students are provided the opportunity to develop a framework for decision making regarding the contemporary major agriculture-related issues, such as water quantity and quality, conservation of natural resources, use of fertilizer and agricultural chemicals, food quality and safety, global climate change, intensive animal production systems, animal well-being, biotechnology, resource management, utilization of public lands, and agricultural policy.

Selected Topics: Production agriculture; ecosystem concepts, dynamics, functions, and change; climate, water, soils, and organisms; animal production systems; animal well-being; crop production systems; environmental quality; pest biology and regulation; food products, processing and safety; biotechnology, agricultural economics, policies, and land use implications; agricultural research.

Distinctive Features: The course addresses a broad array of issues affecting not only agriculture but the general public, such as food supply, environmental impact, land use, and animal well-being. Students present controversial issues related to course topics in teams of four designed to explore and debate the controversies in class forums.

Contact Person: Dr. Kevin Donnelly, Dept. of Agronomy, 550 Ag Hall, Oklahoma State University, Stillwater, OK 74078, Work Phone: (405) 744-7059, Fax: (405) 744-5269

INTEGRATED NATURAL RESOURCE MANAGEMENT
Institution: South Dakota State University
Intended Audience: Upper division majors in the various natural resource management curricula
Disciplines Represented: Wildlife and fisheries sciences, range sciences, park management, environmental management, and plant science.
Personnel: Five faculty, one each from the above areas

General Description: The course brings together students from various natural resource departments to work on a common project. Only a few introductory lectures are used to orient students to the scope and nature of their projects. The primary goal is to develop a management plan for some aspect of natural resource use. The teams are intentionally composed of students from different professional disciplines, who are asked to bring their insights and knowledge from previous learning to the multidisciplinary solution of a problem.

Selected Topics: New topics are introduced, but students are given extensive orientation to how to develop a planning document that includes a mission statement, an expression of philosophy, an inventory of the resources involved, a review of the issues, and management recommendations.

Distinctive Features: The course breaks up the traditional classroom teaching approach (no tests, little formal classroom time) and uses interdisciplinary student teams to explore natural resource management issues. Instructor time is spent in advising teams and reviewing final projects presented in half-hour oral reports to the assembled class. Grades are the same for the whole team for final written reports and final oral reports, but students also evaluate the participation of group members for part of the grade. Students must integrate their own previous learning with the learning of students in other disciplines.

Contact Person: Dr. C.G. Scalet, Wildlife and Fisheries Science, Box 2140B, South Dakota State University, Brookings, SD 57007-1696, Work Phone: (605) 688-6121, Fax: (605) 688-4515

GLOBAL ECOSYSTEMS AND HUMAN INVOLVEMENT
Institution: University of Alberta
Intended Audience: All first-year students in the Faculty of Agriculture, Forestry and Home Economics
Disciplines Represented: Ecology, resource economics, human ecology, agriculture and forestry, resource management, environmental science
Personnel: One instructor/coordinator and four other faculty

General Description: The course is designed to help students understand the interconnectedness of living and nonliving parts within ecosystems, with special emphasis on the interactions of the human and nonhuman parts of ecosystems. Students learn to understand ecological principles and their applications, and to understand the tensions between human aspirations, needs, and desires and the limits of the wider ecosystem. Students learn to accept the challenge involved in developing a balance among these tensions in an effort to promote sustainability of the earth's systems. Students gain an appreciation of the individual's place in the biosphere in geologic and biologic time and develop a worldview and land ethic of resource use.

Selected Topics: Biotic and abiotic components of ecosystems; ecologic principles and applications; ecosystem dynamics, change, development, evolution, structure, function, disruption, and destruction; resource requirements, economics and management; conservation and sustainability, disturbance, restoration, and landscape ecology; agroecology and conservation ecology; tensions between human desires and ecosystem limits.

Distinctive Features: The course is a mixture of lecture, demonstration, laboratory, textbook reading, and discussion. This is a fundamental ecology course for students in occupations that range from land use, such as forestry and agriculture, in a Canadian province where these are major industries, to human ecology and foods and nutritional science.

Contact Person: Dr. M.A. Naeth, Dept. of Renewable Resources, Rm. 751 GSB, University of Alberta, Edmonton, Alberta, Canada T6G 2H1, Work Phone: (403) 492-9539, Fax: (403) 492-4323

Issue Analysis and Problem Solving for Environment and Resource Studies
Institution: University of Waterloo
Intended Audience: Introductory course for majors in environment and resource studies
Disciplines Represented: Biology, systems design engineering, sociology, political science, planning. Course itself uses "transdisciplinary" format
Personnel: Two faculty from Faculty of Environmental Studies

General Description: The purpose of the course is to explore concepts and methods for analyzing issues associated with environment and resource studies, primarily through case examples. The objectives of the course are to:

- introduce analytical approaches for problem definition and problem solving that are appropriate for a wide range of environmental and resource issues;
- illustrate some interrelationships among environment and resource issues that are often perceived to be isolated from one another and "managed" accordingly, but in fact are rooted in ecological, economic, and institutional systems; and
- provide practice in analyzing case examples and in accessing reference and other library information.

Selected Topics: Environment and resource disputes, local environment and resource issues, governmental institutions, corporations and "super companies," social change, a sustainable society, and successful paths to sustainability.

Distinctive Features: Students learn the analytical skills needed for thinking clearly about environmental issues in the context of specific case examples. Students pursue assignments involving the analysis of a "home-town" environmental case, and complete reports on governmental agencies and issues relating to the environment and large corporations. The course is inherently interdisciplinary by use of case examples of ongoing disputes involving multiple interest groups and different uses of resources. It provides brief overview introductions to subject matter pursued in more detail in other courses, e.g., ecology of ecosystems, corporate and government institutions, introduction to sustainable societies, social change, and practical projects on the campus and in the community involving senior students.

Contact Persons: Sally Lerner, Associate Professor, Dept. of Environment & Resource Studies, Faculty of Environmental Studies, Waterloo, Ontario, Canada N2L 3G1, Work Phone: (519) 885-1211, Fax: (519) 746-0292

George Francis, Associate Professor, Dept. of Environment & Resource Studies, Faculty of Environmental Studies, Waterloo, Ontario, Canada N2L 3G1, Work Phone: (519) 885-1211, Fax: (519) 746-0292

Education

Some might make the case that education is itself an interdisciplinary field of study, that it draws heavily upon other fields of study—psychology, sociology, history, administrative science—and makes no disciplinary contribution itself. Others would argue that education is a professional field like other professions, and it is the focus of professional practice in particular kinds of settings that gives education its special character. In any case, education commonly combines some of its own internal subfields in interdisciplinary study, or reaches out to related fields outside of education to create interdisciplinary arrangements. The courses below from the University of Massachusetts, Universidad de las Americas, Harvard University, and New York University provide good examples.

PUBLIC EDUCATION IN TURMOIL: LEGAL AND HISTORICAL PERSPECTIVES FOR CITIZEN ACTION
Institution: University of Massachusetts
Intended Audience: Second-year undergraduates and above
Disciplines Represented: History and education
Personnel: Two faculty

General Description: The future of public education in the United States is at risk. At no time in history have so many come to doubt the ability of public education to prepare the nation's students for productive employment, higher education, and enlightened citizenship. The social and economic changes in recent decades have deepened long-standing divisions in American democracy over the role of public education. The purpose of the course is to provide students with a better understanding of the historic roots, legal dimensions, and policy implications of the current controversies in education so that they will be better able to promote the well-being of our public schools and universities by informed citizen action through their local school committees and state legislatures.

Selected Topics: Public Education Endangered: The Nature of the Current Turmoil; The Origins, Rationale, and Evolution of Public Education in the U.S.; Why Public Education; Issues of Social Class. Issues of Gender. Issues of Race and Ethnicity. When Can Public Schools Restrict Freedom of Expression; Academic and Personal Freedom for Teachers; Religious Freedom and the Public Schools; Contested Curricular Choices; Sex Education; Interest Groups and Education.

Distinctive Features: Historical perspective is provided for key current issues, so that students gain a sense of where the issues came from, what historical factors shaped the issues, and what key legal cases have shaped the parameters of the debate. Students write position papers in which they are expected to research all sides of an issue and present and defend their viewpoint in the context of opposing arguments. A broad final essay exam is used to encourage synthesis of the interdisciplinary material.

Contact Persons: Joyce A. Berkman, Dept. of History, Box 33930, University of Massachusetts, Amherst, MA 01003, Work Phone: (413) 545-6759, Fax: (413) 545-6137

David Schimmel, Dept. of Education, Box 34120, University of Massachusetts, Amherst, MA 01003, Work Phone: (413) 545-1529, Fax: (413) 545-1523

CHILD EVALUATION (VALORACION INFANTIL)
Institution: Universidad de las Americas, A.C.
Intended Audience: Child, clinical, and educational psychologists; speech and language specialists; special education teachers; medical doctors; physical therapists; special education and regular classroom teachers.
Disciplines Represented: Psychology, education, medicine
Personnel: 11 faculty

General Description: The underlying philosophy of the course is to improve attention offered to at-risk populations as well as diagnostic services provided to children with special needs. By presenting the student with practical, low-cost diagnostic tools and by developing a sense of interdisciplinary work, the course tries to form a new breed of professionals able to facilitate the diagnostic process and become proficient in doing team work in a special education setting. The main objective of the course is to develop skills that health and education professionals require in order to establish holistic diagnoses, providing the qualitative and quantitative information needed to determine optimal intervention for children 0-12 years old with special needs in the areas of intellectual, social, motor, and emotional development.

Selected Topics: Identification of developmental disabilities in early childhood, emotional evaluation, language evaluation, identification and evaluation of gifted and talented, evaluation of learning disabilities.

Distinctive Features: The course draws on skills of varied faculty to present and explore various diagnostic and evaluation instruments used in fields related to education, and provides an overview of assessment that enables students to understand the "whole child," ages 0-12.

Contact Person: Guadalupe Vadillo, Universidad de las Americas, A.C., Puebla No. 223, Col. Roma 06700, D.F. Mexico, Work Phone: 525-1575 - 208-0247, x234, x250, Fax: 525-4346 - 511-6040

INQUIRIES INTO TEACHING AND LEARNING I AND II: UNCOVERING WHAT IS, IMAGINING WHAT MIGHT BE

Institution: New York University
Intended Audience: Undergraduates and graduate pre-service teachers
Disciplines Represented: History, philosophy, psychology, sociology, anthropology of education, social policy, curriculum and instruction, multiculturalism
Personnel: Twenty, including one coordinator, five instructors, and fourteen graduate assistants

General Description: Designed as an exploration of the nature of learners and learning, teachers and teaching, knowledge and knowing, and schools and schooling, this course introduces prospective elementary, secondary, and special education teachers to the personal, social, institutional, and pedagogical issues they will encounter as educators. They engage in autobiographical reflection, read, discuss, and write about relevant professional literature, interact with panels of classroom teachers, students, policymakers, and faculty from education-related disciplines, observe in schools, and create portfolios which begin to document their professional development and emerging beliefs and commitments. Among other issues, the course examines the educational implications of cultural, linguistic and intellectual diversity and how personal knowledge shapes teaching and learning.

Selected Topics: Learners and Learning, Teachers and Teaching, Knowledge and Knowing, Schools and Schooling.

Distinctive Features: Five sections of 45 students each are broken into cohort groups of fifteen led by graduate students preparing to be teacher educators, specializing in a range of interests. Collaborative, interdisciplinary planning occurs in weekly meetings with the instructors and with the instructional teams for each section. Creative assignments for students include a learning autobiography, cohort group meetings, observations of field experiences, critical reading and written responses, and learning/teaching portfolios. A sound interdisciplinary introduction to issues that will continue to surface for students throughout their teacher education program.

Contact Person: Marilyn Sobelman, 239 Green Street, Rm. 635, New York, NY 10003, Work Phone: (212) 998-5233, Fax: (212) 995-4198

INCLUSIONARY EDUCATION AND AT RISK CHILDREN: MAPPING
    A PROCESS OF CHANGE
Institution: Harvard University
Intended Audience: Graduate students in Education
Disciplines Represented: Education, Law, Government, Medicine
Personnel: Four faculty from the colleges listed above and guest lecturers

General Description: In recent years courts and legislative statutes have demanded
that public schools become "inclusionary," i.e. include in regular classrooms students
with physical, behavioral, learning, and emotional difficulties who were formerly
placed in separate classrooms or institutions. This reform has created complex
challenges and opportunities for public schools. At stake are the schools' capacity,
and, indeed, the entire society's capacity, to respond positively to increasingly diverse
students who have different learning styles, problems and strengths. This reform also
comes at a time when public schools are increasingly under siege, and when parents
are questioning their commitment to public education. Moreover, this reform comes
at a time of growing concern over the costs of special education; and there is, in fact,
a danger that inclusionary education will disguise elimination of services for children
with special needs. Students in this course are placed in one of several new inclusionary
schools in Boston, and through the course explore these challenges. Taught in
collaboration with Harvard Law School professors, this course pioneers an interdisciplinary approach to exploring this topic, drawing on the perspectives of faculty
members from the Graduate School of Education, the Medical School, the Law
School, and the Kennedy School of Government.

Selected Topics: The legal and social history of inclusion; institutional systems change;
the implications of inclusion models for traditional understandings of normality and
pathology; challenges of inclusionary reform for school and classroom teachers.

Distinctive Features: Students have practicum placements in inclusionary settings
in urban schools and get involved with those schools and their children through legal
advocacy groups, after-school programs, and mentorship programs. All faculty attend
and contribute to all class sessions. The course is cross listed in Law, and students
come from Education as well as fields outside of Education. Students keep detailed
field notes and write case descriptions and analytic papers. The course has been
supported by the Provost Fund for Innovative Education.

Contact Person: Gil G. Noam, Harvard Graduate School of Education, 422 Larsen
    Hall, Appian Way, Cambridge, MA 02138, Work Phone: (617) 496-0636, Fax:
    (617) 495-3626

INTEGRATIVE STUDIES PROGRAMS

Undergraduate students almost always are required to "major" in something,
to accumulate a concentration of academic credits in a particular field of

study, usually an academic discipline. The major is the depth component of undergraduate education. Originally, the major was simply a group of courses that students could take for their specialization. The concept dates back to the University of Virginia in 1825, and the name "group system" was used by President Andrew Dickinson White at Cornell in 1868. The terms "major" and "minor" appear to have been used for the first time in the catalog of Johns Hopkins University in 1877-78. When President Lowell sought ways to reintroduce structure into Eliot's "elective system" at Harvard in the years after 1909, he used the term "concentration."[13]

As the academic disciplines began to dominate the curriculum, the major came to be thought of as it is today—as a disciplinary major. The idea of a disciplinary major has its strengths, of course, and its values are well-argued: it provides an in-depth knowledge of a field and the methods used in that field to generate and transmit knowledge. Disciplinary majors continue to be the dominant pattern today, but in recent years some institutions have developed alternatives supported by reasonable justifications.

Keeping in mind the original meanings of "concentration" and the "group system," one can make the case that the major need not consist of courses only in one discipline. The groups of courses taken for a concentration should, no doubt, add up to something; that is, they should have a cumulative, as opposed to random, effect, but that does not mean, necessarily, that they should all be taken in a single academic discipline or professional field. Using this logic, students at some institutions in the late 1960s began to press for interdisciplinary majors. Several colleges and universities responded by creating area studies programs, "field majors,"[14] and student-created concentrations. Brown University was one of the early leaders in creating interdisciplinary majors. Perhaps the first and best known of the integrative studies programs were the American Studies programs of the late 1950s and early 1960s. It was recognized at that time that getting a good grasp of American life and culture might involve more than the traditional American political history course. The study of America more generally (meaning then the United States) could be enriched, it was thought, by studying American literature, art, philosophy, and religious traditions simultaneously, or at least in an integrated sequence of courses. Often, by drawing on courses already in place in other departments, a college program in American Studies could be developed simply by placing existing courses in a brochure and making a program out of them. Naturally, the programs soon became more sophisticated, drawing on faculty talents to coordinate the courses, identify common themes, eliminate overlap, and devise appropriate advisement and mentoring for students. American Studies and similar programs showed that in-depth knowledge in one field, as Ralph Ross has pointed out, may require knowledge of other fields as well:

> One may study literature, for example, and should see at once that history
> and philosophy, religion and manners are involved in what one reads. . . .
> The events of history are of all kinds, including literary events. If they were
> parceled out to different subject matters, all subject matters would be
> included, for everything has a history, from logic to marriage. . . . Sociology
> has been called the study of society. What, then, do political science,
> economics, and social psychology study? Clearly, parts of society. And if
> sociology omits those parts, how much of society is left for it? Not just
> crumbs from the table of other studies, but somehow not the whole loaf
> either, unless society is really studied as a whole. But that would take a
> joint effort by all the social and behavioral sciences.[15]

Drawing on the crumbs and loaf metaphor used above, one might say that
interdisciplinary programs are somewhere between crumbs and the whole
loaf; maybe "slice" is the best word. But as anyone knows, there is more than
one way to slice a subject—by different angles, different thicknesses, and so
on. Interdisciplinary and integrative programs involve the inventing of new
concentrations that provide a new "slice" of some reality.

The programs listed below are not all majors, although some are, but most
involve, to borrow the phrase from Cornell in the mid-1860s, a "group
system." They are presented here as examples of more complex arrangements
for interdisciplinary teaching and learning involving more than individual
courses. Some do not meet the criterion established earlier for utilizing more
than one teacher in a single course, but their interdisciplinarity and their use
of teams of faculty for planning capture the same spirit. These courses often
use the arrangements described in the first chapter of this book as "cluster
courses" or "learning communities," and the reader interested in this topic is
reminded again to consult *Learning Communities: Creating Connections Among
Students, Faculty, and Disciplines.*[16] The arrangements described here are
characterized by a high degree of inventiveness, some being experimental,
others more established. What holds them together is a common concern for
finding ways to integrate various types of study in interdisciplinary formats.

In the examples that appear below, the customary pattern of describing
single courses is abandoned to include descriptions of entire programs. In
some cases, individual courses are still described briefly, but usually in the
context of a wider program. The titles here refer to programs, and when
courses are described, they are usually (but not always) interdisciplinary,
team-taught courses, as those terms are used throughout this book. The
examples come from University of King's College, Elmhurst College, Tufts
University, Northwestern University, University of British Columbia, Harvard University, the University of Wisconsin—Green Bay, Marshall Univer-
sity, Wayne State University, and Sarah Lawrence College.

CONTEMPORARY STUDIES PROGRAM

Institution: University of King's College
Intended Audience: Serves as interdisciplinary major option for honors students
Disciplines Represented: Political philosophy, critical theory, history and philosophy of science, women's studies, and literature
Personnel: Eight faculty, four each at University of King's College and Dalhousie University

General Description: The purpose of the Contemporary Studies Program is to bring together several disciplines and traditions of inquiry to make sense of the contemporary period as a whole. Serving as an undergraduate foundation for further study of some aspect of contemporary life or simply as a course of study for developing insights for students into the nature of the world in which they live, the Contemporary Studies Program provides a series of interdisciplinary courses that focus on twentieth-century European and North American culture. Examples of courses include the following: Development in the 20th Century; The History and Philosophy of 20th Century Science and Technology; Culture, Politics, and the Post-Colonial Condition; The Deconstruction of the Tradition in the 20th Century, The Place of Women in Contemporary French Critical Theory; and From Symbolism and Surrealism to the New Novel and Beyond. The Program includes a capstone honors seminar, a concurrent lecture series, and opportunities for independent reading in contemporary studies.

Distinctive Features: Because a high value is placed on studying the past in many colleges and universities, often with little or no emphasis on the twentieth century (now almost past), it is refreshing to see a whole program devoted to the interdisciplinary study of the present. The course involves collaboration among faculty in an array of disciplines across two related institutions. It combines in-depth study of various topics with a synthetic overview, thus providing a foundation for further study or simply an innovative option within liberal education.

Contact Person: Elizabeth Edwards, Director, Contemporary Studies Programme, University of King's College, Halifax, Nova Scotia, Canada B3H 2A1, Work Phone: (902) 422-1271 x148, Fax: (902) 423-3357

LINKED LIVING COURSES PROGRAM

Institution: Elmhurst College
Intended Audience: First-year students
Disciplines Represented: English composition, psychology
Personnel: Two professors, residence hall director

General Description: Students who test into second-level English composition—above average, but not honors students—and who wish to study general psychology at the same time, are registered together in these cluster courses and placed in the same residence hall. (Students meet two general education requirements in this way.) The two courses are designed to provide a "double dose" of critical thinking and writing skills, including skills in critical analysis; research; documentation of sources; summarizing, drafting, revising, and organizing ideas; applying criteria; and developing surveying and interviewing skills. Both professors explicitly address these skills in their classes, and attend each other's classes, acting as quasi-students, resource persons, and connection-makers. In the writing course, which immediately follows the psychology class, writing assignments from the previous hour are clarified and addressed, and writing assignments are linked to the lectures and discussions of the psychology class. Students in the linked program also interact with each other in the residence hall by forming study groups.

Distinctive Features: The program extends the simple clustering of courses by linking two cluster courses to the residence setting. It focuses on providing academic skills needed for later success in college in a context where peers can support each other in the learning process and develop a close relationship to faculty they work with in both classes. Students and faculty report high satisfactions with the course and plans are under way for linked courses for nonresidential and transfer students.

Contact Persons: Dr. Ann M. Frank Wake, Elmhurst College, Dept. of English, Box 22, 190 Prospect Avenue, Elmhurst, IL 60126, Work Phone: (708) 617-3135, Fax: (708) 617-3735

Dr. Jane A. Jegerski, Elmhurst College, Dept. of Psychology, 190 Prospect Avenue, Elmhurst, IL 60126, Work Phone: (708) 617-3585, Fax: (708) 617-3735

AMERICAN STUDIES PROGRAM (Course described is Ecology of the Americas: An Introduction to American Studies)
Institution: Tufts University
Intended Audience: Undergraduate majors
Disciplines Represented: Biology, chemistry, drama, education, English, film studies, urban and environmental policy
Personnel: Nine faculty who organize into two teams to offer the course in alternate years

General Description: In 1992 Tufts established a new Center for Interdisciplinary Studies, encompassing 10 programs. The programs are at the BA level where a student can earn a degree in Interdisciplinary Studies. One of the oldest programs in the Center is American Studies, but "American" is more broadly defined to include North and South America and the studies include disciplines from the sciences as well as the more common history and American literature. To introduce students to interdisciplinary studies and the broader way of looking at the Americas, the faculty created a course that focuses on ecology as a way of examining historical changes and contemporary issues. The course explores transformations of the environment from pre-Columbian times to the present in both North and South America. The study focuses on aspects of the urban environment, including Mayan civilization, and contemporary life in Sao Paulo, Rio de Janeiro, and Los Angeles. The course poses the problem of constructing a just and sustainable future for the Americas.

Distinctive Features: American studies is part of a larger Interdisciplinary Studies umbrella, and the introductory course brings together faculty from different disciplines. Ecology of the Americas introduces students to a broader, global approach to thinking about the Americas, and brings together the past, present, and future in a probing exploration of the urban environment.

Contact Person: Saul Slapikoff, American Studies Program, 107 Eaton, Tufts University, Medford, MA 02155, Work Phone: (617) 628-5000 x2311, Fax: (617) 627-3032

INTEGRATED ARTS PROGRAM (Course described is Art Process)
Institution: Northwestern University
Intended Audience: Undergraduates supplementing their major with a minor
Disciplines Represented: Theater, art, and music in the Art Process course
Personnel: Six drawn from above disciplines

General Description: The Integrated Arts Program is a minor and can be taken only in conjunction with a formal major in one of the schools. The College of Arts and Sciences, in which the program is housed, defines minors as "areas of study in recognized but newly emerging fields that are not formal majors in departments or programs." These programs are usually curricular innovations crossing established disciplines to focus on particular themes that are best explored in an interdisciplinary or multidisciplinary way. The Integrated Arts Program involves the required A-level course, Art Process; selection of two of four B-level courses that introduce students to modes of theater, art, music, and dance; selection of two of the thirteen C-level advanced courses offered in various departments; and completion of the team-taught Performance Seminar and an aesthetic philosophy course, Towards a Theory of the Arts.

The introductory course, Art Process, is taught by six faculty from the School of Music, the School of Speech, and the College of Arts and Sciences. The course is divided into three, three-week units devoted to theater, art, and music, plus one culminating week to explore issues common to all the arts and issues separating the arts. The course has an experiential studio base plus field visits to galleries, concerts, and recitals.

Distinctive Features: The program uses the larger framework of minors in conjunction with majors to permit and support interdisciplinary studies. The Integrated Arts Program achieves its interdisciplinary goals through team-taught introductory and capstone courses, and by permitting student election of courses available in a wide range of disciplinary homes. The program offers a clever blending of different forms of interdisciplinary study in a single program.

Contact Persons: Carol Simpson Stern, Ph.D., Director, Integrated Arts Program and Dean of the Graduate School, Northwestern University, Graduate School, 633 Clark Street, CROWN 1-502, Evanston, IL 60208, Work Phone: (708) 491-8502, Fax: (708) 491-5070

Alan Shefsky, Secretary, Integrated Arts Program, Northwestern University, 1979 South Campus Drive, Evanston, IL 60208, Work Phone: (708) 491-2576, Fax (708) 497-2019

INTERDISCIPLINARY STUDIES (Course described is Science One)
Institution: University of British Columbia, Canada
Intended Audience: First-year students intending to major in a science discipline or take several courses in science
Disciplines Represented: Biology, chemistry, physics, and mathematics
Personnel: Four professors, two sessional lecturers, one director, one secretary, and several guest lecturers

General Description: From first year to Ph.D., the options for interdisciplinary study are many at the University of British Columbia. The Faculty of Arts offers many routes for students to explore a wide range of interdisciplinary study. There are first-year and majors programs for undergraduates and a graduate program in Comparative Literature. Other interdisciplinary M.A. and Ph.D. programs are available through the Faculty of Graduate Studies. Students can also pursue interdisciplinary interests by taking Arts Studies courses that are specially designed to be interdisciplinary or by completing a minor in related subjects or series of courses that complement their major. Examples of interdisciplinary concentrations include Canadian Studies, Comparative Literature, Environmental Studies, Ethnic Studies, International Relations, Medieval Studies, Modern European Studies, Nineteenth Century Studies, Women's Studies, and the integrated General BA Program. All of these programs are sponsored by the Faculty of Arts and are coordinated by an Associate Dean for Interdisciplinary Programs and Curriculum.

One of the most creative efforts in interdisciplinary studies at the University of British Columbia is not a major or concentration, but a large integrated core course that provides foundational studies for anyone wishing to major in one of the sciences. Launched in 1993, Science One is a major pedagogic change in the classic first-year curriculum for science majors. The Program is built around an academically rigorous 21-credit course, which covers the equivalent of first-year biology, chemistry, mathematics, and physics in an interdisciplinary, integrative approach. Science One is structured as a "community" in which both the students and the instructors learn together. An important part of the program is the "home base," which is an open concept room with offices on one end, and an informal conversation pit and study area with large tables and a large blackboard on the other. Rather than supplying students with a compendium of facts, the program teaches students how to acquire knowledge. All factual information in Science One is covered at the level of the most rigorous first-year course offered in each discipline. The students can therefore integrate seamlessly into the second year in any one of the 21 Faculty of Science departments or programs. With proper choice of electives, they can also switch into a variety of other areas, such as business administration, economics, applied science, engineering, or environmental studies. For students interested in a medical career, Science One gives them the necessary first year prerequisites. A strong conceptual thread runs through the year. At any time, faculty integrate at least two of the disciplines. Where three or four of the disciplines interconnect smoothly, units are introduced that are treated in depth in one or two weeks. Examples of five such units are:

1) Scaling and allometric properties (biology, mathematics, physics)
2) Waves (biology, chemistry, mathematics, physics)
3) Growth and decay (mathematics, biology, chemistry)
4) Photosynthesis (biology, chemistry, physics)
5) Mass extinction and the ways of science (geology, astronomy, chemistry, microbiology, physics, statistics and probability).

Science One also uses several guest lecturers who give lectures, lead workshops, raise issues in panel discussions, and talk about their experience as scientists. These presentations raise the students' awareness of the variety of science disciplines; give them a realistic feel for what scientists do day to day in academia, the public sector, or industry; and help them put science into a social and cultural context.

Distinctive Features: The University of British Columbia is an impressive example of a major Canadian university that has created organizational and curricular structures to position itself to support faculty and students in interdisciplinary studies. A wide variety of programs are provided at many different levels for integrated programs as well as team-taught interdisciplinary courses. Science One is a bold experiment in integrating introductory studies in basic science disciplines and mathematics. Something must be working right to create a close-knit community of science scholars: Students created a club and a T-shirt marked SOS—Science One Survivors, so that they can remain in touch in their second year.

Contact Persons: Dr. Juliette A. Benbasat, Science One Program, 6356 Agricultural Road, Rm. 464, University of British Columbia, Vancouver, British Columbia, Canada V6T 1Z2, Work Phone: (604) 822-9876, Fax: (604) 822-5551, E-mail: science 1@unixg.ubc.ca

Dr. Graeme Wynn, Associate Dean, Faculty of Arts, 1866 Main Mall, University of British Columbia, Vancouver, British Columbia, Canada V6T 1Z2, Work Phone: (604) 822-6700, Fax: (604) 822-6607

Concentration in Environmental Science and Public Policy

Institution: Harvard University
Intended Audience: Interdisciplinary concentration
Disciplines Represented: Several disciplines in a variety of schools and colleges
Personnel: Faculty and graduate students from across the university

General Description: The concentration is designed to provide a multidisciplinary introduction to current problems of the environment. It is founded on the premise that the ability to form rational judgments concerning many of the complex challenges confronting society today involving the environment requires both an understanding of the underlying scientific and technical issues and an appreciation for the relevant economic, political, legal, historical, and ethical dimensions. It offers students an opportunity to specialize in a specific area of either natural or social science relating to the environment. The concentration is administered by the Department of Earth and Planetary Sciences. It is overseen by a standing committee functioning as a board of tutors including representatives from other departments of the Faculty of Arts and Sciences and from other schools as appropriate to ensure the requisite breadth of the program. Enrollment in the concentration is limited, providing opportunities for in-class discussion and for informal student-faculty interactions. The design of the concentration is reviewed annually by the board of tutors with a more formal report due to the Faculty each five years following the date when the concentration was first introduced.

All students have to satisfy a core of requirements in biology, chemistry, earth and planetary sciences, economics, government, and mathematics. Depending on preparation, students are encouraged to substitute more advanced courses for those required and take elective courses in their main area of interest. Students in the junior year take a seminar envisaged as the central integrating component of the concentration. The seminar covers a number of current environmental issues, comprehensively and in depth. It involves graduate students and faculty from a number of departments in the Faculty of Arts and Sciences and from several of the professional schools, including the Kennedy School of Government, the Law School, the Divinity School, the School of Public Health, the Business School, and the Graduate School of Design. Topics covered so far include policy issues relating to depletion of stratospheric ozone, conservation of wetlands, regulation of toxic waste and tropical deforestation, but change from year to year. In the senior year, students wishing to graduate with honors are expected to write a thesis applying skills and knowledge gained in their course experience to a specific environmental issue.

Distinctive Features: The concentration offers rigorous preparation in several basic sciences, which provides the groundwork for advanced study of environmental policy issues. Work in the sciences and social sciences is integrated in a junior year team-taught public policy tutorial designed for discussion of current environmental issues emphasizing not only scientific but also political, legal, and ethical dimensions.

Contact Persons: Lorraine Tringali, Administrator, Environmental Science & Public Policy, Hoffman Laboratory, 20 Oxford Street, Cambridge, MA 02138, Work Phone: (617) 496-6995, Fax: (617) 495-8839, E-mail: espp@geophysics.harvard.edu

Prof. Ulrich Petersen, Head Tutor, Dept. of Earth and Planetary Sciences, Harvard University, Cambridge, MA 02138, Work Phone: (617) 495-2353, Fax: (617) 495-8839, E-mail: petersen@geophysics.harvard.edu

INTERDISCIPLINARY PROGRAM IN INFORMATION SCIENCES (Courses described are Visual Information and Information Problems)
Institution: University of Wisconsin—Green Bay
Intended Audience: Majors in the program
Disciplines Represented: For the two courses described these include Visual Information: statistics, psychology, mathematics, and communication; Information Problems:computer science and communication
Personnel: Three faculty, Visual Information; Two faculty, Information Problems

General Description: The University of Wisconsin—Green Bay, founded in 1969 as an innovative institution around an environmental theme, has a long tradition of interdisciplinary programs. One of these is in Information Sciences, where the curriculum goes beyond the typical computer science program to address broader issues in accessing, manipulating, displaying, and interpreting information. Two lower level courses are designed to introduce students to this interdisciplinary way of approaching information science. In a course on Visual Information, a mathematician with background in image digitization and statistics joins a psychologist with interests in vision, perception, and aesthetics, and a media specialist in production techniques, to help students explore the elements that are part of an effective visual presentation and to understand the potential power of information presented visually. Another course, offered to students early in the program is Information Problems, taught by two faculty on a rotational basis from a pool that includes a computer scientist, a communications specialist, a linguist, and a media specialist. Students work in problem-solving teams on assigned projects to use an array of tools to transform data into information.

Distinctive Features: The program breaks out of the more narrow interests of computer scientists and communications experts to address the larger questions about what information actually is and how it can best be presented. Team-taught interdisciplinary courses offered early in the program introduce students to an interdisciplinary concentration of immense practical significance in today's world.

Contact Person: Clifford Abbott, TH331 UWGB, 2420 Nicolet Drive, Green Bay, WI 54311, Work Phone: (414) 465-2451, Fax: (414) 465-2890

BASIC HUMANITIES DEGREE PROGRAM
Institution: Marshall University
Intended Audience: Undergraduate majors
Disciplines Represented: Classical studies, philosophy, religious studies
Personnel: Department faculty

General Description: The Basic Humanities Program provides an alternative major to students interested in the interdisciplinary study of humanities. The goal of the program is to provide a means for students to develop an understanding of themselves and their cultures through the exploration of texts—the basic philosophical, religious, and literary/artistic works that continue to shape human cultural experience. Students take three interdisciplinary, team-taught courses that serve as the core to the program: Orientation in Humanities, Basic Humanities, and Humanities Seminar. In addition, students select three period courses from the Ancient World Track or Modern World Track, courses regularly offered by the three participating departments. Students also "contract" for five additional courses offered either by the participating departments or by other humanities disciplines. The program is shaped by the student under the guidance of at least two faculty advisors.

Distinctive Features: The orientation course in the program introduces the disciplines and the idea of interdisciplinary studies while building basic skills in reading and interpreting a text through spoken and written discourse. The Basic Humanities course focuses on humans as symbol-making animals who create their own realities and explores how postmodern assumptions and concepts uncover the ways humans constitute and encounter their realities. The Senior Seminar focuses on topics of current interest in the humanities.

Contact Person: Dr. Charles O. Lloyd, Marshall University, Classical Studies, Huntington, WV 25755, Work Phone: (304) 696-4642, Fax: (304) 696-6565, E-mail: lloydc@muvms6.wvnet.edu

INTERDISCIPLINARY STUDIES PROGRAM
Institution: Wayne State University
Intended Audience: Adult Learners in College of Lifelong Learning
Disciplines Represented: Several, depending on course topics
Personnel: Faculty, adjuncts, guest lecturers, videos

General Description: The College of Lifelong Learning provides several options within its Interdisciplinary Studies Program. Rather than delivering courses in a team-taught format, teams of faculty carefully plan courses, develop detailed syllabi, and then individually offer the courses "on their own" as free-standing courses taught by one professor. Examples of these courses are Human Life and the Changing Environment, essentially an interdisciplinary health and wellness course; Changing Life on Earth, part evolution and part cell biology; and Media in America: Money, Influence and Power, a course on newspaper and television journalism.

Distinctive Features: Faculty in the College of Lifelong Learning, who may not be able to coordinate schedules to teach together, collaborate extensively in planning courses, learn from each other, and then teach from a common syllabus.

Contact Persons: *Media in America,* Dr. James Michels, Wayne State University, 474 Justice Bldg., 6001, Cass Avenue, Detroit, MI 48202, Work Phone: (313) 577-4612, Fax: (313) 577-8585

> *Human Life & Changing Environment* and *Changing Life on Earth,* Dr. Clifford Maier, Wayne State University, 461.1 Justice Bldg., 6001 Cass Avenue, Detroit, MI 48202, Work Phone: (313) 577-4612, Fax: (313) 577-8585

PROGRAM OF INTERRELATED, INTERDISCIPLINARY COURSES AT SARAH LAWRENCE COLLEGE

Institution: Sarah Lawrence College
Audience: Seniors and selected graduate students.

General Description: Seniors at Sarah Lawrence College are offered a program of interdisciplinary courses. Although similar to the occasional "capstone" courses described later, these seminars constitute a program of interrelated courses extending over two semesters, cooperatively planned by faculty, and supplemented by a monthly colloquium featuring faculty and guest speakers. Designed primarily for seniors the program is open to selected graduate students. The courses described briefly here are representative of those typically offered.

Distinctive Features: The program involves fourth-year students in advanced studies in their disciplines and divisions without being excessively specialized, while extending their liberal education, and includes a unique blend of further, in-depth study and perspective-taking analysis. Interesting options are available throughout the program on a variety of topics created by bringing together faculty from appropriate disciplines in unique ways. Courses are enriched by being linked with colloquium presentations by other faculty and guests.

ANTIQUITY TO THE REFORMATION. A study of "pious images" in art and literature. The focus of the course in the first semester is on how the social and political forces of late sixteenth-century Italy shaped the making of religious images, particularly in the work of Michelangelo and Leonardo. In the second semester, the focus is on the impact of Reformation theology on English literature in late Elizabethan and seventeenth-century culture. The colloquium features speakers from the fields of literature, philosophy, art history, religion, classical and romance languages, and history.

Contact Person: Joseph Forte, Ph.D., 895 West End Avenue Apt. 4B, New York, NY 10025, Work Phone: (914) 395-2657, Fax: (914) 395-2666

EROS IN LITERATURE AND PHILOSOPHY. Three courses are associated with this colloquium, one a year long course on Eros and Text, and two semester-long courses, Eros and Writing and Eros and Tragedy. These courses, each in their own way, explore different aspects of the relationship of desire, romance, and erotic experience to writing, how Eros is expressed in literature, and how the understanding of Eros is shaped by and mediated by understandings gained through literature. In addition to course and colloquium participation, students are also involved in small reading groups where they read texts and present their critical interpretations to the class.

Contact Person: Belle Brodzki, Ph.D., 30 Cooper Lane, Larchmont, NY 10538, Work Phone: (914) 395-2415, Fax: (914) 395-2666

INEQUALITY: SOCIOLOGICAL AND ECONOMIC PERSPECTIVES. This interdisciplinary senior seminar in the social sciences examines inequality by race, class, and gender, and provides students an opportunity to combine more in-depth study in theory and methodology with policy-oriented practice. The focus of the first semester is on how power, privilege, and other status differentials intersect with ideologies about racial inequality. In the second semester, the focus is on economic inequality, the theoretical and methodological controversies in economics on the topic of inequality, and public policy debates that emerge from these disagreements.

Contact Person: Marilyn Power, Ph.D., 88 Clove Road, New Rochelle, NY 10801, Work Phone: (914) 395-2658, Fax: (914) 395-2666

SENIOR SEMINAR ON CULTURAL STUDIES. This interdisciplinary sequence involves the study of culture and representation: culture broadly understood as the human construction of life, and representation as the realm of words and images and the construction of mean. In the full semester, the focus is on structures of interpretation and involves scrutinizing literary, visual, cultural, and linguistic frames of meaning. In the second semester, the focus is on probing how anthropologists "write" culture by inscribing human social practices through various frames of analysis and interpretation. Searching questions are raised about the methods of anthropology from a cultural studies perspective.

Contact Person: Angela Moger, Ph.D., 25 Wesskum Wood Road, Riverside, CT 06878, Work Phone: (914) 395-2368, Fax: (914) 395-2666

WOMEN'S AND GENDER STUDIES

In recent years, some new areas of study have developed in the curriculum that take as their organizing principle a theme or topic that grows out of a social concern, for example, the treatment of women, the concerns of minority groups, or the need for developing global understanding. Although study and scholarship in these areas may be motivated by an underlying political concern, the range of things studied is very broad, and will vary with regard to the agenda of those who study and teach, from wishing to create deeper understanding, to hoping to cultivate activism and foster change, both in attitudes and behavior. These "new arrivals" in the curriculum grew out of social movements of the 1960s, with roots going back, of course, to earlier times. Besides sharing a common concern for injustice and oppression, these curricular movements all faced a common dilemma: whether to create separate programs, or whether to infuse their concerns into the "regular" curriculum, or both. Each of these areas discovered that, as new areas of study, they needed to draw upon existing tools of scholarship and available faculty from the disciplines. Eventually, they created new literatures and new methods of scholarship especially relevant to their concerns. It is not surprising that these areas have created, as one of their curricular expressions, interdisciplinary, team-taught courses.

Perhaps the best recent summary of the purposes and scope of women's studies programs is the report under the sponsorship of the Coordinating Council of the Women's Studies Association that appears in *Reports from the Fields*.[17] As noted in the report, "the central organizing category of analysis in women's studies is the concept of gender," and the programs are usually "built from a variety of curricular building blocks." Most programs are made up of a series of "cross-listed" courses drawn from the disciplines, but "virtually all women's studies programs supplement cross-listed courses with interdisciplinary or transdisciplinary courses sponsored by the women's studies program itself."[18]

The concept of women's studies courses goes back to the late 1960s, with credit for the first complete program going to San Diego State University in 1970.[19] The number of courses grew through the 1960s so that by 1970 there were over 100 women's studies courses, and by 1971, more than 600. In a decade, that number had grown to 350 programs and 30,000 courses.[20] Increasingly, women's studies has become more than a body of information and has become established as "an approach, a critical framework through which to view all knowledge," that stresses "dialectical ways of thinking that emphasize making connections of all kinds and holding together things that seem contradictory." For example, "the introductory course typically is organized thematically to introduce students to some of the key feminist issues such as identity formation, cultural representations, work, family, sexuality, violence, class stratification, and racial and cultural diversity. Studying such topics requires an interdisciplinary approach that teaches students to connect their inquiry across several disciplines."[21] Although women's studies courses have usually invited the participation of men, even though the focus has been on women's issues, some courses have been conceived of more broadly to address gender issues affecting both men and women. The examples presented below illustrate several different types of courses.

An interesting example of a course that stresses gender issues more broadly is offered at the University of Hartford. It examines gender formation and influence through the life cycle for both males and females.

SEX, SOCIETY, AND SELFHOOD

Institution: University of Hartford

Intended Audience: General education core, but open to first-through fourth-year students

Disciplines Represented: Communication theory, cultural studies, education, psychology, rhetoric and composition, and sociology

Personnel: Eight to ten total divided into teams of three

General Description: The course begins at birth and moves through childhood, adolescence, and into adulthood. It explores such areas as family dynamics, education, work, leisure, and the popular culture in order to investigate the kinds of roles that are being encouraged for men and women and boys and girls to take up in our culture. The course is designed to explore how (or whether) those roles are changing as we move into the twenty-first century. What kinds of options do males and females have within our culture. What ranges of behaviors and beliefs overlap for men and women in our culture? What kinds of contradictory messages does our culture give about the roles we "should" take up? Students' personal experiences growing up as a gendered being form the center of the course. Students are asked to think about certain issues, to begin, for example, by remembering the kinds of toys they played with as a child. By examining other people's experiences in the class and by looking at published work on the subject, a broader perspective is established. Students are asked to analyze many objects in American culture that are infused with values about gender—from TV to songs and films—objects that, before this course, may have simply have been taken at face value.

Selected Topics: Child's Play: Ideology and the Construction of Gender in Baby and Childhood Playthings, Products, and Entertainment. Up Close and Personal: Girls and the Fairy Tale. All in the Family: Psychodynamics' in the Home and the Construction of Gender. Anything You Can Do, I Can Do Better: Comparing Boys' and Girls' Cognitive Abilities. What They Didn't Teach Me at School: The Role of Gender in Shaping Gender Roles. Dominant Representations of Women: Masochism, the Body, and Femininity. Representations of Men: Sports, the Body, and Masculinity. Gender and Work: Gender and Status.

Distinctive Feature: The program examines both male and female gender formation, and is a definite contrast to "feminist" courses, being designed with the purpose of attracting both men and women to the course in ways that feminist courses often do not. The program makes intentional efforts at integration of disciplinary perspectives and encourages students to use material from one discipline to examine material from another. It is also writing intensive, assigning students to write a gender-focused autobiography that is developed and revised as the course proceeds, requiring students to reconsider material studied earlier in the course in light of material studied later.

Contact Person: Kathleen McCormick, Dept. of Rhetoric, Language and Culture, University of Hartford, West Hartford, CT 06117, Work Phone: (203) 768-4415, Fax: (203) 768-5043

Women's Interests and Concerns

Other courses are more clearly feminist in their orientation, and although men are welcome in these courses and could certainly profit from them, these courses are more clearly directed to the interests and concerns of women. Because women's studies is itself an interdisciplinary field of study, it is not surprising that the introductory survey courses designed to introduce students to the field are also frequently interdisciplinary. The course at Williams College serves as a good example of an interdisciplinary introductory course at the undergraduate level. The course from the University of Southern California is a good example of an advanced introductory course for graduate students.

INTRODUCTION TO FEMINIST THOUGHT

Institution: Williams College
Intended Audience: Women's studies students or general elective
Disciplines Represented: Literature, history, philosophy, psychology, political science, economics
Personnel: Three or four faculty

General Description: This course is designed to initiate students into the pleasures, pains, and perplexities of critical thinking about gender. The intent is to survey a wide variety of thinkers and issues—historical and contemporary, theoretical and practical. Above all, the course is intended to establish the tremendous diversity of thought under the general rubric of "feminism," to introduce students to contemporary debates within feminism, and to offer tools of analysis for future work.

Selected Topics: What is feminism? Why theory? Liberal Feminism, Marxist and Socialist Feminism, Radical Feminism/Standpoint Women at Work, Women and the Family, Women's Words/Women's Power, The Lesbian Continuum, The Body Politic, Sex and Love, Reproductive Freedom.

Distinctive Features: The course offers a breadth of exposure to many topics with an interesting balance of lecture, discussion, and reading of key texts. Students meet in study groups before class to generate questions for discussion. Students are assigned group projects on key topics and are graded as a group for this exercise.

Contact Person: Jana Sawicki, Stetson Hall, Women's Studies, Williams College, Williamstown, MA 01267, Work Phone: (413) 597-2305, Fax: (413) 597-4088

FEMINIST THEORY (cross listed as Feminist Legal Theory)

Institution: University of Southern California
Intended Audience: Law students and graduate students from a variety of disciplines and professional fields

Disciplines Represented: Law, sociology, and the fields represented by the students

Personnel: Two professors, one from law, one from sociology

General Description: This course explores major perspectives and contexts for feminist theorizing and includes a "map" of feminist theories, major analytic traditions, categories, claims, and debates. The focus is on the deployment of these theories in contexts such as law, labor, sexualities, and cultural representations. The goal is to understand the theories, learn how contexts have influenced them, and how they have influenced contexts.

Selected Topics: Women as a Category of Analysis: Claims of Sameness and Difference and the Difference It Makes; Gender and Relationships of Dominance; Gender and Epistemology: What do Women Know? How Do they Know It? How Do We Know About Women? Theories and the Practice of Representation. Postmodernism and the Problem of Practice.

Distinctive Features: A beginning class at an advanced level for graduate students interested in interdisciplinary perspectives on feminist theory. Papers focus on analyses, reflection, and commentary on the extensive assorted readings.

Contact Persons: Judith Resnick, University of Southern California Law Center, University Park, Los Angeles, CA 90089-0071, Work Phone: (213) 740-4789, Fax: (213) 740-5502

Barrie Thorne, University of Southern California, Sociology Dept., Kaprielian Hall 358, Los Angeles, CA 90089-0071, Work Phone: (213)740-2791

Advanced Topics

Other women's studies courses explore advanced topics. Some employ great inventiveness in bringing together distant fields to explore unusual themes, such as those developed at the University of Dayton, the University of Southern California, the University of Oregon, Miami University (Ohio), and the University of Michigan.

FOCUS ON WOMEN

Institution: University of Dayton

Intended Audience: Required of Women's Studies interdisciplinary minors but lectures free and open to the public

Disciplines Represented: Topic changes each year as do disciplines represented

Personnel: Faculty coordination and guest lecturers from diverse disciplines

General Description: Seminar Topic for 1993 was Science, Technology and Gender Issues. The seminar examines the androcentric bias in the way science is conceived and pursued, and explores ways in which this bias can be corrected to attract more women and minorities into the fields of science and technology. In 1994 the seminar topic was Women Creating Culture. Students explored some of the many ways in which women have contributed to the development of culture as gatherers, healers, artists, and organizers, as well as mothers and wives. Lecturers focused on women artists and composers, midwifery, lesbian culture and women's gifts to creative approaches to ministry.

Selected Topics: For 1993 the topics included Issues of Gender-Bias in the Study of Science, Reproductive Theories in Female Medicine, Women Subjects in Scientific Testing, Women's Contributions to Science and Technology, Careers in Science, Objectivity and Values in Science, Modern Technology and the Environment, and Product Design for Women in the Workplace.

Distinctive Features: Many disciplines are brought to bear on a unifying theme. Seminar topics change each year as a new subject is invented around feminist concerns. Integration takes place through the imaginative arrangement of topics by the course coordinator.

Contact Person: Judith G. Martin, SSJ. Ph.D., University of Dayton, Women's Studies Program, Dayton, OH 45469, Work Phone: (513) 229-4285, Fax: (513) 229-4330

HUMOR IN WOMEN'S LITERATURE AND MUSIC
Institution: University of Oregon
Intended Audience: Intermediate to advanced seminar
Disciplines Represented: English and music
Personnel: Two women faculty

General Description: Humor in Women's Literature and Music examines how laughter, literature, and music as modes of expression intersect in American women's writing and music of the twentieth century. Together, faculty and students explore distinctive ways that contemporary women writers and composers use such types of humor as the following: surprise (the unexpected, incongruent), satire (ridicule of human folly or foible with an intent to educate), parody (application of a manner or technique of a well-known writer/composer), caricature (exaggeration of characteristic details), and merriment (good humor, pleasure, or delight). The course is also designed to explore the relationship of women's uses of humor to this country's central cultural and political movements since 1950.

Selected Topics: The literature is by Terry McMillan, Rita May Brown, Megan Terry, Katherine V. Forrest, Kathleen Alcala, Gloria Naylor, et al. The music examined is by such contemporary women composers as Vivian Fine, Joan Tower, Cathy Berberian, Pauline Oliveros, Anne Le Baron, Susan McClary, et al. Selections fit the categories of humor under general description.

Distinctive Features: Designed as a seminar, the course focuses on listening to key musical works and reading representative texts for class discussion. Offered through the Humanities Center and intended for a general audience, this course is an exploration of women's issues through the creations of women intended as humorous.

Contact Person: Dr. Monza Naff, Robert D. Clark Honor College, University of Oregon, Eugene, OR 97403, Work Phone: (503) 346-5414, Fax: (503) 346-2220

WOMEN AND THEATER: THE POLITICS OF REPRESENTATION

Institution: Miami University

Intended Audience: Second-year students in Interdisciplinary Studies (Western College Program)

Disciplines Represented: Drama, literary criticism, film criticism, feminist theory, psychoanalysis, history, anthropology

Personnel: Two faculty and up to three assistants

General Description: In this course, students read, interact with and respond to texts drawn from drama, literary criticism, film criticism, feminist theory, psycho-analysis, history, and anthropology in a number of creative and provocative ways. Course goals include, among others, increasing students' familiarity with a variety of dramatic forms; teaching them to integrate theoretical materials with various forms of expression; enriching their understanding of the relationship between artistic prod-ucts and cultural agenda; helping them to examine societal patterns of power and assumptions about suitable roles and behavior for women; developing their skills as critical thinkers and "resistant readers"; and training them to read and critique a visual text. Throughout the semester, students actively engage course texts and themes by participating in a wide variety of hands-on, inquiry-based, visual, textual, and artistic activities, interactive and multi-media lectures, improvisatory exercises, and interdisciplinary writing assignments, and by attending local theatrical perfor-mances and dress rehearsals. Moreover, students collaborate with one another inside and outside of class to design, interpret and act out original and text-derived scenework which they present to their peers. The highlight of the course occurs near the end when students create and perform elaborate personal and visual responses to the course's cross-disciplinary themes, writings, and activities. This course considers women and feminist issues from a cross-section of traditional and nontraditional disciplinary perspectives; it exposes students to the creative productions of lesser known white, black, Chicano, heterosexual, and lesbian women playwrights, and it involves an experimental and experiential (visual, textual, and performance-ori-ented), collaborative and student-centered pedagogy.

Selected Topics: Representing Women on Stage and Screen, Women Playwrights, Exploding the Canon, Women and Madness, Women and Violence

Distinctive Features: The course offers a unique pedagogy stressing active involve-ment of students. It is offered within the School of Interdisciplinary Studies and is designed to connect meaningfully to a broad audience of both male and female students who may initially lack interest in or be resistant to acting, performance, feminism, and multi-cultural or sexuality issues.

Contact Person: Sally Harrison-Pepper, School of Interdisciplinary Studies, (Western College Program), Miami University, Oxford, OH 45056, Work Phone: (513) 529-5672, Fax: (513) 529-5849, E-mail: harrison-pepper_ sally@msmail.muohio.edu

WOMEN'S REPRODUCTIVE HEALTH

Institution: University of Michigan
Intended Audience: An upper-level undergraduate course offered as a follow-up to "Perspectives on Women's Health"
Disciplines Represented: Medicine and nursing
Personnel: Two professors and numerous guest lecturers from medicine and nursing

General Description: The course explores the medical, social and political aspects of Women's reproductive health. Medical, nursing, public health, and feminist perspectives are presented on key issues.

Selected Topics: Prenatal Care, Teenage Pregnancy, Sexually-Transmitted Disease, and Menopause.

Distinctive Features: Students are exposed to the dialogue and debate across disciplines and are expected to discuss the personal relevance of issues explored. The course has its home in Women's Studies in the College of Literature, Science, and the Arts, but almost all of the faculty are from other colleges.

Contact Persons: Timothy R. B. Johson, Professor of Obstetrics, University of Michigan, Ann Arbor, MI 48109, Work Phone: (313)763-0983, Fax: (313) 763-5992

Carolyn Sampsell, Associate Professor—Nursing, University of Michigan, Ann Arbor, MI 48109, Work Phone: (313) 747-0142, Fax: (313) 747-0351

Multicultural Themes

Some courses on women introduce a multicultural element. (See Multicultural and Ethnic Studies below.) Not all women, of course, are the same, and some have had very different experiences conditioned by their cultural and ethnic background. To acknowledge this difference and to explore the nature of these different experiences, the University of Michigan has designed a woman's studies course that invites comparison.

DIFFERENCES AMONG WOMEN

Institution: University of Michigan
Intended Audience: Undergraduate students interested in Women's Studies

Disciplines Represented: Psychology, history, women's studies
Personnel: Two faculty from women's studies with a disciplinary base in psychology and history

General Description: Central questions addressed in the course include the following: When do people sexed female identify themselves with collectivities called, for example, "women of color?" "working mothers?" "Americans?" "African Americans?" "lesbians?" What kinds of life experiences—family ties, nationality, sexual practices, discrimination, political activism, religious affiliations, degrees of affluence or impoverishment—tend to consolidate what kinds of identifications? How are these life experiences and identifications interconnected and dependent upon one another and upon the life experiences and identifications of people sexed male? How, in particular, has the history of the U.S.—a multiracial collectivity characterized by profound inequities of race, class, and gender — created and been created by such experiences and identifications?

Selected Topics: History of Women Thinking about Differences; Theorizing Categories of Difference; Sites of Difference; Theorizing Difference and Domination; Local Knowledge/Global Visions; Making a Difference

Distinctive Features: Students work in pairs on anthologies of women's writings to prepare critical papers on how differences among women are understood. An interesting mix of guest lectures, student presentations, readings, and discussion is used to explore differences from an interdisciplinary perspective.

Contact Persons: Andrea Hunter, Psychology and Women's Studies, University of Michigan, 5063 ISR, Ann Arbor, MI 48109, Work Phone: (313) 763-2481, Fax: (313) 747-4943

Susan Johnson, History and Women's Studies, University of Michigan, L-317 Winchell, Ann Arbor, MI 48109, Work Phone: (313) 763-7862, Fax: (313) 747-4943

MULTICULTURAL AND ETHNIC STUDIES

Although definitions for multicultural and ethnic studies vary from campus to campus, "what the programs have in common is a specific or comparative focus on groups viewed as 'minorities' in American society." Although European immigrants have from time to time been thought of as minorities, "groups of color" have become the focus of most ethnic studies programs, that is, "'the unmeltable ethnics' or ethnics without options regarding whether to invoke their ethnicity."[22]

Ethnic studies were born from the student movements of the late 1960s, and were part of a larger agenda that included demands for "equal access to higher education, changes in the curriculum, the recruitment of more professors of color, and the creation of ethnic studies programs."[23] Beginning with strong organized pressures to create "Black Studies" programs, other programs, representing the interests of other minority groups, were also soon developed. Today there are over 700 ethnic studies programs or departments in the United States, with an array of national professional associations, including organizations for Black, Chicano, Asian American, Puerto Rican, and American Indian Studies, as well as the National Association for Ethnic Studies.[24] Some view the present status of these programs with alarm, but for opposite reasons. Some people say that in spite of strong efforts by ethnic studies advocates, the curriculum remains "Eurocentric," with diversity concerns still largely marginalized. Others say that "the academy currently is purging the curriculum of its historic canon and replacing it willy-nilly with non-Western, ethnic and gender studies." In a reflective response to this rhetoric, based on a nationwide survey of 196 colleges and universities, Arthur Levine and Jeanette Cureton suggest that neither view fits the facts, and that there has been a "quiet revolution" in which multicultural studies have found several appropriate niches within the existing curriculum.[25] The results of the study show that more than one-third of all institutions have a multicultural general education requirement, that at least one-third of all colleges and universities offer course work in ethnic and gender studies, and that more than half have introduced multicultural themes into departmental course work.[26] One trend in larger universities today is the integration of separate African-American, Chicano, and Asian American studies programs into larger ethnic studies programs that stress collaboration and comparative studies. Examples include programs at the University of California, Berkeley; the University of California, San Diego; the University of Washington; the University of Colorado at Boulder; and, one of the oldest "combined" programs, at Bowling Green State University in Ohio.[27]

As they developed, ethnic studies programs, like women's studies programs, had to create both curriculum and methodology, and in doing so, they drew upon existing disciplinary resources while creating interdisciplinary courses and curricula. Black studies programs (referred to variously as "Afro-American," "African and Afro-American" and "African" studies, depending on the emphasis given to the specifically American experience),[28] provide an interesting example of how interdisciplinary approaches developed. The study of the African-American experience has a longer, formal history, perhaps, than other ethnic studies programs, including an earlier creative phase by some of the earliest black academics (including the foundation by Carter G. Woodson of the Association for the Study of Afro-American (formerly Negro) Life and History in 1915); a second stage, dominated by European and white American scholars; a third stage, beginning roughly in the mid-1960s in which black and white scholars from a variety of disciplines began to create interdisciplinary studies and programs; and now a fourth stage in which "Africana studies has achieved legitimacy and has become

institutionalized within American higher education," now being characterized by "theoretical refinement and more sophisticated analysis and interpretation."[29] On the other hand, as others pointed out, programs continue to
exist "on the fringe or periphery of the 'regular' liberal arts curriculum."[30] At
their best, black studies programs challenge the existing curriculum. As
Johnnetta B. Cole notes,

> Black Studies challenges what is taught in the liberal arts curricula of
> America's colleges and universities; to whom and by whom it is taught;
> how it is taught; and why it is taught. These challenges represent a
> sweeping critique, followed by plans, proposals, curricula, and projects
> designed to begin to correct certain fundamental problems in American
> higher education."[31]

In developing the point about "how what is taught is taught," Cole notes that
a change in pedagogy is required:

> the loyalty to disciplines over knowledge, the territoriality of departments,
> and the sanctity of specialized, indeed professional versus general educa-
> tion are questioned. The call is for far greater dependence on an interdis-
> ciplinary approach.[32]

What Cole has said about black studies programs applies equally well to other
ethnic studies programs. What they provide is often a challenging "revision"
of the curriculum as well as an opportunity to examine old questions in a new
way through interdisciplinary perspectives.

Although courses on the experience of various minority groups abound in
various ethnic studies programs, they are often taught from a single disciplinary perspective, for example by a sociologist specializing in ethnic relations or
an American historian. Occasionally, an interdisciplinary approach is achieved
when scholars in differing fields bring their disciplines to bear on the same
material and time periods. This type of interdisciplinary collaboration, in this
case between a sociologist and literature professor, is illustrated by the course
at Elmhurst College described below. An interdisciplinary course on the
Chicano Movement is represented by the University of New Mexico. The
University of Arizona and the University of California—Los Angeles offer
courses in American Indian studies. The University of California—Sacramento offers a course on African studies.

THE AFRICAN-AMERICAN EXPERIENCE IN LITERATURE
Institution: Elmhurst College
Intended Audience: First-year honors students

Disciplines Represented: Sociology and English
Personnel: Two faculty

General Description: Students investigate the experiences of African Americans as depicted in literature for four main historical periods: Slavery (1619-1865), Post Civil War (1865-1954), Civil Rights (1954-1968), and Contemporary (1968-present). Issues such as the social structures, roles, and social interactions for blacks and between blacks and whites are investigated. Students engage in writing and discussion as modes of developing and sharing their understandings of the materials and issues. Objectives include being able to:

- Discuss the experiences of African Americans in each of the four major time periods based on representations of these experiences by black writers.
- Discuss strengths and weaknesses of various literary formats for depicting effectively the experiences of African Americans, for attracting black and white readers, and for aiding social understanding and change.
- Use a variety of written and oral formats to assist comprehension to develop critical thinking and writing skills, and to convey learning.

Selected Topics: Readings include Gates, *Classic Slave Narratives*; Angelou, *I Know Why the Caged Bird Sings*; Ellison, *Invisible Man*; Chapman, *Black Voices*; Bell, *Faces at the Bottom of the Well*. Students are also exposed to and encouraged to view films representative of the four periods.

Distinctive Features: The sociology professor provides content and discussion of socio-historical and cultural issues, and the English professor leads discussion of the literary texts. Small group discussion and evaluation of student work is overseen by both instructors. The course raises larger questions about the relationship of literature and society and the value of a variety of literary forms for their insight into the personal experiences of African Americans in American society.

Contact Persons: Dr. Brenda Forster, Dept. of Sociology, Box 51, Elmhurst College, Elmhurst, IL 60126, Work Phone: (708) 617-3083, Fax: (708) 617-3735

Dr. Ann Frank Wake, Dept. of English, Box 22, Elmhurst College, Elmhurst, IL 60126, Work Phone: (708) 617-3135, Fax: (708) 617-3242

THE CHICANO MOVEMENT
Institution: The University of New Mexico
Intended Audience: Undergraduate students
Disciplines Represented: Sociology, political science
Personnel: Two professors, one each from these disciplines

General Description: This course offers a retrospective examination of the Chicano movement, a social movement that developed within the Mexican-American community during the 1960s and 1970s. Several aspects of the movement are analyzed from a sociological and political standpoint, including movement activists, the movement's structure, and its strategies for social change. The course concludes with an assessment of the social and political consequences of the movement in light of contemporary events.

Selected Topics: Social Movements and Chicano History, Pre-Conditions of the Chicano Movement, The United Farm Workers, The Land Grant Issue in New Mexico, The Chicano Student Movement, The Brown Berets, El Partido de la Raza Unida, The Decline of the Chicano Movement, and Legacies of the Chicano Movement.

Distinctive Features: Provides a valuable social and political analysis of the Chicano Movement as one aspect of Chicano cultural history. Although the course has not been offered recently, other new team-taught courses are on the drawing board for a Chicano Studies minor. The current program is regarded as interdisciplinary in that it draws on the work of specialists in several arts and sciences disciplines, and efforts are under way to develop more collaboration.

Contact Person: Christine Sierra, Dept. of Political Science, Social Science Bldg. 2074, The University of New Mexico, Albuquerque, NM 87131-1121, Work Phone: (505) 277-1098, Fax: (505) 277-2821

AMERICAN INDIAN STUDIES
Institution: The University of Arizona
Intended Audience: Undergraduate students and students fulfilling General Education Program requirements.
Disciplines Represented: History, political science, law, anthropology, and literature
Personnel: Eight professors, teaching each in their area of specialization

General Description: This course examines diversity, successive colonization waves, and conflict between Native Americans and colonizing nations. It also explores the basic concepts and theories used in analyses of personal, social, cultural, political, economic, philosophical, and religious issues relating to Native American experience. Students examine issues of gender orientation, ethnic grouping, race and social class, self-identity, social difference, social status, and the effects of major institutions on individual experiences.

Selected Topics: Who is an Indian? The Hollywood Indian, Indian Country, Demographics and Diversity, Origins, World View, Spirituality, Precontact, Columbus (Encounter and Reaction), Indians and Colonial America, The Cherokees vs the U.S. Removal Policy, Allotment Act, Reservation Policy, Indian Education, Land Cessions, IRA/New Deal, Termination, Relocation, Urban Indians, Sovereignty, Self-Determination, Tribal Government, Art, Dance, Music, Literature, American Indian Women, Economic Development, Gaming, Religious Freedom, Repatriation, Water Rights, and Fishing Rights.

Distinctive Features: This course has a strong social and political issues emphasis and draws on several disciplines to examine how political and social structure has influenced the experience of Native Americans in the past and still today.

Contact Persons: Jay Stauss and Mary Jo Fox, American Indian Studies Program, Harvill 430, Tucson, AZ 85721, Work Phone: (520) 621-7108, Fax: (520) 621-7952

AMERICAN INDIAN STUDIES
Institution: University of California—Los Angeles
Intended Audience: General Education for Freshmen and Sophomores
Disciplines Represented: Law, anthropology, literature, music, linguistics, sociology, theater, etc.
Personnel: Eleven Faculty from the above specialties

General Description: This course provides introductory material about the culture, history, diversity, and contemporary issues of Native North American peoples. The first half of the course presents the diversity of precontact cultures. Selected case studies describe the "ethnographic present" with the intention of introducing the student to a holistic understanding of American Indian cultures and to an under-standing of the range and variation of Native American cultures. Overview of linguistic diversity, archaeological and migration patterns serve as general back-ground. The second half of the course emphasizes the diversity of cultural and political survival among Native peoples. Emphasis is given to understanding changing colonial relations, and the ways in which Indian peoples preserved culture, commu-nity, and political organization within rapidly changing economic, political, and cultural situations.

Selected Topics: Cultures and historical periods (precontact), Native American Religions, Native North American Languages, Comparative Ethnographic Law, South-west Cultures, Dance and Music of California, The Tlingit and Northwest Cultures, The Iroquois and Cherokee: The Northeast and Southeast, Colonial History, U.S. Policy Towards Indians, History and Contemporary Indian Law, Contemporary Tlingit and Northern Cheyenne Communities, Language Preservation and Survival, Indian Images in Film, Contemporary Literature, Native American Identity, Contem-porary Theatre and Media, and The Ethics of Repatriating Sacred Objects and Human Remains.

Distinctive Features: Native North Americans have many diverse cultures, histo-ries, and issues, and much of the course is devoted to interdisciplinary perspectives on cultural, linguistic, historical, and social diversity among Native North Americans. Faculty expertise is drawn from many sources to present a broad, stereotype-breaking overview.

Contact Persons: Duane Champagne, 3220 Campbell Hall, UCLA AI Studies
Center, Los Angeles, CA 90024, Work Phone: (310) 825-7315, Fax: (310)
206-7060

Carole Goldberg-Ambrose, 2437 Law School Bldg., UCLA College of Law,
Los Angeles, CA 90024, Work Phone: (310) 825-4429, Fax: (310) 206-6489

AFRICA: MYTHS & REALITIES
Institution: California State University—Sacramento
Intended Audience: General education students
Disciplines Represented: Humanities, Social Science
Personnel: Ten Africanist professors, each in his/her area of specialization

General Description: This is an interdisciplinary course which serves as an introduction to African Studies. It examines the most common myths found in both
popular and academic literature about Africa and its people.

Selected Topics: Caste, Class, Clan, Race, and Ethnicity in Africa, Languages of
Africa, Politics of Africa, African History, African Economy, African Art, African
Religions and Philosophies, African Culture, Communication in Africa, African
Justice Systems, and Literature in Africa.

Distinctive Features: The purpose of this course is to introduce Pan African Studies.
It is intended to introduce students to the context from which Pan African Studies
arose, including the Western intellectual tradition, while also taking into account
substantive objections to Pan African Studies as a legitimate academic discipline.

Contact Persons: Dr. Alexander Kimenyi, Cal State University—Sacramento,
Ethnic Studies Center, 6000 "J" Street, Sacramento, CA 95819-6013, Work
Phone: (916) 278-6645, Fax: (916) 278-5156

Dr. David Covin, Cal State University—Sacramento, Ethnic Studies Center,
6000 "J" Street, Sacramento, CA 95819-6013, Work Phone: (916) 278-6645,
Fax: (916) 278-5156

Cultural Interface

Some multicultural courses explore what takes place when cultures interface.
What happens when so-called "civilized" cultures interface with "less-well-
developed" cultures? How does the more dominant culture see the less-
developed, and how are both cultures influenced by this encounter? This can
take place through a broad international encounter that crosses the seas or
when a dominant culture encounters and responds to an ethnic sub-culture.
Two courses, in quite different ways, draw upon the skills of anthropologists
and literature professors to explore what happens when one culture encoun-

ters another, and what happens when one culture studies another. The courses offered at Mills College and Sarah Lawrence College provide provocative illustrations.

Tribal Cultures in Fact and Fiction

Institution: Mills College
Intended Audience: First-year undergraduates
Disciplines Represented: Anthropology, comparative literature
Personnel: Developed as team-taught for three years, but due to budget restrictions, now offered by the anthropologist alone

General Description: The course is an examination of the ways in which tribal and traditional cultures/peoples have been portrayed in anthropological as well as literary texts. Through critical readings, students seek to uncover the cultural assumptions, prejudices, and fantasies that have influenced the writers' perceptions and representations. From the discovery of "new" worlds in the fifteenth and sixteenth centuries to present-day plans for the modernization of "developing" nations, European and American writers have been fascinated, frightened, repelled, or inspired by those peoples they have alternately called "savage" or "primitive." Native peoples of Africa, the Americas, Australia, the South Pacific, and Asia became important metaphors for philosophers and fiction writers, and from the accounts written about them by travelers and missionaries a new scientific discipline, anthropology, was born. What can the representations by these observers tell us about relationships between cultures, between objectivity and subjectivity, between fiction and a science of the "other"? The course includes texts written by European and American authors about tribal cultures, asking such questions as What is the source of the author's data? What is the author's hidden agenda? How accurate are the portrayals? And will the real "Primitive" please stand up?

Selected Topics: Class sessions focus on reading texts and articles, such as Montaigne, "Of Cannibals"; Jefferson, "Notes on Virginia"; Golding, *The Inheritors*; Melville, *Typee*; Mead, *Coming of Age in Samoa*; Deloria, *Custer Died for Your Sins*; and others.

Distinctive Features: The course employs social science and literary perspectives to examine cultures that are different in level of development to raise the larger issue: What is "civilized" and what is "primitive"?

Contact Persons: Christian Marouby, Associate Professor, French, Mills College, 5000 MacArthur Blvd., Oakland, CA 94613, Work Phone: (510) 430-2215, Fax: (510) 430-3314

Ann Metcalf, Associate Professor, Anthropology, Mills College, 5000 MacArthur Blvd., Oakland, CA 94613, Work Phone: (510) 430-2341, Fax: (510) 430-2304

ETHNOGRAPHY AND LITERATURE

Institution: Sarah Lawrence College
Intended Audience: Third- and fourth-year students with background in literature or anthropology
Disciplines Represented: Anthropology, literature
Personnel: Two faculty

General Description: Ethnography has recently been referred to as a "curious genre of fiction" and, in a variety of ways, ethnographic and literary representations of other cultures have increasingly come to overlap and intersect. We have "ethnographic novels," culturally situated fictions (including Ruth Underhill's *Hawk Over Whirlpools* among the Papago, Oliver Lafarge's *Laughing Boy* among the Navajo, and Adolph Bandelier's classic on the Pueblo Indians, *The Delight Makers*) by authors who have also published formal "scientific" ethnographies on the same peoples. We have as well, today, ethnographic "dialogues" (for example, between Dennis Tedlock and the Zuni), ethnopoetic translations (such as those of Dell Hymes), and "discourse analyses" of speech styles (such as those by Keith Basso with Western Apache)—all refinements of ethnographic method with a focus on "oral literature." In another aspect, those peoples who were once only written about, now write back—and often in fictional or autobiographical forms (e.g., Leslie Silko, from Laguna Pueblo; James Welch, a Blackfoot; and N. Scott Momaday, a Kiowa) that make creative use of their cultural milieus and experience. All this grants us a particular opportunity to raise interesting questions about literary and ethnographic representation in the Americas, and to consider the hopes (and fears) of social science and the possibilities (and limits) of art.

Selected Topics: Discussion of works cited in general description.

Distinctive Features: The course examines ethnographic studies and fictional voices coming from the same culture, and provides an opportunity for comparing directly the similarities, differences, and overlaps from two seemingly unrelated, but related, disciplines.

Contact Person: Peter Whiteley, Ph.D., 140 Cabrini Blvd., Apt. 116, New York, NY 10033, Work Phone: (914) 395-2623, Fax: (914) 395-2666

INTERNATIONAL STUDIES

Although most educator's would agree that students need to learn more about other countries and cultures, there is no general consensus on how to achieve this. The traditional means to broadening international understanding has been through foreign language study, area specializations in history, geography courses, and, where they existed, international studies programs and majors. Today, there is a new awareness of the larger movement toward the "internationalization" of almost everything, including the development of a "global economy." The question of how to increase international awareness is being raised across the curriculum, and in previously unlikely places, such as business and engineering.[33]

As with other curricular movements, internationalization has its historical roots. Indeed, there was a rich period of American higher education, involving an intense interchange between the United States and Europe, not only of scholars, but of ideas about how higher education should be structured; many current practices are derived from this "international influence," such as the graduate school, the lecture method, and the independent scholar-researcher.[34] American higher education has always involved the study of foreign languages and classical writings from European scholarly traditions, but today the desire for "international knowledge" extends far beyond European boundaries and classical texts; what is desired today is more practical knowledge about how to function effectively in the global village.

Sarah Pickert, in the ASHE monograph entitled *Preparing for a Global Community*, has assembled a stimulating review of the different ways that colleges and universities have attempted in recent years to internationalize the curriculum. Among these are a revival and revitalization of foreign language study, core courses (general education) that address or incorporate international themes, the infusion of international topics into disciplinary courses, interdisciplinary studies, courses or programs in international relations, global education, peace studies, various aspects of ethnic studies, and the incorporation of international perspectives in professional programs.[35] Many of these efforts require at least modest interdisciplinary connections, and some involve full-blown interdisciplinary courses and programs.

"Internationalization" is itself, no pun intended, a "global" concept, and as such, suggests, in its essence, multiple perspectives. What people study when they examine other parts of the world can be history, culture, religion, literature, art, music, economic and political systems, geography, law, business practices, and so on. Depending on the focus of the inquiry, two or more disciplines are often combined. In other words, international themes and topics become almost natural interdisciplinary subjects.

One type of international studies course is the broad introduction to non-Western civilizations. Most of these courses require a team, because few faculty are trained as specialists in several cultures, except, perhaps, for a few world historians. A course from Syracuse University that focuses on cultivating an understanding of the present situation in selected countries around the world is described below. The thread that runs through the course is economics. How do various communities around the globe participate in or not participate in the emerging global economy?

GLOBAL COMMUNITY

Institution: Syracuse University

Intended Audience: First- and second-year undergraduates. Meets liberal arts core requirement

Disciplines Represented: Anthropology, economics, geography, history, political science, social science, sociology, writing program

Personnel: Eight faculty, one writing assistant

General Description: The course introduces students to some of the communities and segments of communities that constitute our world, to the evolving global economy, and to various cultural and communal adaptations and rejections of the established world order. The course aims to enable students first to hear a variety of the "voices" trying to shape our world, and secondly to examine their own aspirations and the contributions they can make to the global communities in which they will live out their lives. Travelling in a generally westward direction, the course begins with the global economy molded in the West, and then moves to the economically powerful yet culturally unfamiliar societies of Greater China and Japan. The course proceeds to communities rooted to various degrees in the religion of Islam, and then to those, drawn mainly from South Asia, which question participation in the global economy, before coming back to our own communities. In each of the units into which the course is divided, we seek to identify and understand the predominant voice, but also listen for contending and subordinated voices. In terms of class organization, Global Community has an unusual structure designed to give students the combined benefits of small classes and of a multinational, multidisciplinary faculty. Students are assigned in groups of no more than 15 to one professor, and meet twice a week in their group in a small classroom. But all the groups meet together each week on Wednesdays in the Maxwell auditorium for lectures and discussion by the course faculty. Occasionally in the evening we show films or videos, which are to be treated on the same basis as required reading.

Selected Topics: Economic Nationalism. Multinational Corporations, Regimes, Multinationals, and International Institutions. The Economic Giants: Japan and Greater China. East Asian Alternatives: Can One Have a Free Market Economy without Democracy? The Iranian Revolution: Causes and Outcome. Asian Islam: The Case of Indonesia.

Distinctive Features: The course offers selective snapshots of the contemporary global community with appropriate historical and cultural background. It integrates a large number of disciplines and areas of study as needed. The course is also "writing intensive," emphasizing critical thinking skills.

Contact Person: Professor Peter Marsh, Maxwell Undergraduate Teaching Grant, 306F Eggers Hall, Syracuse University, Syracuse, NY 13244, Work Phone: (315) 443-3061, Fax: (315) 443-9085

Area Studies

Another type of international studies course is the area studies course designed to provide an acquaintance with a particular area of the world. Courses like this often bring together faculty from different disciplines, for example history, art, and literature, to examine different aspects of a foreign culture. The course at Ithaca College is a good example of a team-taught area studies course. Sometimes a deeper acquaintance with an area is achieved by traveling to the area and actually living, studying, and working there. The course at Goshen College illustrates how an interdisciplinary team of college faculty and local educators approach area studies through a travel course.

INTRODUCTION TO JAPANESE CULTURE
Institution: Ithaca College
Intended Audience: Sophomores and juniors without prior knowledge about Japan
Disciplines Represented: History, art history, literature, anthropology, philosophy, religion, and economics
Personnel: Two faculty supplemented by guest lecturers

General Description: An introduction to Japanese culture is an all-purpose first course on Japan, capable of standing alone, or as a class that prepares students for a variety of upper-level offerings on Japan available at Ithaca College. An interdisciplinary approach is used to discuss trends and patterns in Japanese culture. For example, the secular, religious, and aesthetic manifestations of patterns in Japanese are explored as a recurring way of dealing with outside influences. These patterns become evident in a general chronological sequence of historical events. Students are expected to develop a deeper understanding of Japanese culture that moves beyond cliches and headline generalizations that have, for years, plagued Americans' response to Japan. Developing the ability to form intelligent questions pertaining to any aspect of Japanese society is another goal.

Selected Topics: Topics include the typical historical subdivisions plus such topics as addressing stereotypes, economic growth, the arts in Japan, and continuity and change.

Distinctive Features: Both professors attend all lectures, often commenting on each other's lectures or developing "co-presented" lectures. Sometimes the same material or object of art is examined from different perspectives. Besides lecture, the professors collaborate in developing discussion exercises that encourage students to be active participants in examining the differences between Japanese culture and more familiar cultures.

Contact Person: Professor John R. Pavia, Dept. of History, Ithaca College, Ithaca, NY 14850-7283, Work Phone: (607) 274-3035, Fax: (607) 274-2474

STUDY-SERVICE TERM

Institution: Goshen College
Intended Audience: Second- and-third year undergraduates
Disciplines Represented: Foreign language, intercultural communication, social
   science, humanities, natural science
Personnel: Faculty member and spouse or assistants supplemented by local
   lecturers and language teachers.

General Description: The Study-Service Term is a program designed to immerse students for three months in a culture significantly different from that of the United States as a part of their general education at Goshen College. The first seven weeks of the term are spent in more structured study of the language and culture of the host country. The faculty leaders (a GC faculty member and spouse or assistant) use local resources and a variety of teaching-learning methods, including lectures, discussion, field trips, journal writing, readings, special projects and examinations. During the last six weeks of the term, the student works alongside host nationals in a field/ service-learning assignment, usually in a rural area. Throughout the term, students live in homes of the host country and eat at least two meals daily with their "families." There is a prerequisite of level 102 in the language of the host country.

The student normally receives 13 credit hours distributed as follows:

> Foreign Language, 4 hours; Intercultural Communication, 3 hours; Social Science, 3 hours; Humanities, 2 hours; and Natural Science, 1 hour. Current SST locations are in Costa Rica, Dominican Republic, Côte d'Ivoire, Germany, and Indonesia. Other recent units have operated in China and Guadeloupe.

The goals of the international education program are integrally related to the following desired educational outcomes of Goshen College:

- Intercultural openness, the ability to function effectively with people of other world views.
- Effective communication in another culture.
- Active and strategic thinking, emphasizing proficiency in self-directed learning.
- A healthy understanding of self and others.

Selected Topics: Representative topics and activities include conversation and grammar classes in the language of the host country, conversation with families, intercultural communication; economic, social, political and historical realities of the host country; attendance at cultural events and museums; journal writing; awareness of flora and fauna; visits to national parks; lectures on cloud forests and volcanoes; and visits to a tropical garden and snake farm.

Distinctive Features: The program integrates formal learning and experience-based learning on-site in the host country through total involvement in living, learning, and service. The program is directed at development of the student as a whole person. Students earn a block of 13 credits for Study-Service Term.

Contact Person: Dr. Wilbur Birky, 1700 South Main, Goshen, IN 46526, Work
    Phone: (219) 535-7346, Fax: (219) 535-7319

Cultural Comparison

Some courses in international studies stress comparison. Because certain
phenomena are different from culture to culture, they invite comparison. For
example, all societies have developed legal systems. To what extent are these
systems similar or different? The course in Comparative Legal Systems at the
University of Texas—Austin provides a good example of an interdisciplinary
format used to invite comparison.

COMPARATIVE LEGAL SYSTEMS
Institution: University of Texas—Austin
Intended Audience: Undergraduates in the honors program
Disciplines Represented: Classics, Asian studies, and history
Personnel: Three professors from these departments

General Description: This course is designed to introduce students to three classical
traditions in law, the legal traditions of Classical Greece and Classical India, and the
early common law period of the Common Law in England.

Selected Topics: What is the structure of the legal system? What is the role of
courts, judges, jurors, and lawyers? How does the legal system relate to and interact
with other institutions in society? What is the connection between religion and law?

Distinctive Features: This course is taught by three authorities on three very
different legal systems. They address cultural and political history as it pertains to the
law. They plan together, teach together, and develop evaluation exercises together.
In combination they try to give students a knowledge of each of the three systems, an
understanding of law in general, and a comparative perspective on our own legal
system. They achieve this by combining assignments and having the students write
two papers on two of the three areas. The final take home exam is a comparative study
in which students explain how all three systems would each deal with a specific
situation.

Contact Person: Michael Gagarin, Classics, Wagner 123B, C3400, University of
    Texas—Austin, Austin, Texas 78713, Work Phone: (512) 471-8864, Fax: (512)
    471-4111

Cultural Themes

Another type of international studies course focuses on one event or theme,
such as the Holocaust, the break-up of the Soviet Union, the Vietnam War,
or Human Rights. An example of a theme course is found at Mississippi

University for Women. The tragedy of Vietnam is explored through key nonfiction readings, novels, and recent films about Vietnam. Another theme course on human rights is offered on the graduate level at the Univeristy of Denver.

VIETNAM IN FILM AND LITERATURE

Institution: Mississippi University for Women
Intended Audience: Special topics seminar in history, majors and elective students/cross-listed as upper level seminar in American Literature
Discipline: English, history, literature, film
Personnel: Two faculty, limited number of guests

General Description: An exploration of the Vietnam War through nonfiction books, novels, and films. This is an interdisciplinary course designed to explore the history of the American experience of the Vietnam War. Although history, literature, and film study constitute the core of the course and reflect the primary areas of focus for the course, attention will also be given to sociology, economics, psychology, and popular culture. The emphasis will be on film and literature as devices for representing and for coming to terms with the Vietnam War as a culturally disruptive event in American history.

Selected Topics: Nonfiction literature such as narratives. Also, examples of films and novels studied are Baker, *NAM*; Hearden, *The Tragedy of Vietnam*; Herr, *Dispatches*; Webb, *Fields of Fire*; and films, such as *The Green Berets*; *Go Tell the Spartans*; *Good Morning, Vietnam*; *Born on the Fourth of July*; and *Rambo II: First Blood Part II*.

Distinctive Features: The course focuses on a particular historical event and important cross-cultural tragedy by combining vivid portrayals in film and novels with analytical readings. Students are challenged to write thoughtful analyses and personal reactions.

Contact Person: Dabney Gray, P.O. Box W-1634 MUW, Columbus, MS 39701, Work Phone: (601) 329-7392, Fax: (601) 329-7297

INTERNATIONAL HUMAN RIGHTS LAW AND POLICY

Institution: University of Denver
Intended Audience: Graduate students in international studies, law, social work, theology, and business
Disciplines Represented: Law and international studies
Personnel: Two faculty, College of Law, Graduate School of International Studies

General Description: This course provides both a legal and international policy perspective on human rights issues. Students from a variety of professional programs examine human rights policy, do extensive reading, and prepare publishable research papers.

Selected Topics: International Treaties, Commissions, Committees, and Courts; Writing Petitions and Memoranda; Cultural and Political Context of Human Rights Issues; Factors in International Policy Making.

Distinctive Features: Two teachers in different colleges (Law and International Studies) discovered they were each teaching a course on "International Human Rights." One course had a legal emphasis; the other stressed cultural and political context and issues of policy. Having worked together previously on an NEH summer program that brought together human rights specialists from around the country and resulted in an edited book, *Human Rights and Third World Development*, the two professors took up the challenge of making their two courses into one, integrating their interests, knowledge of the literature and teaching methods. When one professor retired, the other continued on alone, but with the interdisciplinary perspective learned from interaction with his colleague.

Contact Person: Ved Nanda, Director of International Legal Studies, College of Law, Lowell Thomas Law Bldg. F205, University of Denver, 1900 Olive Street, Denver, CO 80220, Work Phone: (303) 871-6276, Fax: (303) 871-6001

CAPSTONE AND INTEGRATIVE COURSES

A new kind of course has appeared in recent years, the capstone course, sometimes designated "integrative seminar." These courses are like general education courses, and sometimes appear as part of the general education curriculum; but unlike general education courses, which are usually thought of as introductory or foundational, these courses are advanced, and usually are taken at the end of a student's course of studies. These courses are designed for advanced students, who have already completed most of their major. The main purpose of these courses is to integrate the work done within the major or to relate that work to fields outside the major or both. Sometimes these courses are called "capstone" (as in "the finishing stone of a structure") or simply "integrative seminars." In some instances, the purpose of integrative seminars is to provide students an opportunity not only to reflect on their major, but to pull together and reflect on their entire undergraduate experience. Occasionally this is a required common learning experience involving all students.

The idea of the capstone seminar was given visibility and support in the recent report of the Association of American Colleges and Universities, *The Challenge of Connecting Learning*.[36] One of the report's recommendations was that:

> the end of the major ought to be a time for integrating knowledge, concepts, and capacities from the different parts of students' learning experiences. Programs can support this work by establishing structures, such as the capstone course, which allow broad reflective and critical

views of the field of concentration or bring together students from adjacent fields to explore their similarities and differences.[37]

The rationale for capstone courses appears elsewhere in the report. Briefly, the argument is made that the major provides a "home" for certain kinds of learning, and that the role of the faculty in the major is to give students the intellectual structures and languages that support life in this home. As students progress in their major, they "develop an increased capacity to understand and employ a range of topics and analytical tools, as well as characteristic questions and arguments specific to a domain of inquiry."[38] What students also need to learn, however, is that the discipline provides a "partial perspective."

> Viewed this way, a major requires engagement and disengagement and provides opportunities for both joining and leaving. A student enters the "home" offered by the major in order, finally, to be able to leave it and see it from the outside in, by taking the knowledge, experience, and wisdom gained therein and testing them against the perspectives of other fields and the challenges of the world outside.[39]

Capstone courses and integrative studies are designed to provide a perspective on the major both from within and from without. The examples from Worcester Polytechnic Institute, Sarah Lawrence, Kansas State University, University of Northern Iowa, Dalhousie University, University of Wisconsin—Green Bay, and Earlham College provided illustrations of different types of integrative seminars with varying purposes. They all employ interdisciplinary formats.

LIGHT, VISION, AND UNDERSTANDING
Institution: Worcester Polytechnic Institute
Intended Audience: Seminar for third-year and fourth-year students in science, engineering, and management
Disciplines Represented: Biology, physics, philosophy, psychology, art history, computer science
Personnel: Two full-time and two part-time faculty; planning involved six faculty and four consultants

General Description: The purpose of the course is to allow students to see how developments in science occur in a cultural context, to encourage students to question the traditional boundaries between the sciences and the humanities, and to encourage them to rethink their most unquestioned assumptions about science and about everyday life. The course deals with fundamental experiences of the ordinary world and themes sufficiently broad and important as to have had substantial impact in both the sciences and the humanities. It also has an intrinsic experimental and observational component and a genuinely multidisciplinary structure. Topics focus on the nature of light and vision and the relationship of seeing to understanding. Laboratory experiments range from constructing a perspective picture and reproducing some of Newton's prism observations to carrying out color vision demonstrations on a computer. The course is conducted as a seminar, and students carry out experiments on their own.

Selected Topics: Greek and Arabic theories of vision, the discovery and invention of perspective, seeing and knowing in post-Cartesian philosophy, Newtonian theory of light, the trichromatic theory of color, touch and sight, Goethe's theory of color, Romanticism, Impressionism and Post-Impressionism, photography, Gestalt psychology and avant-garde art, neurobiology of vision.

Distinctive Features: The course stretches across the disciplines from physics to art history and takes seriously the challenge of getting students in the sciences to reach out to and deepen their appreciation of the humanities. It is carefully planned to coax students across the science-humanities gap and to get them to reflect deeply on the philosophical issues relating to perception.

Contact Person: Professor Stephen Weininger, Dept. of Chemistry, Worcester Polytechnic Institute Worcester, MA 01609, Work Phone: (508) 831-5396, Fax: (508) 831-5485

SENIOR SEMINAR PROGRAM
Institution: Sarah Lawrence
Intended Audience: Primarily seniors but open to graduate students
Disciplines Represented: Varies with courses
Personnel: Faculty and guest speakers

General Description: Seniors at Sarah Lawrence are offered a series of interdisciplinary "capstone" seminars. The program consists of cooperatively planned and interrelated courses presented over two semesters by different faculty and supplemented by a monthly colloquium featuring faculty and guest speakers. One example of the senior seminars follows:

> **Senior Seminar in the Social Sciences: The Modern City—Technology, Democracy, and Political Economy**
>
> **Intended Audience:** Fourth-year students with 15 hours completed in the social sciences and interested graduate students
>
> **Disciplines Represented:** Political science, history of science
>
> **Personnel:** Two faculty plus guests
>
> **General Description:** The late twentieth century has given birth to the "megacity." With over 10 million inhabitants apiece, megacities like

Tokyo-Osaka, Seoul, the Los Angeles Basin, New York, Shanghai, Djakarta, and Mexico City are strong magnets for new cultures, new economies, new inequalities, and new conflicts. More than any time in the human past, the economic power directing flow of capital and wealth is centered in the megacities. In turn, megacities are assuming distinct and often unequal roles in the international economy. For world political and business elites, megacities represent a gigantic step forward as they promote rapid shifts and flexibility in production, investment, and labor. For ordinary people—immigrants, factory workers, clerical workers, the urban poor, and others—megacities are the sites where community, the promise of economic growth and of democracy are provided or denied. The politics and economies of different megacities are the foci of this course. What institutions and political assumptions give rise to megacities? Can community, equality and democracy be achieved in places where millions often live and work? Do neighborhoods, workplaces, ethnic or racial ties, or political parties provide meaningful associational ties in the megacity? Is the politics of the megacity inherently undemocratic, resting as it does on the ability of experts and elites to manipulate money, labor, and capital across large spaces and diverse populations? What institutions hold power in and amongst these new cities? Do they grow spontaneously or is there a discernible plan behind their development? How have ordinary people tried to shape the new cities in which they live, and what have been the results?

Selected Topics: North American and East Asian megacities, drawing on the general literature about cities and specific works about New York, Los Angeles, Tokyo, Shanghai, and Seoul. The readings and discussions trace the ways that elites and ordinary people view the city.

Distinctive Features: The course provides students in the social sciences with a way to do advanced work while synthesizing many other interests of their college work into a year-long project. It combines a seminar with colloquia presented by guest lecturers.

Contact Person: Ray Seidelman, Ph.D., 17 Belleview Avenue, Sarah Lawrence College, Ossining, NY 10562, Work Phone: (914) 395-2419, Fax: (914) 395-2666

Contact Person: Anne Lauinger, Ph.D., Sarah Lawrence College, Bronxville, NY 10708, Work Phone: (914) 395-2261, Fax: (914) 395-2666

THE NATURAL RESOURCES AND ENVIRONMENTAL SCIENCES SECONDARY MAJOR CAPSTONE COURSE

Institution: Kansas State University
Intended Audience: Students from other science majors pursuing a secondary major (comparable to a second major or sizable minor)
Disciplines Represented: Civil engineering, landscape architecture, agronomy
Personnel: Three faculty

General Description: The Natural Resources and Environmental Sciences Secondary Major Program provides an opportunity for students in any major to develop a concentration in environmental studies. Students must have pre-requisite courses in mathematics, chemistry, physics, and economics, and must select 15 credit hours from approved courses for the program. Students are also required to take this interdisciplinary capstone course team taught by three instructors from natural sciences, applied sciences, and social science and humanities. Although the topic may change, the focus of the course in the last two years has been on environmental issues relating to wetlands. Faculty and guest speakers explore scientific dimensions of wetlands, government laws and regulations, operations of wetlands, systems approach to planning and management, conflict resolution, and group decision making. As the issues are explored students work in interdisciplinary project teams of four or five students on topics suggested by the instructors. The students refine and prioritize the projects and eventually assign each team to a particular project. Periodic memos, a preliminary oral presentation, final oral presentation, and final written report are required from each team. The course also includes a field visit to a representative wetlands area.

Distinctive Features: The program provides a unique opportunity for a "second major" by drawing on the faculty resources of several disciplines and student expertise assembled from their own primary majors. This integrative capstone course encourages students to apply knowledge from their interdisciplinary major to a final comprehensive project focusing on wetlands environmental issues.

Contact Person: James K. Koelliker, Dept. of Civil Engineering, Seaton Hall, Kansas State University, Manhattan, KS 66506, Work Phone: (913) 532-1578, Fax: (913) 532-7717, E-mail: koellik@ksuvm.ksu.edu

ENVIRONMENT, TECHNOLOGY, AND SOCIETY
Institution: University of Northern Iowa
Intended Audience: Capstone course required for graduation, must have at least third-year standing
Disciplines Represented: Primarily from sciences and social sciences
Personnel: 20 faculty teaching in one semester drawn from a pool of 40

General Description: A lack of recognition of the connectedness of things has been partially responsible for adverse environmental impacts, economic failures, social programs that do not work, and the difficulties in achieving peace. On the other hand, seeing the connectedness of all things has permitted a greater understanding of the natural world plus fruitful approaches in the arts and sciences. One of the goals of this course is to build upon what students have learned in two or three years of disparate courses and to show how well-connected things are in this world. Another goal is to develop a higher degree of environmental literacy. David Orr, who has written on this subject, says educators have failed to teach about how the earth works. "By failing to include ecological perspectives in any number of subjects, students are taught that ecology is unimportant for history, politics, economics, society, and so forth." It is not the purpose of the course to dictate your values and personal positions relating to environmental, technological, and social issues, but to help you learn to think them through. To accomplish this, capstone challenges your assumptions, positions, and values in a number of areas to make you more environmentally literate.

Selected Topics: Madagascar: Five-fifths of Humanity, Earth in Space and Time: A Global View, The Ends vs. Means Concepts, Limits to Growth, Ends and Values, Ecology: A Normative Science?, The Land Ethic, Religion and the Environment.

Distinctive Features: This common learning course at the upper division level is a capstone designed to integrate students' previous work in science and in general education. The course is regarded as a rare requirement at public universities and is drawing attention as an "across-the-board" expectation to develop deeper understanding of environmental issues on the part of all graduates.

Contact Person: Lynn A. Brant, Dept. of Earth Science, University of Northern Iowa, Cedar Falls, IA 50614, Work Phone: (319) 273-6160, Fax: (319) 273-7124

SCIENCE FUNDAMENTALS
Institution: Dalhousie University
Intended Audience: Third-year and fourth-year students with honors standing in the Faculty of Science
Disciplines Represented: All of the science disciplines
Personnel: 25 faculty

General Description: Scientists of the future will have to work jointly on complex problems with others from a wide range of disciplines. For example, an environmental impact study may involve a team of biologists, earth scientists, physicists, engineers, oceanographers, meteorologists, etc. How do they approach problems? True, they are all scientists, but what is their common ground, and can they talk to each other? This course provides a head start on this type of interaction for advanced students looking forward to careers in science. The course objectives are to promote cooperative problem solving in science, to expose students to the practicalities of doing science in the real world, and above all to develop scientific communication skills, recognizing that no scientific investigation is complete until the results have been communicated clearly to the appropriate audience. Mastery of these abilities to think across disciplinary boundaries and to communicate effectively will contribute positively to the success of a scientific career.

Selected Topics: History of Science, Scientific Revolutions, Comparison of Scientific Methods, Methods of Handling and Interpreting Numerical Data, Database Searching Skills, Communication of Scientific Results, Scientific and Technical Writing, Oral Presentations, Journals, Conferences, Electronic Bulletin Boards, Research Environments, Basic vs. Applied Research, Funding, Contracts, Patents, Social Responsibility, Ethical Issues.

Distinctive Features: The course introduces students from several of the sciences to the real-world issues of supporting a career in science. This communications intensive course has four major papers, four minor papers, and four oral presentations, and places emphasis on funding sources and government relations in Canada.

Contact Person: D. Barrie Clarke, Earth Sciences, Dalhousie University, Halifax, Nova Scotia, B3H 3J5 Canada, Work Phone: (902) 494-3438, Fax: (902) 494-6889, E-mail: clarke@ac.dal.ca

Lost and Found: A Senior Seminar

Institution: University of Wisconsin—Green Bay

Intended Audience: Seniors completing a capstone seminar to complete general education requirement

Disciplines Represented: Cultural geography, literature, history, architecture

Personnel: Two faculty

General Description: This course explores objects, concepts, ideas, and ways of living that have been abandoned. To assist in this exploration, the course draws on the disciplines of history, literature, geography, and architecture. The key to this exploration lies in examining objects that have symbolic value but, though abandoned, are still with us. For example, consider the old bank building that is now a store selling satellite dishes; or the word "ROCKET" on the floor of Bill's Pancake House; or the old logging sled in Wabeno, WI. What are the meanings of these objects? To arrive at the meaning of these objects it is necessary to see them, measure them, determine their functions (current and past), and place them in their spatial and temporal context. Walking and bus field trips to selected urban, suburban, and rural locations are required. Visiting these sites provides students with models of research and the opportunity to interview individuals who have some affiliation with the structure and context of the site. In addition to field experiences, student research includes other primary sources, such as the Local History Room of the Brown County Library and the superb Wisconsin State Historical Society Area Research Center situated in UWGB's Cofrin Library. Students become familiar with tax records, plat maps, Sanborn fire insurance maps, manuscripts, court and company records, and village, town, and county records.

Selected Topics: Students read D.W. Menig, *The Interpretation of Ordinary Landscapes*, as well as Michael P. Conzen, et. al., *A Scholar's Guide to Geographical Writing on the American and Canadian Past*; J.B. Jackson, *Discovering the Vernacular Landscape*; J.B. Jackson, *A Sense of Place, A Sense of Time*; J. Jakle, *The Visual Elements of Landscape*; S. Kostof, *America by Design*; R. Von Tscharner, et. al., *New Providence: A Changing Cityscape*.

Distinctive Features: The course connects students to their ordinary surroundings and teaches them to see artifacts of the past in the present. The final project is a "biography of a building."

Contact Person: William G. Laatsch, Dept. of Geography, University of Wisconsin—Green Bay, Green Bay, WI 54311-7001, Work Phone: (414) 465-2355, Fax: (414) 465-2791

❖

PHILOSOPHY OF NATURAL SCIENCE
Institution: Earlham College
Intended Audience: Third-year and fourth-year science majors
Disciplines Represented: Philosophy, chemistry, biology, physics, geology
Personnel: Two faculty

General Description: This course is an introduction to the history of philosophy in general, whereby science students come to see how important the history of philosophy is in understanding the foundations of their own disciplines. It is unusual among philosophy of science classes in focusing on one big question: What constitutes the most adequate scientific explanation? Students read proposed answers to this question in the form of theories from Aristotle through Hume, Descartes, Kant, to more modern positions such as scientific realism and positivism. While the focus on one question allows an order to their inquiry and keeps from overwhelming the students, picking at that thread engages them in the whole fabric of the history of philosophy— epistemology, metaphysics, and ethics.

Selected Topics: Selected readings in the history of philosophy, including Clark and Bakka, *Explanation: An Introduction to the Philosophy of Science*; Kuhn, *Structure of Scientific Revolutions*; and Polany, *Science, Faith, and Society*, etc.

Distinctive Features: Students work in teams through the first half of the course to reach a "consensus" answer to the theme question of the course: What constitutes the most adequate scientific explanation? Why a consensus? Drawing on its Quaker roots and traditions, Earlham college seeks ways to encourage learning from and with others and the building of skills in collaboration. The course has been team taught over 20 years and now has a textbook by the two professors published in 1988, which is used as a textbook for the course.

Contact Person: Len Clark, Drawer 66, Earlham College, Richmond, IN 47374, Work Phone: (317) 983-1318, Fax: (317) 983-1616

ELECTIVES

Most colleges and universities make room in the curriculum for what have come to be known as electives. The idea of "elective" goes back to the mid-nineteenth century when Charles William Eliot, then president of Harvard, began to argue for a certain amount of student choice in selecting courses outside the prescribed classical curriculum. As the college curriculum of the early twentieth century began to settle into place, with its two primary components, general education and the major, each coming to occupy about one-third of the student's time, the remaining third remained open for "electives." At some institutions, elective hours are organized into a pattern for a minor, usually made up of studies closely related to the major; but for many students there is usually some place in their course of studies for free electives, courses that simply happen to be of interest. Because such courses are not required, either for general education or the major, they need to be attractive in order to draw student enrollments. Such courses often reside in the upper division offerings of a department, in honors programs, or in a special term, such as an interterm or summer session. Some of the most interesting courses to surface in the call for examples seem to fit nowhere— they are simply interesting electives. Often they deal with topics that have no apparent utilitarian value and rely on connecting with some natural interest that a student may have. The elective portion of the curriculum is another place to look for interdisciplinary team-taught courses. The courses listed here as examples are from Sarah Lawrence, the University of Michigan, Hobart and William Smith Colleges, Oberlin College, Marshall University, Johnson County Community College, Elmhurst College, and Columbia University.

Sensory Worlds: The Ecology, Physiology, and Psychology of Perception

Institution: Sarah Lawrence College
Intended Audience: Open to anyone other than first-year students
Disciplines Represented: Biology and psychology
Personnel: Two faculty

General Description: Honey bees "see" ultraviolet light that is invisible to humans, bats and dolphins "see" by using echoes from their own vocalizations, and snakes "see" by detecting infrared radiation that we experience as heat. Each organism lives in a sensory world that is shaped by evolutionary forces to reflect those features of the external world that are relevant for its life. What information is selected, and how is it captured by the sensory organs? How is this information represented by the brain/mind to yield a useful description of the environment? What is the relationship of that description to physical reality? Can experience modify preexisting capacities for sensory awareness? Workers from fields as divergent as neuroscience, psychology, philosophy, and computer science are beginning to band together to attempt to unravel these ancient and complex questions. Using methods and insights from these various disciplines, students are given the opportunity in this course to focus on how the brain acquires sensory information and produces mental representations of it. Theoretical analysis is balanced by practical demonstrations intended to reveal the exquisite sensitivity and fascination of the senses.

Distinctive Features: The course brings together a biologist and psychologist to explore recent fascinating work in animal and human perception, the "cognitive psychology" of nonhuman organisms as it provides insight into human perception. The course provides an interesting opportunity for students to explore, through a serious scientific and philosophical inquiry, what is meant by "reality."

Contact Person: Margaret Johnston, D. Phil., 380 Bronxville Road, Bronxville, NY 10708, Work Phone: (914) 395-2245, Fax: (914) 395-2666

WORDS AND MUSIC
Institution: University of Michigan
Intended Audience: Graduate student poets and musicians
Disciplines Represented: Poetry and music composition
Personnel: Two faculty plus an accompanist

General Description: This course brings composers and poets together to collaborate on original works. They study the basic forms of verse in English and the ways in which words and music can be combined. Some projects include setting poems to music, studying various popular song forms, exploring recitation with music, from melodrama to jazz poetry, and exploring how dramatic compositions move in the direction of opera. Performance of student collaborations are a regular feature of the class.

Distinctive Features: Student poets and student musicians collaborate in producing and performing creative works under the guidance of mentors from poetry and music. Various forms of poetry, with differing approaches to meter and rhyme, are explored as students produce illustrative projects. The goal is to find a compatible match between lyrics and song. Students learn about the art forms as well as the joys and difficulties of collaboration. A ratio of one poet to two or three composers works well.

Contact Person: William Bolcom, School of Music, University of Michigan, Ann Arbor, MI 48109-2085, Work Phone: (313) 763-2019, Fax: (313) 763-5097

PIECES OF LANDSCAPE: UPSTATE COBBLESTONES
Institution: Hobart and William Smith Colleges
Intended Audience: Open
Disciplines Represented: Art history and geology
Personnel: Two faculty

General Description: Cobblestone buildings are one of the most distinctive features of the landscape around the Colleges. These beautiful structures were built between about 1825 and 1860. They are constructed of rounded stones set in a lime mortar. The stones were left by the retreat of the glaciers 10,000 years ago; the lime mortar was made from glacial sands and much older local limestones. Working with these indigenous materials, cobblestone masons created a range of buildings, from fancy to utilitarian, but all distinctively "Upstate." This course surveys the geological history of our area to understand why the materials for cobblestone buildings are so abundant. It investigates nineteenth-century social and technological history as well as European antecedents of cobblestone construction to understand how these factors coalesced to produce the cobblestone buildings seen today, as well as the factors that eventually led to the abandonment of cobblestone construction. It studies the techniques, styles, and histories of individual buildings as well as the materials and methods of construction.

Distinctive Features: The course capitalizes on a unique architectural form visible in the region where the campus is located, and draws on the rather different insights of geologist and artist to understand how people used the earth materials available to them to create an unusual architectural form. It includes laboratories and field visits to quarries, canal sites, and buildings. The course culminates in the construction of a modest cobblestone structure.

Contact Persons: Professor Brooks McKinney, Geoscience, Hobart & William Smith Colleges, Lansing 006, Geneva, NY 14456, Work Phone: (315) 781-3819, Fax: (315) 781-3587

Professor Dan Ewing, Art, Hobart & William Smith Colleges, Houghton House 302, Geneva, NY 14456, Work Phone: (315) 781-3489, Fax: (315) 781-3689

THE MEANING OF LIFE
Institution: Oberlin College
Intended Audience: Open
Disciplines Represented: Classics, philosophy, theater, social commentary
Personnel: Two faculty

General Description: This Colloquium is an interdisciplinary inquiry into the meaning of life. The inquiry is directed to this perennial subject of human interest for its own sake, and is supported by readings from philosophy, literature, and drama. The strategy of the inquiry is to discern some of the major issues and concerns that make up the subject, and then to bring analysis and criticism to bear on them. Attention is given to works that speak in salient ways to questions about how one is to live and what kind of person one is to be, and in doing so proffer general conceptions of the meaning of life. The course provides an opportunity to consider the bearing of mortality and of contingencies of various kinds on views about the meaning of life. Also examined is the thesis that life is meaningless and its supposed implications, certain conceptions of the individual that inform major responses to the problem of the meaning of life, and some classical alternative basic attitudes (pessimism, optimism, resignation) as these are associated with such responses.

Distinctive Features: This course explores a developmentally relevant topic, focusing on sublime questions that many students would like to explore but seldom get to, because academic specialization militates against it. This bold examination of meaning through the exploration of carefully selected ancient and modern texts is writing intensive with an emphasis on discussion.

Contact Persons: Norman S. Care, Dept. of Philosophy, Oberlin College, Oberlin, OH 44074, Work Phone: (216) 775-8393, Fax: (216) 775-8124

Thomas Van Nortwick, Dept. of Classics, Oberlin College, Oberlin, OH 44074, Work Phone: (216) 775-8391, Fax: (216) 775-8124

SHAKE, RATTLE, AND ROLL
Institution: Marshall University
Intended Audience: Honors Program Students
Disciplines Represented: History and music
Personnel: Two faculty

General Description: This course describes the roots of rock-n-roll and protest music and analyzes their role in the civil rights and antiwar movements of the 1950s through the early 1970s. Particular attention is given to the inter-relatedness of the movements and the music, i.e., how the music promoted the goals of the movements and how the movements provoked and stimulated the writers, composers, and performers to push the music to new levels of involvement in and discussion of social and political issues. The course relies heavily on video and audio tapes, oral history interviews, readings, guest presentations by local individuals involved in the music or the movements or both, lectures, and class discussions.

Distinctive Features: One of a series of courses designed for honors students, this course requires a major research paper in which students are expected to integrate the disciplines of music and history.

Contact Persons: Robert Sawrey, History Dept., Marshall University, Huntington, WV 25755, Work Phone: (304) 696-3347, Fax: (304) 696-6565

Ann Marie Bingham, Music Dept., Marshall University, Huntington, WV 25755, Work Phone: (304) 696-3147, Fax: (304) 696-3232

IN SEARCH OF SOLUTIONS
Institution: Johnson County Community College
Intended Audience: Open
Disciplines Represented: Changes each time
Personnel: Two faculty per semester, with one new each term

General Description: This course focuses on two topics during the semester and how each topic affects the local, national, and global communities. It complements other courses in the curriculum by combining an emphasis on both specific content and on skill development in the areas of interaction, analysis, syntheses, and conflict resolution. Students study this issue in a historical and contemporary context, de- velop a greater understanding of the issues, and attempt to take a position on the issues. This resolution is subjected to further challenge and dialogue. In this course, the processes of reflecting, researching, analyzing, and evaluating are as important as the content. As points of view concerning the issue are developed, students must articulate and defend these as they are challenged by others and make judgments among alternative options. The first topic is selected by the faculty members, then midway through the semester the students select the second topic to be considered.

Distinctive Features: This course is a free-flowing, ever-changing mechanism for examining current issues, with an emphasis not so much on the content of the issue but the ways to think about it. It is developmentally relevant for producing more complex patterns of thought on the way to the upper stages of reflective judgment, and provides an opportunity for students to consider the use of evidence in making arguments.

Contact Person: Matt Campbell, JCCC 12345 College, Overland Park, KS 66210, Work Phone: (913) 469-8500 x3274, Fax: (913) 469-4409

VIOLENCE: PERSONAL AND SOCIETAL ISSUES
Institution: Elmhurst College
Intended Audience: January term students can earn either psychology or sociology credit
Disciplines Represented: Psychology and sociology
Personnel: Two faculty

General Description: This course is designed to increase students' understanding of the various forms of violence in current U.S. society. Students examine personal, group, and societal aspects of violence using psychological and sociological perspectives. The course focuses on exploring explanations of the causes of violence, the personal and societal effects of violence, prevention of violence, and social control mechanisms. Readings, lectures, films, debates, guest speakers, and discussions are used to help students understand the topics. Upon completion of this course, students should be able to:

- Describe the major psychological and sociological theories about the general causes of aggression and violence.
- Identify, compare, and contrast the major specific factors associated with common forms of aggression and violence, including bullying, gang violence, sexual assault, family member abuse, murder, ethnoviolence, and war, using both psychological and sociological perspectives.
- Discuss, compare, and contrast approaches for preventing and controlling the various kinds of violence and aggression, as listed above, incorporating both psychological and sociological perspectives.

Selected Topics: Topics include youth violence, acquaintance and family violence, murder, ethnoviolence, bullying, gang activities, and war.

Distinctive Features: Both instructors, a psychologist and sociologist, are present at all class sessions and make a serious effort to integrate psychological and sociological perspectives of each topic. Extensive use of films, debates, and writing assignments sharpens students' ability to construct and justify arguments.

Contact Persons: Dr. Brenda Forster, Dept. of Sociology, Box 51, Elmhurst College, Elmhurst, IL 60126, Work Phone: (708) 617-3083, Fax: (708) 617-3735, E-mail: janej@elmhcx9.elmhurst.edu

Dr. Jane A. Jegerski, Dept. of Psychology, Box 133, Elmhurst College, Elmhurst, IL 60126, Work Phone: (708) 617-3535, Fax: (708) 617-3735

ANIMAL COMMUNICATION
Institution: Columbia University
Intended Audience: Available to undergraduates in Biology— Psychology joint major or as an interesting elective for students with prerequisites
Disciplines Represented: Biology and psychology
Personnel: Two professors, one each from biology and psychology

General Description: This course provides an interdisciplinary introduction to experimental paradigms in animal communication with emphasis on teaching artificial codes to primates, birds, and marine mammals. Interdisciplinary perspectives include communication theory, discrimination theory, language development, and behavioral learning.

Selected Topics: Human Communication; Animal Communication Systems; Animal Intelligence and Cognitive Abilities; Teaching Other Species Nonspecies Specific Codes; American Sign Language with Primates; Computer-Mediated Communications with Chimpanzees; One-Way Communication with Dolphins and Sea Lions; Dolphins and Productive Codes and Interactive Systems, and Philosophical Implications.

Distinctive Features: A stimulating interdisciplinary course within a joint major, but perhaps more attractive as a fascinating elective for students with basic background in biology and psychology and an interest in learning or communication.

Contact Person: Herbert Terrace, Dept. of Psychology, 406 Schermerhorn, Columbia College, Columbia University, New York, NY 10027

CONCLUSION

The courses listed in Part II of this book are only the beginning of a collection of examples. Surely there are many more courses equally well-qualified for inclusion that might have been listed had I known about them. Although the methods used to obtain these examples did not use sampling techniques, as social scientists would use that term, and although the institutions contacted were given great discretion (and used it) in identifying the courses they wished to submit, the collection that resulted is satisfying in its breadth of representation of types of courses, faculty, fields, institutions, and geographical regions.

Fortunately, there is an on-going effort to collect examples of interdisciplinary courses carried on by the Association of Integrative Studies. As mentioned earlier in the chapter on future prospects for interdisciplinary studies, the Association for Integrative Studies (AIS), among its many other activities, keeps an archive of course syllabi, brochures, and other documents on interdisciplinary studies. It is hoped that this book will add to that collection and will stimulate further collection by AIS in the years ahead. If you have an interesting example that others might profit from learning about, or if you are seeking examples not listed in this book, please contact:

Professor William H. Newell, Executive Director, Association for Integrative Studies, School for Interdisciplinary Studies, Miami University, Oxford, Ohio 45056, Work Phone: (513) 529-2213, Fax: (513) 529-5849

As professors, we are socialized to work as specialized independent professionals, and we suffer, again and again, from lack of knowledge, not so much in our scholarly specialties, but in our professional life as teachers. I consider myself to have been in a privileged position to learn from editing this terrific collection of courses. I hope this book is only the beginning of further dialogue, including a whole network of continuing communication among colleagues who care about interdisciplinary courses and team teaching.

NOTES

1. Arthur Levine and John Weingart, *Reform of Undergraduate Education* (San Francisco: Jossey-Bass, 1973), p. 525.
2. Richard Hofstadter and Wilson Smith, eds. *American Higher Education: A Documentary History*, "The President's Commission on Higher Education for Democracy, 1947." (Chicago: University of Chicago Press, 1961), p. 989.
3. Gary Miller, *The Meaning of General Education: The Emergence of a Curricular Paradigm* (New York: Teachers College Press, 1988), p. 183.
4. Clifton Conrad, *The Undergraduate Curriculum: A Guide to Innovation and Reform* (Boulder, CO: Westview Press, 1978), p. 48.
5. Mark Schlesinger, *Reconstructing General Education: An Examination of Assumptions, Practices, and Prospects.* Occasional Paper Series No. 2 (Bowling Green, OH: Cue Project, Bowling Green State University, 1977), p. 39.
6. Arthur Levine, *Handbook On Undergraduate Curriculum* (San Francisco: Jossey-Bass, 1978), p.5.
7. Daniel Bell, *The Reforming of General Education* (New York: Anchor, 1968).
8. Ernest Boyer and Arthur Levine, *A Quest for Common Learning: The Aims of General Education* (Princeton, NJ: The Carnegie Foundation for the Advancement of Teaching, 1981), pp. 11-16.

9. Virginia Smith, "New Dimensions for General Education" Ch. 14 in Arthur Levine, ed., *Higher Learning in America: 1980-2000*. (Baltimore: The Johns Hopkins University Press, 1983), pp. 246-47.

10. Frederick Rudolph, *The American College and University* (New York: Alfred A. Knopf, 1965), pp. 252-53.

11. Arthur Levine, *Handbook on Undergraduate Curriculum* (San Francisco: Jossey-Bass, 1978), pp. 109-10.

12. Donal Schon, *The Reflective Practitioner* (New York: Basis Books, 1983), pp. 3-69.

13. Arthur Levine, *Handbook*, pp. 29-30.

14. *Ibid*, pp. 34-36.

15. Ralph Ross, "The Nature of Transdisciplinarity: An Elementary Statement" in Alvin M. White, ed., *Interdisciplinary Teaching*, New Directions for Teaching and Learning, No. 8 (San Francisco: Jossey-Bass, 1981), pp. 20-21.

16. Faith Gabelnick, et. al. *Learning Communities: Creating Connections Among Students, Faculty, and Disciplines* New Directions for Teaching and Learning, No. 41 (San Francisco, Jossey-Bass, 1990).

17. Association of American Colleges, *Reports from the Fields* (Washington: Association of American Colleges, 1991) p. 207ff. The report was authored by Johnnella Butler and several colleagues with input from and under the guidance of the Women's Studies Association.

18. *Ibid.*, p. 213.

19. *Ibid.*

20. Catherine Simpson, *Women's Studies in the United States* (New York: A Report of the Ford Foundation, 1986.)

21. Association of American Colleges, *Reports from the Field*, pp. 214-215.

22. Evelyn Hu-DeHart, "The History, Development, and Future of Ethnic Studies" *Phi Delta Kappan*, September 1993., p. 51.

23. *Ibid.*

24. *Ibid.*

25. Arthur Levine and Jeanette Cureton, "The Quiet Revolution: Eleven Facts about Multiculturalism and the Curriculum," *Change*, January/February 1992, p. 25ff.

26. *Ibid*, pp. 25-26.

27. Evelyn Hu-DeHart "The History, Development, and Future of Ethnic Studies," p. 51.

28. Darlene Clark Hine, "Black Studies: An Overview" in Robert L. Harris, Jr., *Three Essays: Black Studies in the United States* (New York: The Ford Foundation, 1990), p. 15.

29. Robert L. Harris, Jr., "The Intellectual and Institutional Development of Africana Studies" in Robert L. Harris, Jr. *Three Essays*, p. 7ff.

30. Johnetta B. Cole, "Black Studies in Liberal Arts Education" in Johnella Butler and John Walter, eds., *Transforming the Curriculum: Ethnic Studies and Women's Studies* (Albany, NY: State University of New York Press, 1991), p. 140.

31. *Ibid.*, p. 134.

32. *Ibid.*, p. 136.

33. Sarah M. Pickert, *Preparing for a Global Community: Achieving an International Perspective in Higher Education*. ASHE-ERIC Higher Education Report No. 2. (Washington, DC: The George Washington University, School of Education and Human Development, 1992), p. 11.

34. Frederick Rudolph, *The American College and University,* Chapter 13 "The Emrging University," p. 264ff.
35. Sarah Pickert, *Preparing for a Global Community,* pp. 12-14.
36. Association of American Colleges, *The Challenge of Connecting Learning* (Washington, DC: Association of American Colleges, 1991).
37. *Ibid.,* p. 11.
38. *Ibid.,* p. 5.
39. *Ibid.*

INDEX

●●●●●●●●●

by Janet Perlman

BCS Graphix
JN 103038 Index 7
85% 1.5 BWR ND
ICTT

ISBN 0-89774-887-5

90000